PROBLEMS OF THE MODERN ECONOMY

Changing Patterns in Foreign Trade and Payments

PROBLEMS OF THE MODERN ECONOMY

General Editor: EDMUND S. PHELPS, *University of Pennsylvania*

Each volume in this series presents prominent positions in the debate of an important issue of economic policy

---

THE BATTLE AGAINST UNEMPLOYMENT

CHANGING PATTERNS IN FOREIGN TRADE AND PAYMENTS

THE GOAL OF ECONOMIC GROWTH

MONOPOLY POWER AND ECONOMIC PERFORMANCE

PRIVATE WANTS AND PUBLIC NEEDS

THE UNITED STATES AND THE DEVELOPING ECONOMIES

LABOR AND THE NATIONAL ECONOMY

INEQUALITY AND POVERTY

DEFENSE, SCIENCE, AND PUBLIC POLICY

AGRICULTURAL POLICY IN AN AFFLUENT SOCIETY

Changing Patterns in Foreign Trade and Payments

Edited with an introduction by
BELA BALASSA
THE JOHNS HOPKINS UNIVERSITY

REVISED EDITION

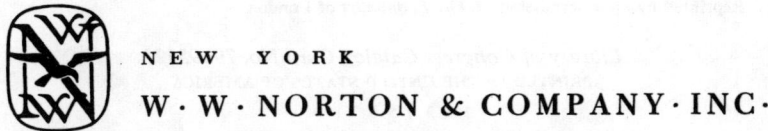

NEW YORK
W·W·NORTON & COMPANY·INC·

COPYRIGHT © 1970, 1964 BY W. W. NORTON & COMPANY, INC.

The Atlantic Case, by Harry G. Johnson. From *The Atlantic Community Quarterly,* (Fall 1967), pp. 371–380. Originally published in and copyright by *New Society.* Reprinted by permission of the author and *New Society.*
American Attitudes Toward Trade Liberalization in the Atlantic Area, by Bela Balassa. This article originally appeared in *Moorgate and Wall Street,* a review issued by Hill Samuel & Co., Limited, 100 Wood Street, London, E.C.2, and is reprinted by permission.
The American Challenge, by Gene Bradley. From *The Atlantic Community Quarterly,* (Winter 1967–68), pp. 520–527. Reprinted by permission of the publisher.
An Answer to *The American Challenge,* by Roger Beardwood, Associate Editor of *Fortune.* Reprinted from the September 15, 1968, issue of *Fortune* Magazine by special permission; copyright 1968 by Time Inc.
Economic Sovereignty at Bay, by Raymond Vernon. From *Foreign Affairs,* (October 1968), pp. 110–122. Copyright by the Council on Foreign Relations, Inc., New York. Reprinted by permission of the author and the publisher.
National Economic Policy in an Interdependent World Economy, by Richard N. Cooper. Reprinted by permission of The Yale Law Journal Company and Fred B. Rothman & Company from *The Yale Law Journal,* Vol. 76, pp. 1273–75, 1278–93, 1296–98.
The International Monetary System and the Reconciliation of Policy Goals, by J. Marcus Fleming. Reprinted with Permission from J. M. Fleming's "The International Monetary System and the Reconciliation of Policy Goals" in George Horwich, ed., *Monetary Process and Policy; A Symposium* (Homewood, Ill.: Richard D. Irwin, Inc.), pp. 244–57.
The Dollar and World Liquidity: A Minority View, by Emile Despres, Charles P. Kindelberger, and Walter S. Salant. From *The Economist,* (February 5, 1966), pp. 526–529. Reprinted by kind permission of *The Economist* of London.
Unfinished Business, by Fritz Machlup. From *Remaking the International Monetary System: the Rio Agreement and Beyond,* Committee for Economic Development, The Johns Hopkins Press, 1968, pp. 96–111. Reprinted by permission of the publisher.
The Threat to the Dollar, by Robert Triffin. From *The Atlantic Monthly,* (February 1961). Reprinted by permission of the author.
The Case for Going Back to Gold, by M. A. Heilperin. From *Fortune,* (September 1962), pp. 108, 152–59. Copyright 1962 by Time Inc. Reprinted by permission of Time Inc.
Exchange-Rate Flexibility, by J. E. Meade. From the *Three Banks Review,* (June 1966), pp. 3–27. Reprinted by permission of the publisher.
Where the Rainbow Ended, from *The Economist,* (December 1960), pp. 1325–1326. Reprinted by kind permission of *The Economist* of London.

Library of Congress Catalog Card No. 79–95521
PRINTED IN THE UNITED STATES OF AMERICA

1 2 3 4 5 6 7 8 9 0

Contents

Introduction vii

PROLOGUE 1

PAUL W. MC CRACKEN · The World Economy at a Fork in the Road 1

PART ONE: Tariffs, Trade, and Economic Integration 11

IRVING B. KRAVIS · The U.S. Trade Position and the Common Market 12
ROBERT E. BALDWIN · Toward the Next Round of Trade Negotiations 27
HARRY G. JOHNSON · The Atlantic Case 39
BELA BALASSA · American Attitudes Toward Trade Liberalization in the Atlantic Area 48

PART TWO: Foreign Investments and the Multinational Corporation 61

JUDD POLK · U.S. Exports in Relation to U.S. Production Abroad 61
GENE BRADLEY · The American Challenge 72
FORTUNE · An Answer to *The American Challenge* 81
RAYMOND VERNON · Economic Sovereignty at Bay 84

PART THREE: Interdependence and National Economic Policies 98

RICHARD N. COOPER · National Economic Policy in an Interdependent World Economy 98
J. MARCUS FLEMING · The International Monetary System and the Reconciliation of Policy Goals 116
JAMES TOBIN · Economic Progress and the International Monetary System 130

vi CONTENTS

PART FOUR: The International Role of the Dollar
and the U.S. Balance of Payments   144

> EMILE DESPRES, CHARLES P. KINDLEBERGER, AND WALTER S.
> SALANT · The Dollar and World Liquidity: A Minority
> View   144
> EDWARD M. BERNSTEIN · Does the United States Have a
> Payments Deficit?   157
> FRITZ MACHLUP · Unfinished Business   161

PART FIVE: Solutions to the International
Monetary Problem   176

> ROBERT TRIFFIN · The Threat to the Dollar   176
> EDWARD M. BERNSTEIN · International Monetary Reserves
> and the Composite Gold Standard   186
> M. A. HEILPERIN · The Case for Going Back to Gold   198
> J. E. MEADE · Exchange-Rate Flexibility   203

EPILOGUE

> THE ECONOMIST · Where the Rainbow Ended   223

Suggested Further Readings   229

Introduction

SINCE THE SECOND WORLD WAR, international economic issues have assumed increasing importance in the United States. In the trade field, there is concern about the effects of European economic integration on U.S. exports and the repercussions of multilateral tariff reductions on American industry. Exports are also affected by the recent upsurge in foreign direct investment since producers have the choice between exporting and investing abroad. At the same time, the growing role of the multinational corporation, together with the increased interdependence of national economies, limit the freedom of policy-makers to pursue domestic economic objectives. These limitations are of especial importance in a system of fixed exchange rates which closes an important avenue for correcting balance-of-payments disequilibria. The slow growth of gold stocks, the use of dollars as foreign exchange reserves, and the continuing U.S. balance-of-payments deficit further complicate the situation and call for a reappraisal of the international monetary system. These outstanding issues of international economic policy—their nature, their ramifications, and possible solutions—are the subject of the present volume.

The book opens with an essay by Paul McCracken, Chairman of the Council of Economic Advisers, written a few weeks before his appointment to the Council by President Nixon. McCracken argues that while U.S. balance-of-payments deficits have helped to "lubricate" the international economic system by providing foreign exchange reserves to other countries, the resulting situation is fraught with dangers. Continuing deficits tend to undermine confidence in the dollar, while the pursuance of conflicting national policy objectives creates strains and stresses in the international economy. To avoid the possible consequences of a world-wide deflation or the increased use of direct controls, McCracken calls for anti-inflationary policies in the United States, increased international policy coordination, an equitable distribution in the burden of defense, and improvements in the international monetary system.

TARIFFS, TRADE, AND ECONOMIC INTEGRATION

In the first essay of Part One, Irving B. Kravis examines the changes which have occurred in the U.S. trade position during the postwar period. These have been due in part to the increased need for imported materials, the massive flow of American capital to Western Europe, and the shortening of the technological lag of our competitors. Integration in Western Europe has further contributed to changes in trade relations for the benefit of European countries, and the emergence of the Common Market as the largest trading unit in the world has challenged U.S. supremacy in international trade negotiations.

Indeed, bargaining between the United States and the Common Market was the dominant feature of negotiations on multilateral tariff reductions in the framework of the Kennedy Round, completed in 1967. The negotiations have led to an average reduction of tariffs on nonagricultural commodities by about one-third, and thus represent a further advance in the liberalization of international trade that was begun in the 1930s. Robert E. Baldwin briefly reviews the process of trade liberalization and indicates some of the problems that need to be solved if the process is to continue. In his opinion, a viable system of trade adjustment assistance to firms and workers adversely affected through reductions in trade barriers is a precondition of further advances in the liberalization of world trade. Baldwin also calls for the use of flexible tariff-cutting techniques, and inclusion of nontariff barriers in the next round of negotiations.

While Baldwin suggests improvements in the process of multilateral trade negotiations, Harry G. Johnson believes that this avenue of trade liberalization holds little hope for the future. He recommends instead that serious consideration be given to the possibility of establishing a North Atlantic Free Trade Area— even if this were not to include the European Common Market. Johnson's paper was written for a British audience, but it fits well the pattern of recent proposals in the United States for establishing such a trade area.

In the next essay, the editor of this volume takes issue with these proposals and advances the view that, under present-day conditions, the establishment of a North Atlantic Free Trade Area is neither desirable nor feasible. He also criticizes the suggestions made for trade arrangements which exclude the European Common Market, arguing that the political and economic objectives of trade liberalization favor the continued application of the multilateral approach.

FOREIGN INVESTMENT AND THE MULTINATIONAL CORPORATION

While the contributions in Part One deal with problems of trade liberalization, in the opening essay of Part Two, Judd Polk suggests that issues of trade policy be considered together with policy on foreign investments since, for U.S. firms, exports and the establishment of foreign subsidiaries are but two facets of decisions on production. Polk buttresses his argument by noting that sales of U.S. subsidiaries abroad are six times larger than exports and recommends that governmental restraints on U.S. direct investments, motivated by balance-of-payments considerations, be considered in this light.

American foreign investments are examined from a different point of view in Jean-Jacques Servan-Schreiber's *Le Défi Americain*, translated under the title *The American Challenge*, of which a summary, written by Gene Bradley, has been reprinted in this volume. Servan-Schreiber regards the penetration of U.S. capital in Western Europe as a manifestation of American superiority in management, organization, and technology. He expresses the view that, if things continue unchecked, "in 15 years, the third industrial power after the U.S. and the U.S.S.R. could well be not Europe but American industry in Europe." To meet this challenge, he urges the formation of large industrial units in Western Europe, the integration of European capital markets, and the creation of an all-European policy of science and technical education.

As a partial answer to Servan-Schreiber, the Editors of *Fortune* note that foreign direct investment is a two-way road: parallel with U.S. investments in Western Europe, there has also been a reverse flow from Europe to the United States. In fact, while American direct investments in European countries amounted to $17.9 billion at the end of 1967, in the same year the value of European direct investments in the United States was $7.0 billion.

In turn, Raymond Vernon takes issue with Servan-Schreiber's proposition that the subsidiaries of American companies tend to overwhelm European industries. He rather places direct foreign investment in the context of the trend toward the multinational corporation. This trend, so Vernon argues, limits the sovereignty of the nation state in economic affairs: not only does the multinational corporation necessarily follow a global strategy on the world level, but its internal transactions appear as international transactions for the nation state. He further raises, but does not answer, the question of whether "sovereign states will learn to live with a decline in their perceived economic power."

INTERDEPENDENCE OF NATIONAL ECONOMIC POLICIES AND BALANCE-OF-PAYMENTS ADJUSTMENT

According to Vernon, the emergence of the multinational corporation is part and parcel of the increased interpenetration and interdependence of the national economies of the industrial countries. The implications of this interdependence for national economic policy-making is the subject of the opening essay in Part Three by Richard N. Cooper. As a result of increased interdependence through trade and capital movements, notes Cooper, differences in the national economic policies of the industrial countries are soon translated into balance-of-payments disequilibria and, at the same time, reduce the effectiveness of these policies in reaching domestic objectives. The situation is aggravated by inconsistencies in the policy objectives of individual countries, thus leading to international competition in economic policy which adversely affects all participants.

Cooper's discussion on the interdependence of national economic policies has relevance for the system of fixed exchange rates as it exists today. J. Marcus Fleming surveys the development of the system from the time of the Bretton Woods Agreement which set up the International Monetary Fund (IMF), with the objective of providing loans to finance temporary balance-of-payments deficits. Fleming submits that while this system functioned without much difficulty until the early 1960's, the increased mobility of capital, disparities in the degree of cost inflation, and the growing precariousness of the structure of international liquidity, along with the slow growth and the subsequent decline in the monetary gold stock, have created strains and stresses in subsequent years. With individual countries placing domestic objectives ahead of balance-of-payments considerations, and committed to maintaining fixed exchange rates, restrictions and direct controls have been used to correct deficits instead of permitting adjustment through changes in domestic incomes and prices.

But what are the possibilities for balance-of-payments adjustments under a system of fixed exchange rates? Having surveyed the principal mechanisms of adjustment, James Tobin concludes that they work at a slow pace so that "major imbalances are likely to take years to eliminate, unless they are corrected by measures which hamper economic growth or restrict world commerce." These conclusions have lead Tobin to suggest that there is need for increasing international liquidity in order to provide ample time for adjustment.

THE INTERNATIONAL ROLE OF THE DOLLAR AND THE U.S. BALANCE OF PAYMENTS

The view is generally held that the problem is not just the slow growth of international liquidity but the precariousness of a system of liquidity which in part consists of national currencies. Thus, U.S. balance-of-payments deficits, while contributing to international liquidity, also weaken the confidence in the dollar. In the opening essay of Part Four, Emile Despres, Charles P. Kindleberger, and Walter S. Salant take issue with this view. They submit that the use of the dollar as an international currency makes it inappropriate to apply existing definitions for measuring the balance-of-payments deficit of the United States. The authors concentrate their fire on the so-called liquidity definition used by the U.S. Department of Commerce, which measures the deficit as the sum of changes in reserves and in short-term liabilities to foreign private holders of dollars. Accordingly, financial intermediation involving the inflow of short-term, and the outflow of long-term, capital would give rise to a deficit under the liquidity definition, although it is only a manifestation of the role of the United States as a world banker and as such is necessary for financing expansion in Western Europe.

The authors extend their criticism to the definition adopted by a Committee headed by Edward M. Bernstein under which the deficit is measured by net official reserve transactions in the form of gold, foreign exchange, and claims on the IMF. Yet, as Bernstein points out in the following paper, "a reserve transactions deficit either depletes the reserves of a country (and cannot be continued indefinitely) or increases its liquid liabilities and confronts it with the risk of a sudden drawing down of its reserves in the future by conversions of foreign exchange holdings of its currency." Just like a commercial bank, the United States cannot continue to make "loans" in the form of long-term capital if this undermines confidence in its ability to repay short-term obligations in their full value—that is, without necessitating a devaluation of the dollar in terms of gold and/or in terms of other currencies.

Fritz Machlup has little doubt that the U.S. balance of payments is in a deficit and has been in a deficit for some time. In fact, he considers the continuation of this deficit in the presence of a "dollar overhang" from earlier years to be the major reason for recurrent speculation in gold. Machlup further argues that direct measures and selective controls will not cure the deficit, so that a real adjustment is necessary which may necessitate a realignment of currency values.

SOLUTIONS TO THE INTERNATIONAL MONETARY PROBLEM

It has so often been said that the present difficulties on the international monetary scene reflect three basic problems: the liquidity problem—the overly slow increase in world reserves; the confidence problem—uneasiness concerning possible changes in the relative values of reserve assets, such as gold, dollar, and sterling; and the adjustment problem—the slowness of the principal mechanisms for remedying disequilibria in the balance of payments. The distinction of having first indicated the dangers of the present international monetary system belongs to Robert Triffin. In Triffin's opinion, international reserves would need to grow *pari passu* with the expansion of trade, yet the increase in gold production can supply only a portion of the required liquidity. At the same time, it cannot be expected that the United States will continue to contribute to world liquidity by increasing her short-term liabilities since *either* the U.S. balance-of-payments deficit will be remedied and this source of liquidity will thus have dried up *or* the continuation of the deficit will result in a run on the dollar, thereby disrupting the international monetary system.

Besides diagnosing the ills of the international monetary system, Triffin prescribes a remedy: to transform the IMF into an institution resembling in some respects a world central bank. Triffin's views have been much debated and a variety of alternative proposals have been made. But thus far the only progress for increasing international liquidity through collective action has been the agreement on the creation of Special Drawing Rights (SDRs) to be allocated to members of the IMF. Edward Bernstein warns that while the creation of the SDRs will somewhat ease the liquidity problem, the confidence problem will remain since an international monetary system with multiple reserve assets is bound to lead to changes in the holders' preference for these assets. To avoid this, Bernstein suggests the establishment of a Reserve Settlement Account in the framework of the IMF in which countries would hold their reserve assets—gold, foreign exchange, and SDRs—denominated in a composite reserve unit (CRU) and would transfer reserves in the form of CRUs.

Bernstein considers his scheme as a composite gold standard which represents "a natural evolution of the gold standard." M. A. Heilperin, in turn, advocates the restoration of a full-fledged gold standard, accompanied by increases in the price of gold. The discipline of the gold standard would then require remedying balance-of-payments disequilibria through changes in domestic incomes and prices. Most observers think that this would be an overly large price to pay and recommend either increasing liquidity to leave more time for the adjustment process or greater flexibility in exchange rates.

Among the authors of the selections reprinted in this volume, Triffin and Tobin have expressed the view that an increase in world liquidity would permit adjustment to take place in case of imbalances. James E. Meade, on the other hand, believes that greater flexibility in exchange rates would be necessary to remedy balance-of-payments disequilibria. His practical recommendations include widening the band within which exchange rates are permitted to fluctuate from 1 to 5 percent and adopting a sliding parity which would allow annual charges of 2 percent in these limits. Proposals of this sort have been made by several other writers and these are under consideration at the time this volume goes to press.

As an epilogue to the volume, we have appended a modern fable, written by the staff of *The Economist* in 1960, which has not lost either its relevance or its charm. It visualizes a world without gold where the demonetization of gold is followed by the use of IMF deposits as reserves.

PROBLEMS OF THE MODERN ECONOMY

Changing Patterns in Foreign Trade and Payments

Prologue

The World Economy at a Fork in the Road
PAUL W. MC CRACKEN

Paul W. McCracken, Professor at the University of Michigan, is presently Chairman of the Council of Economic Advisers to President Nixon. In this essay, written in October 1968—a few weeks before his appointment to the Council—Mr. McCracken considers the major international economic problems facing the United States and the Free World.

RECENT DEVELOPMENTS in the Free World are raising questions about our ability to realize the promise of continuing growth in the world economy. Indeed, if we do not watch our step, we shall drift inexorably toward a world of competitive deflation and an increasingly restrictive and illiberal international financial and trading system—a world, in short, where economic and monetary forces are nudging nations toward autarchy and economic warfare.

What is the problem? To understand this question, it will be helpful to recall a bit of history.

INTERNATIONAL LIQUIDITY AND THE U.S. BALANCE-OF-PAYMENTS DEFICIT

The present international monetary and financial system was shaped almost a quarter of a century ago at the Bretton Woods Conference. There the decision was made that the world would operate within a system of fixed exchange rates and convertible currencies. This had much to commend it. A world in which currencies are freely and readily convertible into each other at fixed and certain rates of exchange would give a desirable degree of stability and order to world trade and commerce. The chaos of the 1930's associated with inconvertible currencies and growing financial and trade restrictions—a chaos that made its contributions to international political tensions—was still then fresh in our minds.

On the whole, the system has worked well. From 1948 to 1965, world trade more than tripled, and for the industrial nations of the world it almost quadrupled. If the test of the pudding is in the eating, the recipe used at Bretton Woods seemed to have been a good one indeed.

Now in a reasonably stable world a nation's balance of payments will not always be in equilibrium. For a variety of reasons, payments deficits or surpluses will occur from time to time. If exchange rates cannot adjust, each nation must obviously then have international monetary reserves that can be drawn upon to cover these deficits. The vaults of the major industrial nations were, however, bare by the end of the war. How, then, was this system to get into operation?

It was at this point that the world was the beneficiary of a massive piece of luck. Early in the postwar period, the United States began to run deficits in its balance of payments. These other nations, therefore, found themselves with growing holdings of dollars, the money of the world's largest and strongest economy. The U.S. held over 70 percent of the world's monetary gold. And it stood ready to exchange gold for dollars presented to it by any foreign Central Bank or Treasury. These dollars were, therefore, a "natural" for needed international monetary resources, and they were being held abroad in growing amounts because of our external payments deficits. Thus, though no one really planned it all that way, the dollar came to be the major international reserve currency.

PROBLEMS OF AN INTERNATIONAL RESERVE CURRENCY

So long as the world was thirsty for international liquidity, the system worked smoothly. This seeming success—arising, it is worth repeating, from the accident that the world happened to need international reserves when we began to have persisting payments deficits—masked for a time three related and fundamental problems inherent in the system. First, the use of a specific country's money for international reserves poses some difficult problems. Second, to make this system work we must have a far closer and more sophisticated synchronization or coordination of the domestic economic policies of the major industrial nations than anything devised to date. Third, nations attach different priorities to different objectives of economic policy, and this can be the source of major strains. Suppose that we explore each of these in turn.

The use of a specific country's money for international reserves does raise some obvious questions. The French have had a point when they insist that the reserve-currency nation (that is, the U.S.) is not subject to the same discipline as other countries. When another nation runs a deficit in its balance of payments, the depletion of its reserves of foreign exchange or gold forces corrective action. When the U.S. runs payments deficits, it merely pays out more dollars—and other nations must accept them or assume responsibility for jeopardizing the whole system. This system has, however, some unhappy features for the reserve-currency nation also. It means large foreign holdings of dollars, and the United States is thus exposed to whipsaw effects from anything that might trip off a crisis of international confidence. Moreover, the supply of international liquidity grows to the extent the reserve-currency country happens to run deficits in its balance of payments. There is no reason to expect that this would happen to be equal to the growth in world needs for liquidity.

LACK OF COORDINATION OF NATIONAL ECONOMIC POLICIES

The last two years dramatically illustrate the strains experienced by the international financial systems when close synchronization of domestic economic policies among nations does not occur. In 1964, the surplus in our balance of payments on current account was $8.4 billion. Because of large "noncurrent" drains in our external payments (military establishments abroad, capital flows, foreign aid), we must run a large surplus on current account if we are to have any hope of equilibrium in our total balance of payments. This current account surplus declined persistently after 1964, and in the first half of 1968 it was down to a

$1.7 billion annual rate.

That deterioration in our surplus on current account is the single most basic source of the dollar's recent problems. And the source of the shrinking surplus in our balance of payments on current account is largely, in turn, our overly inflationary domestic economic policies after 1964.

For the U.S. economy imports tend to grow at about the same percentage rate as GNP if the latter is growing about 6 percent per year. When GNP begins to race ahead more rapidly, the rise in imports quickly starts to become close to 2 percent for each 1 percent rise in the domestic economy. This is to be expected. When the domestic economy becomes overheated, delivery schedules at home stretch out, and increasingly demand spills over to foreign markets. As our own price level moves ahead more rapidly, domestic sources of supply become less advantageously priced relative to foreign producers. Because the U.S. economy is large relative to our external payments, an inflation in the domestic economy tends to produce a highly leveraged effect on our imports.

We see this clearly in the data. From 1964 to 1967, GNP was actually allowed to rise about 7½ percent per year. This was substantially in excess of the capability of the economy to produce real output. Pressures on the price-cost level mounted. The 13 percent per year rise in imports that we experienced in these three years was, therefore, almost the classic response of our balance of payments to inflationary domestic economic conditions. . . .

At the time we were pursuing overly inflationary monetary and fiscal policies, the economies of the Common Market were somewhat stagnant. The German economy experienced an outright recession in late 1966 and the first half of 1967, and the French economy was sluggish. As a result, U.S. exports to the Common Market showed no gains in 1967, though with normal economic growth we could reasonably have expected as much as $0.5 billion increase in U.S. exports to these nations.

Thus the failure of industrial nations to coordinate their domestic economic policies and to pursue a course of reasonably noninflationary economic growth weakened the U.S. balance of payments by upwards of $6 billion from 1964 to 1967. The U.S. inflation pushed our imports far beyond what might have occurred with more orderly domestic economic conditions. And last year's stagnation in Germany and France probably cost us up to $0.5 billion of exports. It is not at all certain that the system can survive strains of this magnitude.

DIFFERENCES IN NATIONAL ECONOMIC OBJECTIVES

While most nations have the same list of objectives for national economic policy, there are sharp differences among them in the weights or priorities attached to the different items. In the United States, a reasonably stable price level and full employment are both clearly important. In our socio-political milieu, however, we shall lower our sights on employment only reluctantly and only for brief periods in order to show a better record of price stability. Obviously, those marginally positioned in the work force would tend to be the early job casualties from lower employment, and they also tend to be those about whom there is now particularly intense social concern.

How about Germany? Full employment, of course, is also an urgent objective of economic policy there. There are Germans alive today, however, who personally remember the total inflation of 1923 and the severe inflation incident to the last war. To Germans, with vivid memories of the social disorganization that severe inflation can cause, a reasonably stable price level is, therefore, a more urgent objective of economic policy than here.

The result is that Germany's export price performance has been better than that for the U.S. and substantially better than that for the U.K. The cumulative effect of these differential trends inevitably meant an undervalued Deutsche mark and an overvalued pound. This is merely one illustration of what tends to happen as countries attach different priorities to domestic economic policy objectives.

THE DANGER OF WORLD DEFLATION

It is clear that the time has come for constructive action here. We now have a wired-up, two-price gold market, and the uneasy lack of confidence in the dollar earlier this year was relieved more by the debacle in France than by fundamental therapy here.

There is great danger that we may set the course of world economic policy in the wrong direction. Two possibilities are as ominous as they are tempting. First, the world may undergo a spasm of deflation as each major nation tries to strengthen its own payments position by deflating. The trouble is that its reduced imports mean reduced exports for another nation, which must then deflate to curtail its imports, which are perhaps the first nation's exports, which requires the first nation to deflate even further, which . . . (Here is the parallel strategy to that of the 1930's through which we crushed the whole banking system by trying to deflate to the point where only "good" banks remained.)

DIRECT CONTROLS

The second danger is that we shall try to preserve the nominal characteristics of the present system by *ad hoc* direct controls. We now have an elaborate set of controls over U.S. investments abroad. While nominally we stand ready to exchange gold for dollars presented to us by foreign official holders, the U.S. has exerted substantial pressure on these Central Banks and Treasuries not to exercise that option. Early in 1968, the President proposed direct controls over tourist expenditures—the first installment, as was true for control of U.S. investments abroad, being "voluntary." Having proposed direct and discriminatory controls over U.S. tourist expenditures abroad (that is, "imports" of tourist services), the Administration has had difficulty explaining why there should not also be direct controls over imports of steel. And we are not alone here. A major response of the British and the French to pressure on their currencies has been direct constraints on imports—controls that may well be easier to impose than to remove.

This direct-control route is plausible, tempting, and dangerous. It preserves the cosmetics of the system while it takes us down the road toward the breakup of our liberal international trading and financial system. It would, in short, tend toward open economic warfare among nations—just as the promise emerges of greater international commerce and all that this could mean for higher levels of living and lowered political tensions among nations.

THE CHOICE OF POLICIES

What, then, should be done? The test of whether we are on course, or 180 degrees off course, is a simple one. Does our strategy of policy enable us to begin discarding the considerable clutter of direct controls over such things as investment abroad or tourist expenditures or trade generally? Are our actions enabling us to move toward a more liberal international trading and financial system? Only if these questions can be answered in the affirmative can we be sure that we are moving in the right direction.

Anti-Inflationary Policies in the United States · First, it is clear that the United States must exercise a far more sophisticated control over fiscal and monetary policy. We have agonized through budgets whose outlays have overshot the revenue-yielding capability of our tax system at reasonably full employment by as much as $25 billion. This gap, reduced at the count of nine by the Revenue and Expenditure Control Act of 1968, must not be allowed to emerge again. (Indeed, as indicated earlier, we lucked out on this crisis more because of the French debacle than the timeliness of our own fiscal actions.)

Moreover, the Federal Reserve must adhere to a course of slow monetary expansion, and it must stay firmly on this course. The overly large rate of monetary and credit expansion in July and August tended to undercut the effectiveness of the tax increase which the Federal Reserve had itself so strongly (and rightly) urged upon the Congress. This erratic performance has been exceedingly coarse tuning of our economic policy. If one thing is clear from our experience in these difficult years since 1964, it is the urgent need for a steadier and more even-handed management of both the budget and monetary policy. Indeed, without this we cannot be sure of a cooled-down U.S. economy, without which a strong dollar and international economic and financial equilibrium are impossible.

The Price of Gold · Second, what about gold and its price? This question is more dramatic than fundamental. If the characteristics of the market for this commodity were anonymously described to an economist, of course, he would be inclined to say that here is a market in disequilibrium. And history is not entirely reassuring to those who hope that by brute force a disequilibrium market can be preserved indefinitely.

Moreover, some of the arguments against changing the price of gold are really peripheral. The fact that this might reward Bad Guys (for example, Russia or South Africa) is particularly petty. One might as well argue that people should be prohibited from buying Cadillacs because Cadillacs sometimes provide enjoyment for the Wrong People.

At the same time, an increase in the price of gold does not get at our present problems. Gold cannot provide an assured and orderly increase in international liquidity, and it would do nothing to redress strains that arise because nations pursue different policies and different objectives of policy.

International Economic Policy Coordination · Third, new machinery must be developed to give greater importance, visibility, and substance to the synchronization of economic policies among major nations. To the few officials who meet periodically for a discussion of these matters, there may seem already to be substantial activity here. Actually, however, the visibility of these present consultative arrangements is limited, and their actual impact on economic policies cannot be great.

Equitable Distribution of the Burden of Defense · Fourth, the time has come for Uncle Sam to get hard-nosed about some things that cause major leakages in our balance of payments. It is doubtful if the United States can maintain a free and open system of fixed exchange rates and convertibility of the dollar and also assume the full burden of the world's policeman.

The postwar arrangements by which we established a military shield in Europe and elsewhere without bothering to include in the agreements that host nations must at least pay the foreign exchange costs has to be high on history's list of shortsighted actions. We must insist that host nations, shielded by our military facilities, carry the full foreign exchange costs. And "carry" does not mean "lend"—as is the effect of some present arrangements.

Moreover, U.S. output is now shut out of nations enjoying wide access to the U.S. markets. While foreign cars readily enter the U.S., special tax and tariff barriers virtually exclude U.S. cars from foreign markets. Obviously this cannot be tolerated.

Improvements in the International Monetary System · Finally, we must do some candid and dispassionate thinking about where we go if we cannot make the present system work smoothly. We have invested a good deal of effort and two postwar decades in this system launched at Bretton Woods. A substantial amount of institutional machinery has been constructed. Our strategy must be to make the present system work if it is possible. With some therapy along the lines already indicated, the system will certainly work better, and the extent of the improvement might be surprising. We must not, however, underestimate the formidable nature of the task. Nations are still sovereign. Even with better coordination, nations will still differ about objectives of policy. Some contingency thinking here is much in order.

We should then move boldly and directly toward a more liberal world economic policy—toward a more open system. This has been our fundamental objective all along. We should propose an ambitious program for the orderly dismantling of barriers to trade and capital flows throughout the world. This would require a system capable of orderly adjustment to changing stresses and strains among world economies. And a part of this adjustment process should be a capability for orderly changes in exchange rates. Our present system here is too brittle and frozen. It too quickly forces nations into restrictions on trade or international deflation. Proposals for a wider band or a crawling peg deserve careful consideration. An exchange rate is, after all, a price, and there is no divine law about the immutability of any price (including the price of one currency in terms of another). The important objective is to make progress toward a de-escalation of impediments to trade and investment. It would clearly be in this nation's interest. The expansion of world trade would accelerate. And the danger of blocs waging economic and financial war on each other would be reduced.

Clearly, the world economy is now at a fork in the road. Ours is a moment in history as propitious as it is crucial. The good international trading and financial system is one that encourages the relaxation of barriers and impediments to trade and investment. The Free World should see a major expansion of international commerce in the years ahead. Basic domestic forces will continue to nudge the economies of Eastern Europe toward more liberal and open economic policies, in spite of setbacks like the USSR's invasion of Czechoslovakia. We have, therefore, the potential of growing interdependence among and between the two worlds. While understandably preoccupied with immediate problems, we must keep squarely before us these larger objectives.

Part One: Tariffs, Trade, and Economic Integration

The U.S. Trade Position and the Common Market

IRVING B. KRAVIS

Irving B. Kravis is Professor of Economics at the University of Pennsylvania. He was one of the panelists appearing before a Congressional subcommittee who contributed papers to the compendium Factors Affecting the United States Balance of Payments.

IT IS WIDELY appreciated that the terms upon which the United States has participated in world trade during the past century have been favored by unique features of U.S. geography and economic structure. There is reason to fear that some of these past sources of strength may be eroding, owing partly to the continuing revolution in transportation and communication and partly to economic changes both in the United States and in other important industrial countries.

In particular, the economic structure of Western Europe has been moving closer to that of the United States. The United States thus is being made less unique; it is being confronted with keener competition and with a more nearly equal concentration of economic and political power.

The European Economic Community (EEC) or the Common Market has accelerated these developments—some more clearly than others. It may not be amiss, therefore, to try to assess the impact of the Common Market upon the United States against this general background of changing relative positions. This approach shifts attention somewhat from the usual emphasis on the dangers of trade diversion that are created by the rapid elimination of trade barriers within the Common Market and the establishment of a common tariff wall around it. Aside from the fact that trade diversion has already been so widely discussed, there are several reasons for favoring this line of attack.

In the first place, the extent of trade diversion itself will depend largely upon the policy choices made by the EEC and these will in turn be influenced by the whole constellation of political and economic power relationships between the EEC and other countries, particularly the United States. This is the more likely since the common external tariff itself cannot be regarded as unduly protective by American standards. Tariff comparisons are notoriously difficult, but it is probably significant that at the rates prevailing in 1960 the average U.S. duty was higher than the common external tariff for 47 out of 74 chapters of the Brussels classification for which data were calculated by the Committee for Economic Development. Taken in conjunction with the trade-creating effects of the fillip to economic growth given by the Common Market, adverse overall effects on U.S. exports to the Common Market countries will not necessarily follow *automatically* from the existence of the Common Market. Adverse effects may, however, result from the future commercial and economic policies of the Common Market.

Secondly, a discussion of the effects of the Common Market which is concentrated upon trade diversion stresses competition for EEC markets and may omit the important question of competition between EEC and U.S. firms for American and third markets. After all, U.S. exports to the Six account for only about 15 percent of U.S. commodity exports, and they are, of course, small relative to total sales in the domestic market. Furthermore the more basic issues of relative competitiveness are important also in the contest for EEC markets.

ADVANTAGES OF THE UNITED STATES IN WORLD TRADE

The historical advantages of the United States in world trade may be listed as follows:

1. By the happy accident of geography the United States had an abundant supply of the materials which constituted the essential requisites of an industrial civilization. Coal and iron were linked by cheap water transport. There were ample supplies of wood. Copper, lead, and zinc were found in quantities adequate

not only to supply the United States but also to export to other countries. Abundant supplies meant that materials were cheap and gave a corresponding advantage to manufactured goods.

2. Not only was there a supply of abundant metals but there was also a vast expanse of land variegated with respect to climate and soil. Elsewhere in the world where favorable climate and soil are found, the man-land ratio is generally much higher, and therefore less agricultural output is available for export. Almost from the beginning of the Nation until this day, the United States has thus been a major exporter of agricultural products. It is true that the proportion of our exports made up by agricultural products has been much smaller in recent decades than in the 18th and 19th centuries but it nevertheless remains a fact that agricultural exports account for one-fourth of the total nonmilitary exports of the United States.

3. The United States has been a capital-rich country. The availability of cheap or free land made labor expensive from the beginning, and placed a premium on mechanization. Rough comparisons suggest that in the early or middle 1950's the amount of physical capital per worker used by U.S. enterprises was well over twice as great as that used by the leading countries of Western Europe, while the amount of equipment used per worker was almost twice as great. While the connection between factor intensities and comparative advantage may not be as simple as was once thought, the abundance of capital in the United States has undoubtedly been an important source of advantage for the United States in world competition. At the minimum a plentiful supply of capital made it easier for American firms to take advantage of the opportunities for large-scale production and made resources more readily available for research and development.

4. The American economy has had the advantage of bold and imaginative entrepreneurs. The combination of a rich and unexploited continent and a high degree of equality of economic opportunity stimulated a vigorous competitive race. While the visible hand of the entrepreneur engaged in self-aggrandizement not infrequently seemed to operate with greater strength than the invisible hand supposedly promoting the public interest, the ruthless entrepreneurs of the 19th century did serve to bring about the rapid economic development of the country. They left a heritage of vigor in the adaptation to changing conditions that still

permeates American business leadership.

These are the basic factors, but there are two more elements, arising in part at least from some combination of the above, that ought to be mentioned separately.

5. The presence of a domestic market that was both large in size and rich in its capacity to absorb new and high quality products strengthened the export position of the United States. The large American market, combined with the availability of capital and the pressures of competition, stimulated American firms to exploit the advantages of mass production at an earlier date and more extensively that foreign firms. It was the low costs of large size plants that gave the United States the opportunity to enter world markets for many manufactured goods. This was true for standard items such as apparel and farm implements which were produced in other countries by handicraft or small scale manufacturing industries. In addition, however, the wealth of the American market made it possible to cater to a demand for costly and high quality products by developing mechanized methods for their production. This applied not only to consumer durables but also to the improved machines and materials that were required for their production. Countries whose markets would not support the large-scale output of these products imported them from the United States. In a later stage they imported the improved machines and materials.

6. The movement toward the efficiency of mass production may be regarded as part of a broader search for cheaper methods of production and better or new products. In the 19th century, the "build a better mousetrap" motivation stimulated a flow of new inventions that were quickly inserted into the economic process. As research and development problems became more complicated, teams of specialists working with expensive equipment began to be developed in virtually every large firm. The result was that the American economy had a significant margin of technological superiority, and in many lines of production U.S. exports depended not so much upon the ability to quote favorable prices as upon the ability to offer qualities, designs, or basic products that could not be obtained elsewhere.

CHANGES IN THE AMERICAN POSITION

Basic forces operating both in the United States and the world at large seem to be weakening at least a number of these sources of strength in the American position. Let us take them one by one.

1. The advantage of cheap natural materials has been reduced by a number of factors. First of all the voracious appetite of the American industrial machine has chewed up significant portions of the original deposits of many ores. The once rich Mesabi range no longer yields huge quantities of rich ore but mainly the lower grade taconite. Iron ore, like copper, lead, and zinc which the United States once exported to other countries, must now be imported. The new sources of supply—Labrador, South America, Africa, and Asia—are often exploited by international companies in which entrepreneurs from different countries participate, and American buyers have no favored position vis-a-vis buyers from England, Germany, or other countries. Secondly, oil and natural gas have replaced coal as the lowest cost fuel and the availability of cheap Middle East oil has given our chief industrial rivals an important if sometimes embarrassing (for the coal-producing countries among them) opportunity to offset the advantage of cheap energy enjoyed by American manufacturers. Third, the advance of technology has reduced the relative advantage derived from having a domestic supply of raw materials. Part of this has been accomplished by the continuing revolution in transport which has been reducing the time and cost required to move heavy materials. Another part stems from the increasing economy in the use of natural materials in industry; according to one estimate, for example, natural inputs declined from 25 percent of the gross value of manufacturing output in the world's industrial areas in 1938 to 17.6 percent in 1955. An example of this tendency that has adversely affected the competitive position of an American industry is the reduction in the amount of coke required in the operation of blast furnaces; since coke is more expensive in Europe, the change is more favorable for Europe than for the United States.

On the other hand, the American economy has been a leader in the development of synthetic materials including such important products as artificial fibers, synthetic rubber, and plastics. To the extent that the latest variants of these products continue to be available first and most cheaply in the United States an offsetting advantage with respect to materials is enjoyed by the United States. The possession and extent of such an advantage turns upon technological leadership, discussed below.

2. The potential advantages of the United States in world agricultural markets are frustrated by governmental supports and controls. Although the U.S. Government is scarcely an exception to the almost universal tendency of governments to subsidize and protect agriculture, U.S. agriculture would probably be able to enlarge its export surplus in a free world market. In the world as it actually is, the trend toward increased output behind tariff and quota barriers threatens to limit further the ability of American agriculture to export its products.

3. The U.S. advantages derived from the possession of large amounts of capital have also tended to diminish. One reason—which is of recent origin and may prove to be temporary—is that many of the main competitors of the United States (Germany, France, and Japan, but not the United Kingdom) have increased their stocks of capital at a faster rate than the United States. The impact of the differential in growth rates is not, however, nearly so immediate as a different factor which operates so as to minimize the effect of the abundance of capital in the United States. The shrinkage of distance by phone and plane has increased the mobility of capital. The riskiness of investment in Western Europe has been greatly reduced by political stability, rapidly growing markets, strong currencies, and increased familiarity with European laws and business practices. The $18 billion outflow of private long-term capital from the United States during the past decade (exclusive of reinvested earnings) is the equivalent of 2 percent of the value of reproducible wealth of the United States and perhaps one-fifth that of a country such as Germany, France, or England. (Of course only about one-fourth has gone to Western Europe and a much smaller fraction to any one country, and the comparison with the wealth of these countries is intended only to give an impression of the magnitude of the outflow.)

4. Not only capital but also entrepreneurship has become more mobile; modern technology has expanded the geographical span of control to encompass the world. Thus two-thirds of the long-term private capital outflow of the past decade has been in the

form of direct investment. Direct investment is accompanied by American entrepreneurship, production know-how, and product design.

5. The increase in incomes in Western Europe and elsewhere has greatly expanded the size of the market and thus the opportunities for mass production of standard products such as apparel, of more costly items such as automobiles, and finally of the improved materials and machines required to produce the higher quality goods. This can be clearly seen in the automobile industry. One of the keys to the new-found ability of the Europeans to meet U.S. competition is a market now large enough to obtain an economical scale of output. In other parts of the world, such as Latin America, where the same techniques of production are available and wage rates are even lower than in Europe, automobile production costs are still high; the market in these places simply is not large enough to obtain the volume necessary for economical output. The dependence of the European automobile industry upon American materials and machines is also being reduced. Originally, a leading German automobile producer bought sheet steel from the United States because the desired quality was scarce in Europe. Now supplies are improving in Europe and prices are lower, and the German company's business may be kept only by special price concessions on the part of the American mill or as a result of a desire on the part of the auto manufacturer to maintain diverse sources of supply.

6. A number of factors have operated in the postwar period to minimize the effect upon international trade of the technological superiority enjoyed by U.S. industry. Shortly after the war, the U.S. Government, for good reasons, encouraged the export of American techniques to other countries. Thus the latest machinery and methods of production were incorporated in foreign plants often built with U.S. funds. In addition, the policies of foreign governments operated to offset the technological advantages enjoyed by the United States. In the first place, certain American companies which were permitted to sell in European markets found themselves holding large sums of inconvertible currencies. Although they had been accustomed to supplying their international operations from American sources, they thus found it desirable to cultivate European sources of supply. In some cases, this involved teaching European suppliers to meet the quality

requirements and design specifications that formerly had been available only from American sources. Secondly, many American firms found that they could overcome the barriers of tariffs, exchange controls, and Government purchasing policies only by establishing branches, subsidiaries, or licensees in Europe and elsewhere. More recently, of course, such moves into Europe have been motivated by more purely economic factors, such as higher profit margins, tax advantages, low labor costs, and closer proximity to the market, although tariffs and other Government policies still play a role. In any case, these establishments have the advantage of American know-how. According to a British estimate made about a half-dozen years ago, 25 to 30 percent of company-financed research in the United States was directly available to Britain through branches of American firms, and the resources this represented were greater than those spent by British industry as a whole upon research.

The effect of foreign affiliates upon U.S. exports and the U.S. balance of payments is not clear. There is some indication of a negative correlation between the expansion of U.S.-owned manufacturing production abroad and U.S. exports for given industries. Even if this is more firmly established, it is still possible that foreign affiliates stimulate U.S. exports through purchases of capital equipment, materials, complementary products (to fill out lines) and components more than they hurt them. In addition, it is claimed that foreign producers rather than U.S. home companies would win the foreign markets if the U.S. producers did not establish the foreign affiliates. This argument may have long-run validity, but it is weakened at the moment by the fact that the economies of the continental European countries have been working at capacity; it is not apparent therefore that the European producers would have been able to expand to take the business now enjoyed by the American affiliates. Finally, it is pointed out that the foreign affiliates held the balance of payments by giving rise to a stream of dividends, profits, and royalties, but this contention is set aside by some who stress the short-run effects of the immediate investment outlays upon the balance of payments.

Whether inevitable or induced by governmental policies or by the profit seeking responses of individual companies, it seems more probable that the effect of oversea affiliates and licensing will be adverse for the U.S. trade balance. They certainly appear likely to accelerate the speed with which knowledge of advanced U.S. methods is spread throughout the rest of the world.

Of course, these factors work both ways. European affiliates have been established in the United States and there are American companies that have been licensed to produce European and other foreign designs that are superior to those available in the United States. Nevertheless, an increase in the speed with which new products or methods are transferred is more advantageous for less advanced countries than for those that are in the forefront of technological development.

However, the diffusion of knowledge is scarcely likely to become instantaneous, and it would be of interest to know whether the United States is maintaining its past superiority in developing new methods and products. Research and development expenditures of the United States, it is known, are still many times that of other industrial countries, but it is not known whether the difference is narrowing or not. The importance of this question arises from the fact that the monopoly that an innovating country enjoys on a new product is almost always temporary; even without foreign affiliates or licensees, as knowledge of the new product spreads it is sooner or later successfully imitated abroad. In many cases it will turn out that the innovating country does not enjoy a long-run comparative advantage in producing the new product; thus it sees today's exports become tomorrow's imports. This has happened to a long list of American products from sewing machines to transistors. Furthermore, it is possible that the speed with which innovations are imitated or replaced by superior innovations may be increasing.

If the technological gap between the United States and other industrial countries is, indeed, narrowing, an important source of a demand for dollars is being weakened and the maintenance of our trade position being made more precarious. It is extremely difficult to assess what is happening in this area. One can point to important innovations that have recently come from other countries, but the importation of improved methods is not new. Thus, if one cites the recent import of the oxygen processes for steelmaking from Austria, Germany, or Sweden, it is possible to point to the earlier imports of the bessemer and open hearth processes from England and somewhat later, the extrusion process of squeezing cold steel into desired shapes from Italy. In one area, however, U.S. basic research and development work should be far ahead of that of other countries if the returns are at all proportionate to the investments that have been made—viz., atomic science. If this work begins to produce an economic return the margin of U.S. technological leadership may be strengthened.

More generally, rapid growth in output appears to favor innovation, and a maintenance of the recently developed superiority in the rates of growth of the Six and of Japan would not augur well for the United States. Full use of capacity in the United States with the consequent stimulus to investment (foreign as well as domestic financed) and innovation would, on this account at least, be beneficial to the trade balance.

POLITICAL FACTORS

No account of the American position in international trade, however short, would be complete without reference to the way in which it has been fortified by political factors. The relatively small importance of international trade to the American economy and the dispersion of retaliatory power among a fairly large number of trading partners left the United States free to use its great political power to limit or withdraw access to the domestic market whenever foreign producers made inroads that were damaging to American interests. Although the broader political compulsions to which the United States was subjected, especially after the beginning of the cold war, caused this power to be used rather sparingly, the very threat of its use reduced the incentives of foreign producers to make the investment required in many lines of industry to cultivate the U.S. market.

In the last few years, however, the situation has been changing. First, the balance-of-payments difficulties of the United States have for the first time in generations placed it in a position where a sensitive economic nerve was exposed to the good will of other countries. Second, the rise in relative economic power of other countries cannot be ignored. For example, the real gross national product of the five major members of the Common Market expanded from something like 40 percent of that of the United States in 1950 to 55 percent in 1960, and if the United Kingdom is added the change is from 60 percent in 1950 to 75 percent in

1960. The coalescence of other countries into trading blocs, of which the Common Market is the prime example, has enhanced the significance of these changes. Indeed the formation of these blocs may have a more lasting significance than the difference between EEC and U.S. rates of growth since the probability of survival is higher for the Common Market than for the growth gap.

THE IMPACT OF THE COMMON MARKET

The forces working against the U.S. trade position thus arise fundamentally from changes in the technology of transportation and communications and from basic changes in the economic structure of Western Europe. Western Europe has been the chief beneficiary of the enhanced geographical mobility of the elements that historically have been primarily sources of American advantage in international trade. Furthermore, Western Europe proceeds toward Americanization from an internal dynamic as well as from external effects flowing from the United States. As incomes rise, costly and high quality products begin to find domestic markets. Domestic industries arise to cater to these demands, and supplying industries develop to produce the improved materials and the new machines necessary to make the new goods.

These changes were flowing at full tide before the advent of the Common Market at the beginning of 1958, and the new organization has probably added to them only marginally. It is easy to exaggerate the purely economic impact of the Common Market upon its members. The Six were growing rapidly before they joined together as well as afterwards; indeed in the 4 years preceding the Common Market (1953–57) industrial production in the six countries combined expanded by 40 percent and their trade with one another by 78 percent, while in the 4 ensuing years (1957–61) the corresponding percentages were 30 and 64, respectively. The real threat posed by the organization of the Common Market for the trade position of the United States is the greater concentration of economic and political power than had previously existed, particularly since there are built-in factors that may cause this power to be used in ways that will be harmful to American exports.

Before turning to these political aspects, however, let us examine briefly the respects in which the advent of the Common Market brings or accelerates economic changes that weaken the U.S. trade position.

In the first place, the Common Market institutions may have had some effect in producing more rational practices with respect to certain raw materials than might otherwise have been followed. The complete elimination of tariffs and other restrictions on intracommunity trade in coal and steel, achieved under the European Coal and Steel Community (ECSC), reduced transport costs by rationalizing channels of distribution. In coal, for example, mines near national boundaries began to serve areas determined by economic rather than political factors. There are some signs also that the European Communities (i.e., the ECSC, EEC, and Euratom) aided by pressure from the Italians (who have no coal and depend upon cheap oil from external sources), will hasten the process of relaxing restrictions against the import of oil so as to obtain cheap energy supplies despite unfavorable effects on coal. Belgium has surely gone farther in closing down high cost coal mines than she would have been able to do without the political and economic support of the ECSC. Of course, there are some offsetting policies which tend to raise material costs, but these affect mainly tropical products from French-associated areas in Africa and are probably less important in their overall impact upon materials costs than the policies relating to coal and steel.

Secondly, the Common Market has dramatized the European market and made it more attractive to American capital and enterprise. The Common Market thus has tended to accelerate the process by which American enterprise, technology, and capital rather than American goods move across the ocean.

Third, the formation of the Common Market seems to have provided a stimulus to the growth of large size firms. A wave of mergers, affiliations, and understandings has probably led to larger size and lower cost plants, and has increased the degree of product specialization in plants of a given size. It has led also to larger firms which are more strongly placed with respect to research, finance, and foreign marketing than the smaller ones they replaced. The extent and significance of merger movement in the Common Market are difficult to assess. It is conceivable that what is going on is merely an adjustment by business to the new situation created by the prospect of free trade within the

Community. If so, the policy of live and let live, which seems to have characterized Western European business psychology to a greater degree than that of the United States, may soon reassert itself. It is possible that this attitude was as responsible as the inherent limitations of a market of the size of say England or France or Germany for the existence of smaller scale plants than in America. Of course, the EEC has taken steps to implement the anti-cartel provisions of the Rome Treaty, but whether European business will become imbued with a new competitive spirit either through self- or official-inspiration is far from clear. In any case, at the moment there has been a clear gain in efficiency from the rationalization movement that has taken place.

Fourth, the formation of the Common Market has made a contribution to the rate of growth, and thus created a greater market and a greater opportunity for the mass production of standard items and for the large scale production of more costly goods that were almost an American monopoly. In TV and radio, for example, the European market is already on a par with that of the United States in the quality of the product which it can absorb; in most other consumer durables, however, it is 10 to 30 years behind the United States. Of course, the expansion of the European market has been a boon to American exports thus far; it has offset any tendency for trade diversion to hurt U.S. exports. Indeed, U.S. exports to the Common Market have expanded more rapidly than U.S. exports as a whole since 1957 or 1958. However, the European boom can hardly last forever, and when the domestic absorption of European output slackens, U.S. producers may feel the full impact of the new capacities of European firms to produce goods in varieties, qualities, and quantities which formerly could be obtained only in the United States. Many American businessmen fear just this. They feel that their European competitors have been satisfied to follow the price leadership of American firms in the American and sometimes in other markets; this enables European firms, in view of their lower costs, to enjoy high profit margins on their foreign business at a time when their plants are occupied with domestic orders anyway. Of course, if the European countries succeed in maintaining full employment economies with only mild and infrequent recessions further European inroads on markets held by the United States will depend upon the longer-run growth of European capacity.

Finally, the agricultural policy of the Common Market threatens to increase the degree of self-sufficiency of the area by stimulating the expansion of internal production. New export surpluses such as French wheat have already appeared, and if high internal prices are added to the system of variable levies giving preference to Community products, the United States which has been exporting over $1 billion of agricultural products to the Common Market may find itself reduced to the position of a residual supplier especially for grains. Unlike the other factors we have listed, this one involves competition between United States and European producers only for the markets of the Community itself. To the extent that it will affect competition for other markets, it will be unfavorable to the EEC because it will tend to raise the level of costs.

With the possible exception of the last factor, the adverse influences upon U.S. trade that we have discussed thus far have stemmed from economic changes. The most important consequences of the Common Market for the U.S. trade position are, however, likely to flow from a new political fact: For the first time in many decades the United States is faced in the Western World with an almost equal aggregation of economic and political power. The uncoordinated, sometimes conflicting, and often offsetting policies pursued by six governments are being replaced by coordinated decisions reached in Brussels. Even without the addition of new members, the decisions are taken on behalf of countries whose combined importance in world trade already equals or exceeds that of the United States and who provide a significant fraction of the U.S. export surplus. The bargaining power of the Common Market, already substantial, will of course be further increased if Great Britain and other new members and associates are admitted. As the geographical scope of the Common Market is expanded, it will embrace an increasingly diversified area and will become more self-sufficient and less dependent upon external trade than the individual member countries have been. Thus, like the United States, the new entity will have considerable leeway for deciding upon more or less liberal policies.

How will this power be used? Some parts of the answer seem clear. In the first place, the power of the Common Market is likely to be used to retaliate promptly and fully in response to any adverse actions taken in trade matters by another country, including the United States. This has recently been illustrated by the action of the Council of Ministers of the EEC in raising the common external tariff on a half-dozen product groups in reprisal for U.S. increases under the GATT escape clause in the duties on carpets and glass. This type of response may be expected not only because of the natural tendency for partners to support an aggrieved member (Belgium, in the carpet and glass case) against an outsider, but also because of the psychology underlying commercial policy in Western Europe. In the latter connection, it is not much of an exaggeration to describe the postwar history of the dismantlement of trade barriers in Western Europe as a story of careful horsetrading in which no concession was given without extracting one of equal value. In the past, however, retaliatory action by European countries against American protective measures has been infrequent and never so prompt and forthright; countries almost always awaited the negotiation of compensatory concessions from the United States to replace the ones that had been withdrawn. The past patience of European countries may, of course, be attributable to the fact that their quantitative restrictions against American goods were still in effect, and as long as this was the case they could not feel quite so ill treated by U.S. actions. However, it may also have been due in part to the absence of a mechanism such as the Common Market which has the power to retaliate effectively and without the fear of the consequences that a small country acting alone would have.

A second factor affecting the use of the power that the EEC has is the inherent tendency of any large area composed of diverse interests to reconcile conflicts over the resolution of domestic difficulties by shifting as much of the burden of adjustment to outsiders as possible. This is evident in U.S. commercial policy. For example, the extensive protection accorded by the United States to its textile industry, including high tariffs and new legislation authorizing the establishment of import quotas, reflects pressures arising from the failure of domestic consumption of textile products to expand as rapidly as productivity, with the result that employment levels have been declining. In the short history of the Common Market, there are already a number of illustrations of this tendency to resolve difficulties by cutting off the outsider. These include instances of troubles caused by shortages as well as those caused by surpluses. The most important case involving a surplus, which related to coal, developed in the late 1950's. The desirability of a reduction in imports from the United States and other third countries was virtually the only point on which the Six could agree in their prolonged and difficult negotiations on means of meeting the coal crisis. Analogous action was taken in a number of cases involving shortages; for example, last spring the European Commission recommended to the Dutch Government that it permit the normal volume of potato exports to member countries and restrict exports to third countries.

Even if it seems reasonable to suppose that the Common Market will retaliate when the occasion arises and shift the burden of adjustments to third countries when internal difficulties develop, there remains a large and important area of doubt about the way in which the Community will wield the great power which its size and importance confers upon it. Although the Rome Treaty contains a clause stating that the member countries intend to follow a liberal commercial policy (art. 110), the commitment is quite general and could conceivably be subordinated to other objectives of the Six. At the risk of some oversimplification, one might say that there are two schools of thought within the Community on this matter. One school, for which the French are the spokesmen on many issues, takes the view that the Community represents, among other things, a club for the mutual benefit of the member countries at the expense of outsiders. This position has been generally opposed by the Dutch and also by the Germans, both of whom tend to prefer more liberal trading policies for the Community. Of course, the difference is one of degree, albeit an important one, because some element of tariff discrimination in favor of fellow members is the essence of a customs union. While it is true that the conception of the EEC goes far beyond a mere customs union, it is also true that the most immediate practical attraction of the EEC to participants and would-be participants is its customs union feature.

Toward the Next Round of Trade Negotiations

ROBERT E. BALDWIN

Robert E. Baldwin is a Professor of Economics at the University of Wisconsin. In this essay, written in September 1967 for the Subcommittee on Foreign Economic Policy of the Joint Economic Committee of the U.S. Congress, he surveys the history of multilateral trade negotiations and makes recommendations for making future negotiations more effective.

IT IS WELL TO BEGIN a discussion of future trade legislation by recalling that the official name of the recently concluded Kennedy Round is the sixth round of General Agreement on Tariffs and Trade (GATT) trade negotiations. In other words, unique though these negotiations have been in several respects, they represent but one of a series of trade liberalization efforts that originated 20 years ago. Indeed, one must go back a third of a century to the Trade Agreements Act of 1934 in order to put the Kennedy Round in proper perspective. At that time, as a result of the Tariff Acts of 1921 and 1922 and then the Smoot-Hawley Act of 1930, tariffs were at their highest levels in the nation's history. However, since the first Trade Agreements Act, the United States has become the leader in a significant worldwide reduction in duty levels. Although simple averages are notoriously poor indicators of the restrictive effects of tariffs, a rough notion of the extent of these liberalization efforts can be obtained by pointing out that the average (weighted by trade volume) duty level in 1934 was 48 percent whereas it will be around 8 percent after the Kennedy Round reductions.

The purpose of this paper is to review briefly the history of the negotiations that have brought about this liberalization and then to focus upon certain problems these negotiations have failed to solve adequately. It will be argued that further significant progress in reducing protectionist levels is dependent upon a more successful handling of these problems.

AN OUTLINE OF PREVIOUS NEGOTIATIONS

The Period 1934–45 · The period between 1934 and 1967 can be divided conveniently into three subperiods as far as the history of U.S. commercial policy is concerned. The first extends from 1934 to 1945; the second from 1946 to 1961; and the third from 1962 to the present. In 1934, the President was given the power to undertake trade negotiations with other countries for the purpose of securing reciprocal tariff reductions that, on our part, could go as far as cutting then existing duties in half. Prior to the original Trade Agreements Act, efforts to secure reciprocal tariff reductions had not met with much success. The executive branch had sought to conclude formal treaties with various countries on several occasions but only three ever were ratified by both parties—the last being with Cuba in 1902. Obtaining the necessary two-thirds majority vote of the U.S. Senate in most cases proved to be an impossible task, since it was necessary to specify the particular items proposed for duty reduction in each case. This difficulty was avoided under the 1934 legislation by giving the President considerable power to undertake reciprocal reductions covering a broad range of items. Since 1930, the Congress has not passed a tariff act, but instead granted the President the authority on successive occasions to continue to reduce (and to raise) the general level of duties.

The trade agreements concluded between 1934 and 1945 were bilateral in nature. Thirty-one agreements were negotiated between these years. The technique employed was that the two parties concentrated upon reducing duties on those items for which each tended to be the principal supplier for the other. The mutual tariff reductions agreed upon were then generalized to all traders with both parties. This approach had both advantages and disadvantages. The main drawback was that, by extending the duty cuts to all countries, nonparticipants were able to increase their exports to the two countries without also opening up their economies to greater imports. In view of the existence of widespread unemployment in most countries during this period coupled with the notion of reciprocal concessions contained in the legislation, efforts to avoid this "free ride" aspect of bilateral negotiations were made by confining the cuts between two countries to a small number of items in which each was the other's main supplier. Items for which there was no single overwhelming supplier or countries who were not major suppliers of any item tended to be neglected. Even between two countries, where the principal-supplier trade was highly unbalanced, it was impossible to reduce one party's tariffs the same percentage as the other's and still achieve an acceptable balance of concessions for each. On the other hand, the bilateral technique with its concentration upon principal-supplier items permitted a movement toward freer trade without requiring the consent of all major trading nations. Clearly, during the thirties it would have been impossible to proceed on any other than the step-by-step basis actually adopted.

The Period 1945–61 · At the end of World War II, there was a widespread desire to deal on a cooperative, multilateral basis with economic problems that had important international repercussions. Consequently, the opportunity arose for undertaking tariff negotiations not on a country-by-country basis over time but on a multilateral basis at a given time. The arrangement in which this opportunity was seized and made workable was the GATT. In 1947, 22 nations completed a multilateral tariff cutting exercise that resulted in concessions on nearly two-thirds of total world trade. The United States negotiated under the additional 50 percent cutting power that Congress had granted the President in 1945.

Besides establishing an organization through which periodic multilateral tariff negotiations designed to reduce duty levels could be undertaken, the GATT set forth a code of commercial policy. The most-favored-nations principle is the cornerstone of the GATT. The first article of the Agreement specifies in detail that each nation shall grant nondiscriminatory treatment to the products of all other contracting nations with regard to import and export duties and subsidiary charges, rules, and formalities in connection with importation and exportation, and internal taxes and other internal regulations. A second basic principle is the general prohibition of quantitative restrictions as a protective device. Except under special circumstances, only customs duties can be used for this purpose.

The United States participated in two additional rounds of

tariff negotiations within the GATT framework under the 50 percent cutting authority granted in 1945. One was held at Annecy, France, in 1949 at which 10 more countries became contracting parties to the General Agreement and another at Torquay, England, in 1950–51. In 1955, the Congress again gave the President additional tariff cutting authority but considerably less than it gave in 1934 and 1945. The new authority permitted him to reduce duties by an additional 15 percent over a three-year period. With these powers the United States participated in the fourth round of GATT negotiations in 1956. This session at Geneva dealt with the accession of Japan to the GATT.

The negotiating session prior to the recent Kennedy Round was the so-called Dillon Round (named after the then Secretary of the Treasury) in 1960–61. This was the first negotiation held after the formation of the European Economic Community (EEC). The objective of the United States was to obtain a reduction in the common external tariff of the EEC in order to offset at least partially the trade diversion caused by reducing duties within the EEC toward zero. Consequently, in 1958 Congress gave the President the authority to reduce duties by another 20 percent.

The five rounds of negotiations under the GATT between 1947 and 1960–61 represent an outstandingly successful example of productive international cooperation. Not only were tariffs among the industrial nations reduced significantly but the highly restrictive structure of quantitative controls erected for balance-of-payments purposes at the end of the war were gradually dismantled.

The Period 1962–67 · After the disappointing Dillon Round, however, a view began to develop to the effect that the traditional technique of bargaining was inadequate for achieving further significant liberalization of world trade. The technique employed within the GATT was item-by-item bargaining in an essentially bilateral series of simultaneous negotiations. It was argued that this negotiating method tended to limit both the scope and depth of tariff reductions. Domestic pressures within each country were, it was claimed, more successful in excluding many items on the basis of particular reasons than would be the case if an across-the-board tariff-cutting approach were used.

In addition, it was noted that, when one country excluded important items in a particular industry, other participants tended to exclude for bargaining purposes their important import items in the same industry. The outcome tended to be a negotiation confined to items in which no severe import competition problem existed in any country and therefore in which no one was particularly interested. Participants also adopted the restrictive bargaining attitude of giving up as little as possible in return for as much as possible.

Given these apparent drawbacks of the item-by-item approach coupled with the growing diversionary effects of the EEC on outside trade as internal duties were decreased, the Kennedy administration sought the power to undertake a sweeping negotiation, especially with the EEC, that would bring about a significant cut in duty levels among the industrial nations. The outcome of these efforts was the Trade Expansion Act of 1962 followed by the Kennedy, or sixth, round of GATT negotiations. The essential authority granted under the Trade Expansion Act was the power to reduce duties by 50 percent over a five-year period. A unique feature was the authority to cut duties to zero on items for which the EEC and the United States accounted for at least 80 percent of world trade. The act also contained language permitting the President to negotiate on nontariff barriers.

The history of the four years of negotiations in the Kennedy Round is too well known to require more than a few sentences. In terms of what the United States hoped to accomplish, the results cannot be regarded as other than disappointing. The average cut is more like one-third than one-half. Since Britain was not admitted to the Common Market, the 80-percent provision pertaining to United States–EEC trade became irrelevant. No significant progress was made in beginning to dismantle the complex set of controls that protect important sectors of agriculture in most industrial countries. The nontariff-barrier field also received little attention. However, despite the length of the negotiations and the wide gap between expectations and accomplishment, the Kennedy Round will be regarded in the future as a considerable success. For, compared with previous GATT tariff-cutting exercises, this round stands out as the one involving the deepest average tariff reduction.

PROBLEMS FOR FUTURE NEGOTIATIONS

The last two rounds of GATT negotiations have, however, made it increasingly clear that certain key problems must be dealt with more adequately if further liberalization efforts are to be successful. In a real sense, these problems have arisen because of the very success of previous liberalization efforts. These efforts have eliminated the protection that was largely superfluous and increasingly cut into those areas where significant resource reallocation effects are produced by the reductions. We must deal with the hard core of protection from now on, if further expansion of world trade is to be encouraged. In doing so, several difficult problems must be met. Three of the more important ones are as follows: (1) Achieving a better balance between consumer and producer interests in economically vulnerable industries; (2) Mitigating the restrictive effects of nontariff barriers; (3) Making the negotiating process more effective in achieving its goal of trade liberalization.

1. Achieving a Better Balance Between Consumer and Producer Interests in Economically Vulnerable Industries · This is the key domestic problem in any tariff-cutting exercise. Yet it is one that has not been adequately handled since the first Trade Agreements Act of 1934. The issue can be simply stated. Since the time of Adam Smith, economists have been able to show that —setting aside infant-industry and term-of-trade effects—it is possible for a country to raise its real income level under free trade compared to a system of tariff protection. However, although the gain to consumers in the form of lower prices is more than enough to compensate the producers of protected products from any loss they suffer, in practice such compensation is not made. In industries where workers and employers can readily find alternative employment, the adverse effects of tariff cuts are minor. But in industries where employment and profits are already declining because of increased imports or competition from some other domestic or foreign industries; where the workers are older, less skilled, and less educated than most workers; and where the areas in which the industries are located are depressed generally, then the costs of greater import competition can be high for a small group. It is true that even under these conditions there is usually a net gain in the sense that the gainers from lower prices could conceivably compensate those losing their employment. However, in the actual situation where compensation is not made, it is understandable for members of both the legislative and executive branches of the Government to give greater weight to the large loss suffered by a few people than the more-than-offsetting gain distributed very thinly over many people. Obviously, the typical legislator knows that he is likely to lose votes on balance if he sacrifices the losses of the few for the greater, but thinly spread, gain to the many. But instead of this representing a regrettable fact of politics—as some seem to suggest—I suspect it reflects the actual value judgments of the people in general. In other words, the general public does regard a larger gain spread over many people as inferior to a smaller total loss that falls on a relatively few. However, they would prefer even more a situation where those who were severely hurt economically were given the resources needed for their successful adjustment and where there still remained a consumer gain.

In the past this problem has been handled mainly by refraining from cutting duties on those industries that might suffer a severe loss or by refraining from cutting to the level where such losses would be incurred. President Roosevelt and Secretary of State Cordell Hull pledged themselves not to cut in industries where substantial injury would be caused. In postwar trade legislation, the notions of the peril point—that is, the duty level below which substantial injury would be caused—and of the escape clause—that is, a modification of a previously granted tariff concession due to injury-causing increased imports—were introduced to handle the problem. Finally, in the 1962 act provisions for adjustment assistance in the form of extended unemployment payments, retraining and relocation allowances, low-interest-rate loans, technical advisory services, and so forth, were introduced in order to meet the problems connected with a 50-percent, across-the-board cut.

This trade adjustment assistance portion of the Trade Expansion Act represents a major innovation in dealing with the balance problem between consumer and producer interests. However, the provision is phrased in such narrow terms that in practice it seems unlikely to be an important source of adjustment assistance.

The assistance provided is also on a meager scale. What is needed to deal with the tariff-cutting problem as well as—even more importantly—with the broad problem of adjusting to technological progress within the domestic economy is a general adjustment assistance act. Otherwise, we shall soon arrive at that level of tariffs where substantial potential overall gains remain but where, because of the hardships imposed upon some in obtaining these gains, they are not tapped.

2. *Mitigating the Restrictive Effects of Nontariff Barriers* · Besides having to deal with the hard core of tariff protection, we are increasingly becoming aware of the restrictive nature of nontariff obstacles to trade. Nontariff barriers that were superfluous in their restrictive impact when duty levels were high have become effective deterrents to increased trade as these duties have declined. An added reason why these barriers are likely to become more significant is the probable tendency for countries to introduce new nontariff devices and to enforce old ones more vigorously in order to offset the internal adjustment burdens of tariff restrictions under the Kennedy Round.

An elaboration of the many nontariff barriers that are important in world trade today would require a lengthy paper in itself. The typical classification divides them into the following groups: (1) quantitative controls and state trading; (2) government procurement policy; (3) customs valuation and practices; (4) antidumping legislation and practices; (5) border tax adjustments. Actually, this list covers only a portion of the laws, rules, practices (public and private) distorting trade in a manner that discriminates between domestic and foreign producers. All of the above measures distort trade in a direct and obvious manner. But businessmen have become increasingly concerned with trade distortions brought about indirectly by laws, practices, taxes, and subsidies aimed at domestic activities. These include: (6) domestic subsidies, for example, maritime and other transportation subsidies, agricultural subsidies, research and development subsidies, and special tax benefits; (7) domestic taxes and regulations; and (8) monopolistic practices in private product and factor markets.

Although it is easy to recognize the trade-restricting effects of nontariff barriers, it is a much harder task to suggest how best to reduce these effects on a worldwide basis. The Kennedy Round has not produced much progress along these lines. The tariff-reducing aspects of the negotiations were so difficult and time consuming that it was not possible to launch a major effort to reduce nontariff barriers. However, enough was learned to realize that these are much more difficult to deal with than duties. A major reason for this is because import protection or export promotion is not the main purpose of many of these trade-distorting measures. For example, in parts of agriculture, the coal industry, and the textiles field, nontariff barriers are often only an incidental part of a set of measures designed to ease the adjustment of sectors that are depressed for reasons quite unrelated to import competition. In other cases, the trade distortions are byproducts of measures designed to meet goals that may conflict with economic efficiency in a narrowly defined sense. The various nontariff measures designed to promote national defense fit this category. Similarly, policies whose objectives are to redistribute income, for example, minimum wage legislation, or to increase national prestige, for example, the space program, fall into this grouping.

Clearly, one cannot expect nations to abandon these goals simply for a more rational distribution of world resources devoted to foreign trade. There may be opportunities to modify some of these goals over a long-run period of time, but short-run policy usually must take them as "given." The best that can be done under these circumstances is to try to eliminate needless conflicts among policy measures. For example, the approach followed by most countries in meeting the agricultural problem needlessly sacrifices the benefits of economic efficiency. Temporary income-support payments coupled with measures to attract excess resources out of agriculture are much preferable on efficiency grounds and yet also can prevent undue distributive hardships. The same points apply in such industries as coal and textiles. Maintenance of adequate defense capacity in certain industries also can often be achieved in a manner that does not sacrifice the gains from international trade.

The changes required to obtain these trade benefits are primarily modifications in domestic policies. Easing trade restrictions will only be a byproduct of these domestic changes. This means, of course, that negotiations with the purpose of modifying simultaneously both internal and external policies are necessary. As the Kennedy Round discussions of the world agricultural problem have indicated, successful negotiations of this type are, however, most difficult to achieve. Thus, we face a formidable task in any further efforts to expand significantly the benefits of trade. Some of the most serious distortions in world trade are the indirect consequence of domestic policies, yet these are the kinds of measures that are the most difficult to modify. Only if there is a general desire among the major trading nations at the highest political level to modify these policies will such negotiations succeed. Furthermore, it may be that the main push of any efforts to change these domestic measures must be directed initially more at harmonization than at significant liberalization. Suggestions to standardize and harmonize various trade restricting measures on a sector approach have met with some success in the present negotiations and may be a useful approach for future negotiations. Then, as harmonization is achieved, it may be easier to reduce the trade-restrictive impact of domestic policies.

3. Making the Negotiating Process More Effective ·

(a) *The reciprocity problem*—As John Evans has pointed out so well in his book for the Council on Foreign Relations, *U.S. Trade Policy—New Legislation for the Next Round,* Harper & Row, 1967, the notion of reciprocity as interpreted in the actual negotiations has hampered the move toward trade liberalization. In these negotiations, each party tends to regard any tariff cut by himself as bad and any cut by other parties as good. Consequently, unless each party is convinced that its exports will increase as much as its imports, it pulls back some of its offers to achieve this objective. This in turn sets off a chain of further withdrawals producing the end result that the country with the smallest offer tends to set the standard cut. The principal-supplier technique helps to avoid this in part but the general tendency is clear.

Countries with initially low average duties are put in an especially difficult position. They may be prepared to cut completely to zero, but they know that higher duty countries will consider reciprocity to be achieved before they themselves reach a zero level. Thus, the former countries could be left with zero duties of their own and no bargaining power to use in order to obtain further tariff reductions from other countries.

It probably must be taken as a given constraint of any tariff-cutting exercise that the cuts should not result in any significant increase in a country's balance-of-trade deficit. Moreover, given the unwillingness to use other policies for balance-of-payments adjustment purposes, this means that the direct and indirect effects of the multilateral tariff cuts by themselves must not cause a significant export-import imbalance. However, this general constraint still leaves considerable latitude to the negotiators. Moreover, studies made thus far seem to indicate that as far as the United States is concerned rather significant changes in U.S. versus foreign offers produce only a small net effect on the U.S. balance of trade. The feedback effects are very strong. Yet negotiators easily become caught up in the give-and-take spirit of bargaining sessions and tend to forget the larger purpose of the whole exercise. The result is that some of the benefits to all countries from trade expansion tend to be sacrificed.

(b) *Tariff-cutting techniques*—The interesting aspect of this problem is that the negotiators are not under any legislative directive to adopt this narrow view of reciprocity but have tended to establish it themselves. This perhaps means that the nature of the negotiations should be changed. Indeed, this was one of the initial objectives of the Kennedy Round. Instead of item-by-item bargaining, an across-the-board cutting procedure was to be followed. Implicit in this was the notion that approximately equal percentage cuts (weighted by trade volumes) would achieve reciprocity. We have learned in the Kennedy Round, however, that such a simple technique cannot stand up to the economic and political realities of any negotiation.

In the future, we should try to follow simple tariff-cutting techniques that minimize the negativeness of item-by-item bargaining, but we must also be highly flexible with regard to alternative techniques. The objective is to reduce duties without causing undue hardships domestically. With a vigorous adjustment assistance program coupled with the notion of achieving a general balance of concessions, we can best implement this goal by using a variety of techniques. This might involve some general percentage formula for most items, sector-by-sector negotiations in certain areas, and item-by-item in others. This is the procedure eventually followed in the Kennedy Round. Had it been followed from the beginning, the negotiations might long ago have been completed. In short, we need a balance between simple tariff-cutting procedures and direct negotiations in sensitive areas. In the Kennedy Round, we initially were too rigid on a particular simple tariff-cutting formula; namely, the linear-cut concept. A greater willingness to consider sympathetically other types of cutting formulas might have accelerated the negotiations and deepened the average cut. Yet, all items cannot be covered by simple rules. Negotiations on particular sectors still will be needed. However, if one starts out by trying to negotiate all cuts on an item-by item basis, this, too, will lessen the average tariff reduction.

The Atlantic Case

HARRY G. JOHNSON

Harry G. Johnson is Professor of Economics at the University of Chicago and the London School of Economics and Political Science. In this essay, first published in the May 18, 1967 issue of New Society, *he argues the case for establishing a North Atlantic Free Trade Area.*

THE GOVERNMENT HAS NOW MADE its formal application for United Kingdom membership in the Common Market. Yet the alternatives remain relevant. The road to Rome is paved with complex negotiating problems; and even if these are eventually successfully surmounted, the question will remain of what form relations between the reconstituted Europe and the other advanced industrial countries should take. This article examines the merits of the most obvious positive alternative to membership in the Common Market, the formation of a North Atlantic Free Trade Area.

In a very important sense, the notion of an Atlantic free trade area had its genesis over 20 years ago, in the planning for postwar international economic reconstruction that produced the International Monetary Fund, the World Bank, and the General Agreement on Tariffs and Trade (GATT). The designers of GATT had in their minds the vision—however remotely it might lie in the future—of a system of free international trade, to be established gradually by negotiation of tariff reductions among the leading industrial powers—which were then as now the North Atlantic nations. This vision acquired concreteness and immediacy with the formation of the North Atlantic Treaty Organization (NATO). In the minds of many NATO supporters, economic integration in the fields of trade and international finance was a logical corollary of military partnership; but as it turned out, the concept of economic partnership was stillborn. Instead, the continental European countries proceeded to develop a much narrower and more exclusive form of economic integration, which culminated in the formation of the European Common Market.

At that stage, Britain attempted unsuccessfully to encompass the movement towards continental European integration in a broader, more outward-looking, and looser scheme for a European Free Trade Area, the survivor of which effort is the present-day European Free Trade Association (EFTA).

The successful initiation of the European Common Market, with Britain and the other EFTA countries firmly excluded (at least for the time being), threatened to bring to an abrupt end the progress that had thus far been made in negotiating nondiscriminatory tariff reductions through GATT, and to divide the Western world into mutually exclusive trading blocs. This division would have been sharpened if Britain had been successful in her second attempt at integration with the continental European countries: the Macmillan application for admission to the European Economic Community (EEC). The United States under President Kennedy made an imaginative response to this danger—the Trade Expansion Act, 1962.

THE "KENNEDY ROUND"

This assumed that Britain would succeed in gaining entry to the EEC. The passage of the act was preceded in the United States by much discussion of the desirability of providing economic underpinnings for the Atlantic Alliance; and the key provision of the act was designed to empower the administration to negotiate what would have amounted to a free trade area in major industrial products between the United States and Europe, though without the overt discrimination against the less developed countries of the world that is involved in a customs union of the European Common Market type. This was the so-called "dominant supplier authority," which empowered the President to negotiate the complete elimination of tariffs on industrial product groups in which the United States and the Common Market countries between them conducted 80 per cent or more of Free World trade.

The abrupt rejection of Britain's second attempt to come to terms with the EEC unfortunately knocked the lynch pin—the dominant supplier authority—out of the Trade Expansion Act, since without Britain in the Common Market few industrial products remained qualified for negotiation under that authority; and the American administration was forced to fall back on its second string, its authority to negotiate up to 50 per cent tariff cuts across the board.

Initially, it was believed that such a bargaining approach would be an attractive enough proposition to the EEC. But the negotiations in the so-called "Kennedy Round" have been difficult and protracted—and for a year were suspended owing to internal disagreement in the Common Market over their common agricultural policy. This week the "Kennedy Round" negotiations have belatedly succeeded in reaching an agreement; but the terms fall far short of what was originally intended and it is clear that this particular exercise will never be repeated.

It is in the light of this experience—fundamentally, an experience of frustration of progress towards freer world trade along GATT lines by the inward-looking protectionism of the EEC—that the proposals being advanced for a North Atlantic Free Trade Area should be understood.

Those people who are concerned with maintaining and reinforcing the progress towards reduction of barriers to trade that has been made since the Second World War have been searching for several years for a new approach. The aim is to enable the nations that agree on the desirability of freer trade to continue to work towards it in the stage after the "Kennedy Round," without being impeded by dependence on the assent of the Common Market countries, and if possible by means that would be more attractive to the Six than the "Kennedy Round."

There is a great variety of alternative approaches available, including regional common markets, preferential arrangements, conditional most-favored-nations negotiations, and the sector-by-sector freeing of trade recently favored by the Government of Canada. But consideration of these alternatives strongly suggests the superiority of a free trade arrangement, and specifically of a free trade arrangement to be based initially on free trade among the EFTA countries, the United States and Canada, but to be open-ended in the sense of envisaging the eventual participation of Australia, New Zealand, and Japan and, if they so choose, the Common Market countries—in which case the arrangement would effectively have established a system of world free trade.

NATIONAL AUTONOMY

In the first place, this proposal is consistent with the rules of GATT, to which the prospective members are all contracting parties.

In the second place, a free trade area preserves the autonomy of member-countries on their tariff policies towards non-participants. There is no need to unify commercial policies against outsiders, or to jettison long-standing economic relationships with outside countries derived from political and cultural ties. Still less is there any need while doing so to pretend that one is "safeguarding the essential interests" of such countries. There is also minimal need for coordination of other economic policies, and such coordination as might be necessary could be worked out in the light of experience.

Third, a free trade area is a purely commercial arrangement, carrying no obligation of eventual political federation or union, but only a commitment to exercising national autonomy reasonably and in good faith. This is an important practical political point: while nations may delude themselves into believing that they will automatically assume leadership in a political federation, the other members will be equally determined to prevent them from being successful, with resulting political tensions.

Fourth, and with reference to the economic consequences, complete free trade within a reasonably large international market area has an advantage over partial free trade in the world market (the state of affairs so far established under GATT, and likely to be the situation under GATT-style tariff bargaining for a long time ahead). It guarantees maximum freedom of access to the large market and therefore permits enterprises to exploit the economies of specialization, division of labor, and large-scale production in a really large competitive market.

This consideration has been important in recent thinking about trade policy alternatives in Canada, where a great deal of economic research has confirmed that the benefits that might accrue to Canada in this way are substantial. It has also been an important element of the case for British entry into the Common Market. Indeed, as recent examination of that case has shown, any economic argument for entry has to rest on faith that the benefits from increased economies of scale that may open up will be sufficient to offset the concrete net disadvantages of membership to Britain's trade and the costs of participating in the Common Market's agricultural policy. This must be an exercise in faith, because no economic research comparable to what has been done in Canada has yet been produced in this country. But if this is the basis of the case for joining the Common Market, there is an even stronger case on the same grounds for seeking free trade with the world's richest market and most technologically advanced economy, the United States.

ALTERNATIVES FOR BRITAIN

The obvious—and rational and intellectually defensible—line to adopt at that point would be:

1. What Britain has really been seeking in her quest after Europe has been, in economic terms, not integration with Europe as such, but the opportunity to compete in a larger market in order to increase the efficiency of her industries.

2. The countries of the Common Market were a natural first choice on the basis of history and geographical propinquity. But Britain has a worthy second string to her bow, comprising the overseas English-speaking countries and the other peripheral countries of Europe with which she has already succeeded in working out free trade arrangements.

3. While a free trade arrangement on this basis would involve additional problems for British policy, it would in various ways be a more comfortable and congenial joint enterprise. Similarly, it could be argued in political terms that, while Britain could hope for a position of political leadership in Europe, based essentially on the quality of British political civilization and the depth of British political experience, those same qualities are equally an asset in the Commonwealth and in the United States.

Adoption of these arguments would necessitate recognizing that Britain has in an important sense been hoping for something for nothing from admission to the EEC—economic strengthening plus unearned political leadership—but such recognition would probably in itself be an important step towards facing the country's real economic and political problems (which are in all probability not nearly so agonizing as the popular arguments for rushing into Europe at any cost imply).

Thus it will remain essential to consider seriously the proposals for the formation of a North Atlantic Free Trade Area. The greatest obstacle to such consideration is that the proposals are too sensible—they lack the sex appeal of a hazardous enterprise in political seduction—and hence tend to be dismissed out of hand by those who are asked to think sensibly about problems they are accustomed to handle by emotional reactions. Three such instinctive negative gut-reactions are commonly encountered in any discussion of the proposals.

The *first gut-reaction* is that it is a waste of decent people's time to discuss the proposals, since it is obvious that the United States would never participate in such arrangements.

U.S. ECONOMIC POLICY CHANGES

It is always dangerous to assume that one can predict other countries' policy positions, and especially to assume that these cannot be revised in the light of changing circumstances. It is particularly so with respect to the foreign economic policy of the United States, which changed rapidly and to Britain's advantage on several occasions since the war. Two examples will serve as illustration. At the end of the war, many people here were convinced that the United States was determined to force Britain to her economic knees by insisting on strict free enterprise and cash on the barrelhead. Yet, within a remarkably short space of time, the difficulties of European economic recovery led the United States to invent and legislate the Marshall Plan. In the late 1950s, it appeared that the United States had lost interest in the pursuit of freer trade and was drifting into protectionism. Yet by 1962 it had devised and passed the Trade Expansion Act.

Three aspects of the passage of the Trade Expansion Act are especially relevant to present circumstances. First, the swing of American public opinion towards a freer trade policy was extremely rapid. It was the result of intensive thinking by all sorts of people, none of whose names had ever been mentioned in the British papers as either influential or even as thinkers. Moreover—what is a characteristic of any democratic system, but is almost invariably ignored when one looks at a foreign government—many of them were Republicans and not Democrats. These Republicans were simply fulfilling their obligation as members of a democracy to prepare themselves to provide an alternative government, or simply fulfilling their obligation as elected representatives of the public to arrive at the best judgment they could on the problem at hand. The same process is going on now in the United States. All sorts of people are thinking about the problem in hand: what is to be done after the Trade Expansion Act expires.

Second, most of those who were thinking in preparation for the Trade Expansion Act were thinking, not of what would be in the American national interest only, but of what the Europeans with whom they expected to bargain wanted.

In such a context, it would have been foolish in the extreme for the Europeans to adopt the position: the Americans will never listen to us, so we should say nothing about what we would like. On the contrary, good international neighborliness requires a country to formulate its national interest with respect to the policies of other countries as clearly as it possibly can.

FOUNDATION FOR NAFTA

Third, if the Trade Expansion Act had been successfully negotiated, it would have established the equivalent of a free trade area over the North Atlantic region for the major industrial products. There is thus a foundation in past American thinking on which a North Atlantic Free Trade Area might be built in future.

The *second gut-reaction* against the proposals is that a North Atlantic Free Trade arrangement would be fatally dangerous to Britain, because the result would be that the Americans would simply take over British industry.

It hardly needs pointing out that this argument is totally inconsistent with the first one quoted. Either the United States will be interested in the proposals, or it will not. If it is not interested through sheer political inertia, it cannot at the same time be intensely interested through economic cupidity. The fear of American takeovers is apparently widespread, but it rests largely on confusion about the politics and economics of international investment.

Control of enterprises located in Britain by corporations with head offices located in the United States is *not* the same thing as "domination" of the British economy by the American Government. The American Government does not own the corporations: they are owned by shareholders, and run by managements, who are primarily interested in the profits that efficient operation alone will provide; and efficiency has not so far been declared contrary to the British national interest. Further, if there is fear that American private enterprise will operate against Britain's national interest, one should recall that the British Government has—and has exercised for many years—the sovereign power over enterprises operating in this country, regardless of ownership.

For every buyer there must be a seller. American "takeovers" are to the same extent British "sell-outs." Why do American companies want to take over? Presumably because they believe they can manage the business more efficiently and profitably than the existing owners.

The process of competition, in which poor managements and poor technologies are replaced by better managements and better technologies, is an international one. British enterprises face competition and takeovers not only from American corporations but also from Europeans, Japanese, Canadians, and Australians. But, similarly, efficient British enterprises are "taking over" firms in other countries, and are annoyed by restrictions on their freedom to do so. Concentration on the alleged dangers of American takeovers is mostly a convenient way of ignoring the fact that we are moving into an era of genuinely international competition.

NORTH ATLANTIC TRADE AREA ANALYZED

The *third gut-reaction* to the proposals for a North Atlantic Free Trade Area is to assert that they are "completely impractical." The use of the word "impractical" in this context is like the appeal to "patriotism" in other contexts—a high-sounding excuse for refusing either to think oneself or to admit the thinking of others. If a proposal is sensible it is almost invariably also practical, in the sense that if intelligent men are set to work on the problem of how to make it operational, they will usually come up with a reasonable answer. The British Government is in fact now embarked on its third exercise of this kind, with regard to the Common Market. Yet, less than a dozen years ago, majority opinion in this country was rejecting the whole idea of a European common market as "impractical." Thus, these three grounds for rejecting consideration of the North Atlantic Free Trade Area alternative will not stand up to serious examination.

American Attitudes Toward Trade Liberalization in the Atlantic Area

BELA BALASSA

In this essay, first published in the Moorgate and Wall Street Review *(Spring 1967), the editor of this volume takes issue with the position that establishing a North Atlantic Free Trade Area is superior to multilateral trade liberalization. The essay utilizes the findings of his book,* Trade Liberalization among the Industrial Countries: Objectives and Alternatives.

FOR SEVERAL YEARS NOW, discussions in the United States on trade liberalization among the countries of the Atlantic area have centered on the Kennedy round of tariff negotiations.

With the completion of the Kennedy round, one should consider the alternatives open to U.S. policy-makers in the field of trade policy. One possibility is to continue with periodic negotiations under the most-favored-nation clause on an across-the-board basis—in effect, a succession of Kennedy rounds. Another, more revolutionary, solution that has been proposed in recent years is to establish a free trade area encompassing the industrial countries of North America and Western Europe. Finally, proposals have been made for trade arrangements—in the form of preferential tariff reductions or a free trade area—including the United States, Canada, and the European Free Trade Association (EFTA) countries. Japan may also be considered for membership under a free trade area arrangement but, for simplicity's sake, I will disregard this possibility here.

ECONOMIC AND POLITICAL OBJECTIVES OF TRADE LIBERALIZATION

In a choice among alternative arrangements, the first question to be answered is what objectives—economic and political—these policies may serve. Among economic objectives, increases in national income should be mentioned first. National incomes may rise following the liberalization of trade because trade leads to a more efficient allocation of resources, it permits producing on a large scale in a wider market, and contributes to greater manufacturing efficiency and technological change through intensified competition in a larger area.

None of these sources of gains are of much importance in the United States. Foreign trade amounts to about 5 percent of U.S. national income and, under realistic assumptions, we can hardly expect that it would increase by more than one-tenth if tariffs among industrial countries were eliminated. And while this is not a negligible magnitude—it is only slightly smaller than the American foreign aid expenditure—the resulting gain in economic welfare would be only a fraction of the increase in trade.

Neither should one overestimate the beneficial effects of Atlantic trade liberalization for the United States balance-of-payments due to the elimination of discrimination against American exports in the Common Market and EFTA. My calculations point to the conclusion that this discrimination would affect about one-fifth of American exports of manufactured goods to Western Europe—not exceeding one-half billion dollars on a 1960 basis. The resulting change in the U.S. balance-of-payments would be relatively small, and it could be fully offset if manufacturing prices in Western Europe were to rise by about 3 percent relative to U.S. prices. In fact, a change of this magnitude has taken place since 1959 in both the Common Market and Britain.

Moreover, most industries already exploit all possible sources of economies of scale in the large American market, and hence the widening of the market through increased trade may bring additional gains in a few cases only. The main benefits of trade liberalization for the U.S. economy may, then, come as a result of intensified competition and by avoiding a shift toward protectionism. Examples of the effects of foreign competition include the decision of American car producers to introduce compact cars, and the process of modernization under way in the U.S. textile industry. On the other hand, if no efforts are made to liberalize trade, the alternative may well be increased protectionism rather than the maintenance of the status quo. Political and economic relationships are hardly ever in a position of stable equilibrium but have the tendency to move in one direction or another. Thus, in the absence of pressures for the liberalization of trade, protectionist counterpressures may gain force in this country as well as abroad.

This conclusion is based on certain assumptions regarding political processes, and in view of the relatively small gains obtained from trade liberalization, political objectives assume primary importance in the United States in making a choice among alternative trade policies. Increased cohesion in the Atlantic alliance is usually mentioned as the major political objective of the United States in her relationships with European countries. But is "cohesion" a goal *per se*, relating solely or principally to internal matters, or is it a means to serve external objectives? While internal objectives such as the safeguarding of democratic institutions in European countries and the avoidance of future military conflicts between France and Germany were of considerable importance in the postwar period, it would appear that the principal objectives of the countries of the Atlantic area are found in their relationships with the outside world. These objectives include the strengthening of the West *vis-à-vis* the Communist countries, the furthering of democratic institutions throughout the world, and the raising of living standards in less developed areas.

"Cohesion" in the Atlantic area, then, will serve a useful function inasmuch as it contributes to the attainment of the above objectives. This involves a common understanding on basic principles in dealing with internal and external problems as well as the minimization of conflicts. Correspondingly, trade arrangements should aim at greater cohesion in the Atlantic alliance by contributing to harmonious economic development and lessening the possibility of conflicts within the area. At the same time, attention should be paid to the preoccupation of Europeans with integration in Western Europe and with the present asymmetry in U.S.–European relations. Finally, in making a choice among alternative arrangements, consideration will have to be given to the implications of these arrangements for the developing countries. Aside from humanitarian considerations, improvements in the economic well-being of these countries would contribute to their political stability and permit avoiding an explosive situation in the international sphere that would result from a further accentuation of differences in living standards between rich and poor countries.

PROPOSALS FOR AN ATLANTIC FREE TRADE AREA

In the past, proposals for Atlantic or, at least, U.S.–British, integration came chiefly from the United Kingdom. In the last year or two, however, suggestions for establishing an Atlantic Free Trade Area have been made in American political and academic circles. These suggestions have rarely reached print, an important exception being the statement by Senator Javits, a Republican Vice-Presidential possibility in 1968, who called for "a treaty of free trade and economic cooperation with the UK, other EEC and EFTA nations, Canada, New Zealand and Australia, and other industrialized countries of the OECD which agree to adhere to the new rules of trade of [a] Free Trade Area."[1] Another free trade area proposal has come from the Canadian-American Committee which considers a U.S.–Canadian–EFTA free trade area as a first step towards this objective.[2]

In claiming the superiority of free trade areas over reciprocal tariff reductions under the most-favored-nation clause, the proponents of an Atlantic Free Trade Area have given emphasis to the internal effects of integration and have often neglected its impact on third countries. Indeed, since in a free trade area tariffs on substantially all goods are abolished, the resulting increase in trade will be greater than in the case of less comprehensive tariff reductions. Also, pressure groups representing special interests may restrict the scope of reductions in duties if the negotiations are conducted on an item-by-item or an industry-by-industry basis. Finally, so the argument goes, while the assurance against the reimposition of duties in a free trade area would induce producers to fully utilize the opportunities provided by the elimination of tariffs, this would not be the case if tariff reductions were carried out under the most-favored-nation clause.

There is much substance to these observations: smaller cuts in tariffs, protectionist pressures, and uncertainty would tend to limit the expansion of trade in multilateral tariff negotiations.

1. Jacob K. Javits, "The U.S. Role in Britain's Economic Crisis," Speech at the Savoy Hotel, London, November 8, 1965. Cited in Sperry Lea, "Americans for Free Trade," *The Round Table*, January 1967, p. 11.
2. *A New Strategy for Canada and the United States*, A statement by the Canadian-American Committee, sponsored by the National Planning Association (U.S.A.) and the Private Planning Association of Canada.

But, in judging the relative merits of the two alternatives, several further questions need to be raised—some political and others economic.

To begin with, in U.S.–European relationships we presently lack the degree of solidarity that would be necessary to permit dispensing—once and for all—with the use of protective measures. The U.S. Congress does not seem inclined to accept the removal of duties on products where American producers are assumed to be uncompetitive, and a plan for an Atlantic Free Trade Area would run into objections in European parliaments, too.

In Western Europe, many would consider the elimination of tariffs on trade with the U.S. as a backward step in the process of greater independence from the United States on the grounds that the economic basis for the unification of Europe would thereby be undermined. In the European Economic Community (EEC) itself, the external tariff is regarded as a unifying element—a sign of the Common Market's identity—and suggestions for abolishing tariffs are looked upon with suspicion. It has also been argued that there is need for maintaining the common external tariff in the EEC in order to permit specialization to take place before confronting American competition. Thus, it is said that, in the case of a full and immediate removal of tariffs, science-based industries in the Common Market countries (and in Britain) would be at a disadvantage compared to their American counterparts because of differences in market size and the direct and indirect Federal support to U.S. firms. On the other hand, periodic tariff reductions that maintained a balance between the requirements of protection and the need for foreign competition would contribute to the development of these industries in Western Europe.

Periodic tariff reductions have the further advantage that they permit a "learning process" to take place on the part of entrepreneurs, labor unions, and legislators with respect to the effects of trade liberalization on domestic industries. Their actual experience with tariff reductions may allay the fears of those who demand continued protection on the grounds that wages are lower in Western Europe than in the United States—or that productivity is higher in the United States than in Europe. Businessmen, as well as governments, will observe in practice that trade liberalization does not lead to the decline of national industries and that the adjustment to freer trade is considerably easier, and the losses suffered by domestic firms smaller, than commonly assumed.

The French experience with trade liberalization is especially illuminating. While in 1958 the French Patronat had opposed the establishment of the EEC, a few years later it came to favor continuing participation in the Common Market. At the time of the 1965 French Presidential elections, the majority of businessmen apparently joined the opposition, largely because of their fear that De Gaulle's actions would lead to the breaking up of the Community. It has also been reported that entrepreneurs in France now object less to tariff reductions on trade with the United States—long considered to be the most formidable competitor of French industry—than they opposed the freeing of trade with neighboring countries a decade earlier.

The argument in favor of the gradual approach is further strengthened if we consider that the chances of reaching an agreement increase when especially sensitive industries are excluded from the negotiations. At the same time, the procedural difficulties of tariff bargaining are greatly reduced if negotiations are carried out on an across-the-board basis. The procedure employed in the Kennedy round conforms to these requirements: the negotiating parties have reached a preliminary agreement on a flat rate of tariff applicable to all nonagricultural sectors, with exceptions to be negotiated at a later time.

But what about the advantages which a free trade area arrangement has over m.f.n.-type tariff reductions due to the fact that the former—but not the latter—entails a commitment to refrain from reimposing tariffs and other barriers to trade? While the risk associated with possible future reimposition of restrictions will indeed influence entrepreneurial decision-making, the contrast between the two approaches should not be overdrawn since the outcome will depend on the *credibility* of any commitment. Thus, in view of the use of import surcharges in the United Kingdom in the years 1964-66, and the new British approaches toward entry into the Common Market, the degree of credibility is rather low in EFTA, which fact restrains the adaptation of producing and marketing facilities to a larger market area. In the Atlantic context, too, the credibility of any commitment will largely depend on the degree of solidarity among the participating countries. At the same time, procedures can be worked out that reduce uncertainty in trade among independent national economies without establishing a free trade area.

It is suggested here that, in order to lessen uncertainty in international trade, it would be desirable to establish a "code of good conduct" which would regulate the actions of the trading partners in regard to tariffs, quotas, and subsidies. To begin with, countries would relinquish the right to raise tariffs or impose other forms of trade restrictions in the event that particular industries are adversely affected by increases in imports. Escape clauses would be provided only for cases where certain, mutually agreed upon, conditions are fulfilled, and would permit the application of temporary measures of adjustment assistance rather than tariffs and quotas. The code of good conduct should also strengthen existing provisions against domestic subsidies and dumping, the objective being to avoid the need for countervailing measures on the part of the importing countries.

By reducing uncertainty in trade relations and facilitating the process of domestic adjustment, the proposed scheme would contribute to the expansion of international trade and increase the attractiveness of the gradual approach to the liberalization of trade. Uncertainty in international trade would be further reduced if tariff procedures were simplified since the risk of incurring unforeseen costs and penalties, and the possibility of the invalidation of transactions, tend to restrict the extent of international specialization. This purpose would further be served if the United States and Canada accepted the Brussels Tariff Nomenclature, and all other countries achieved uniformity in regard to the subheadings of the BTN.

I come now to the implications of the choice among alternative arrangements for the developing countries. Under the most-favored-nation clause, tariff cuts are extended to all General Agreement on Tariffs and Trade (GATT) members and hence developing countries automatically benefit from reductions in duties undertaken by the industrial nations. On the other hand, an Atlantic Free Trade Area would discriminate against outsiders since the elimination of tariffs on inter-area trade provides an advantage to producers in partner countries over third country producers.

Thus, while the developing countries would automatically gain if the industrial nations reduced tariffs under the most-favored-nation clause, they would suffer discrimination in the event that an Atlantic Free Trade Area were established. This discrimination would hinder the transformation of the economic structure of these countries by restricting demand for many of the goods they actually export and making it more difficult for them to introduce new export products. In turn, the lowering of tariff barriers would improve the possibilities of the developing countries to export processed goods and thereby contribute to their industrial development.

The establishment of an Atlantic Free Trade Area would, then, run counter to the objective of raising living standards and contributing to economic and political stability in the developing countries. And, aside from its economic effects, such an arrangement would not fail to have unfavorable political repercussions since it would be regarded as a "rich man's club" by these countries. The adverse political effects may, in fact, overshadow the immediate economic consequences.

But could special concessions be offered to the developing countries to offset the losses due to tariff discrimination? While suggestions to this effect have been made by, for example, the Canadian-American Committee, I have considerable doubts about the political feasibility of such a scheme. Experience indicates that the national legislatures of the industrial countries tend to regard compensatory measures as a form of foreign assistance and are reluctant to increase commitments. Thus, while they may be prepared to accept the "side effects" of multilateral tariff reductions which automatically benefit third countries, it appears questionable that they would be willing to undertake unilateral obligations, even though these would serve the purpose of compensating for the discriminatory effects of an Atlantic Free Trade Area.

At the same time, developing countries are likely to find any compensation offered for the loss of potential future benefits under the present system inadequate. In fact, these countries may consider the establishment of an Atlantic Free Trade Area acceptable only if it is accompanied by a unilateral elimination of duties on the part of the industrial countries. We would then arrive at a modified situation of free trade, with tariffs on manufactured goods maintained in less developed areas. While this solution has much to commend it, national legislators are unlikely to find it acceptable. It could, however, be approached through a succession of Kennedy round-type tariff reductions.

TRADE ARRANGEMENTS WITHOUT THE EEC?

Another alternative would be to aim at trade liberalization among the United States, Canada, and the EFTA countries on a preferential basis or in the form of a free trade area. Proposals to this effect were originally made for the eventuality that the Kennedy round remained unsuccessful because of the resistance of the Common Market.[3] More recently, the establishment of a free trade area among these countries has been proposed as a genuine alternative, irrespective of the outcome of the Kennedy round.[4]

In the event that negotiations in the framework of the Kennedy round were to break down, the Committee for Economic Development suggested that the United States should reach a trade agreement with a smaller group of countries, even if this meant jettisoning the principle of nondiscrimination. Further, Henry Reuss, an influential member of the Joint Economic Committee of U.S. Congress, has raised the possibility of making the application of the most-favored-nation clause conditional on reciprocal concessions ("conditional" m.f.n.)—an action that would presumably be undertaken by a group of nations including the United States, Canada, and the countries of EFTA. A variant of this proposal also appears in a study by Randall Hinshaw, prepared for the Council on Foreign Relations.

Conditional m.f.n. is a flexible device since it would permit the exclusion of sensitive industries from the negotiations and would also allow for subsequent changes in the geographical scope and/or the commodity composition of tariff reductions, but flexibility has an important drawback inasmuch as the participating coun-

---

3. Cf. Committee for Economic Development, *Trade Negotiations for a Better Free World Economy*, Washington, 1964; Henry S. Reuss, *The Critical Decade*, New York, McGraw Hill, 1964; and Randall Hinshaw, *The European Community and American Trade*, New York, Praeger, 1964.

4. Canadian-American Committee, *A New Trade Strategy for Canada and the United States*, Washington, 1966; and Sperry Lea, "Americans for Free Trade," *The Round Table*, January 1967.

tries could restrict tariff reductions to industries where they have little to lose, so that much of the expansion of trade might take place at the expense of outsiders.

A further consideration is that EFTA countries have a much greater interest in freeing trade with the Common Market than with the United States. In 1965, the exports of these countries to the EEC amounted to $7.0 billion and imports to $9.6 billion, while the corresponding figures for trade with the United States were $2.4 and $2.6 billion. The discrepancy is especially pronounced in the case of the Continental EFTA countries whose exports to the Common Market were $4.3 billion and imports $7.0 billion, whereas trade with the United States hardly exceeded one billion dollars in either direction. The corresponding figures for the United Kingdom are $2.7 and $2.6 billion (with the Common Market) and $1.4 and $1.5 billion (with the United States). Last but not least, the EFTA countries would benefit from the lessening of discrimination against their industries which is due to the establishment of the Common Market.

It appears likely, therefore, that if the member countries of EFTA were to reach an agreement with the United States to reduce tariffs under conditional m.f.n., they would attempt to make similar arrangements with the Common Market. The EFTA countries would have the best of both worlds in such an event—just as the United Kingdom meant to have it in 1958 in proposing the establishment of an all-European free trade, while maintaining Commonwealth preferences. By contrast, the United States might ultimately lose since the greater relative importance of their trade with the Common Market could be expected to induce the EFTA countries to enter into more comprehensive arrangements with the EEC than with the United States. Such an arrangement would also be attractive to the Common Market nations—in part because they fear the competitive powers of the EFTA countries less than those of the United States, and in part because of the reduction of discrimination in EFTA against their exports.

Objections against conditional m.f.n. further gain in strength if we consider that, once the Pandora's box of discriminatory traiff reductions is opened, individual countries may also enter into discriminatory agreements of varying scope and the specter of retaliation is raised. Finally, since the modification of Article 1 of GATT concerning the most-favored-nation clause requires the concurrence of all member countries, the possibility exists that this General Agreement be abrogated and the progress toward freer trade halted.

To escape the latter result, Randall Hinshaw has suggested that countries entering into preferential arrangements should establish a two-tariff system: "a preferential tariff, bound by an agreed ceiling, which would apply to participants; and a nonpreferential tariff, not bound by the ceiling, which would apply to nonparticipants."[5] But by permitting rates of duties on imports from participating countries to vary between nil and the agreed-upon tariff ceiling (Hinshaw suggests the figure of 10 percent), the two-tariff system would provide an opportunity to choose rates with a view to their trade-diverting effects. Moreover, countries or country groupings might negotiate a tariff ceiling at varying levels with different trading partners.

Reuss and Hinshaw further consider the possibility of establishing a free trade area with the participation of the United States, Canada, and EFTA, and a proposal to this effect has also been made by the Canadian-American Committee. Establishing a free trade area is not open to some of the objections levied against the applications of the conditional m.f.n. clause, and it is compatible with GATT rules. Still, such an arrangement is open to criticism on several counts. To begin with, as indicated above, the countries of EFTA would find it more advantageous to enter into a trade arrangement with the Common Market than with the United States. It stands to reason, therefore, that the EFTA countries would contemplate participating in a free trade area with the United States only if the chances of reaching an accommodation in a European context were nil.

But the latter assumption can hardly be made since, even if De Gaulle were to again oppose the entry of the United Kingdom and other EFTA countries into the Common Market, it would be inappropriate to base a policy on the assumption that such a decision is irrevocable. At the same time, the chances for an accommodation between the two trading groups would probably be jeopardized if the EFTA countries entered into a free trade area encompassing the United States and Canada. While

---

5. Hinshaw, *op. cit.*, p. 175.

the American proponents of the scheme usually emphasize the drawing power which such an arrangement would exert on the Common Market, the chances are that this would instead create two hostile blocs and perpetuate the division—this time between North America and part of Western Europe on the one hand, and the Common Market on the other.

Proposals of this sort are likely to be regarded as an application of the principle of *divide et impera* on the part of the United States and would not fail to create resentment among the supporters of European unity. At the same time, given the imbalance in political and economic power-relations in a U.S.–Canada–EFTA grouping, the importance of the EFTA countries (including the United Kingdom) on the world scene would decline, and they could be easily taken as satellites of the United States. This imbalance in power-relations would hardly be conducive to Common Market participation at some later date and, instead of serving the objective of greater cohesion in the Atlantic area, the scheme would tend to contribute to a hardening of divisions within Europe and within the Atlantic alliance.

CONCLUSION

I have dealt in this paper with alternative trade policies that have been proposed in the United States for the post-Kennedy round period. It would seem to me that, under present-day conditions, the establishment of an Atlantic Free Trade Area is neither desirable nor feasible. The countries on the two sides of the Atlantic are not yet ready to assume the real or imaginary risks such an arrangement may entail, and they do not possess the degree of solidarity that would be necessary to its coming to fruition. The major European countries are also likely to oppose such a scheme on the grounds that it would interfere with the process of political and economic integration in Western Europe. The developing countries, too, would be opposed to it because of the discriminatory effects it would entail.

As regards to trade arrangements with the participation of the United States, Canada, and the countries of EFTA, "conditional" m.f.n. has decided economic and political disadvantages; nor does the establishment of a "truncated" Atlantic Free Trade Area have much to commend it. For EFTA countries, trade relations with the Common Market are of much greater importance than trade with the United States and Canada, and participation in a U.S.-led free trade area is bound to reduce the chances for an accommodation between the two European trading groups. Also, whatever gain the United States might derive from closer relationships with some of the countries of Western Europe, she would probably have to pay the price of alienating other nations of the area.

In turn, tariff reductions under the most-favored-nation clause would reduce the discriminatory effects of European integration for U.S. exports and would meet the objections that removing tariffs would interfere with the consolidation of the Common Market. It would also serve the political objectives of the Atlantic alliance by making a European union more open and lessening discrimination against developing countries. Finally, gradualism in lowering tariffs would make it possible to exclude especially sensitive industries from the negotiations and would permit a "learning process" on the part of business, labor, and national legislatures that promises to facilitate future reductions in duties.

Part Two: Foreign Investments and the Multinational Corporation

U.S. Exports in Relation to U.S. Production Abroad

JUDD POLK

Judd Polk is Research Director of the United States Council of the International Chamber of Commerce. In this essay, written in September 1967 for the Joint Economic Subcommittee of the United States Congress, he considers the implications for policymaking of the establishment of the foreign subsidiaries of U.S. firms.

TRADITIONALLY, THE UNITED STATES, like other countries, has, viewed its trade with other nations as the main indication of its concrete economic interest in the outside world. Trade policy in broad historic sweep has moved from preoccupation with the problems of defending particular industries against foreign competition to general acknowledgment of the mutual interest of all nations in freer trade. In this century, the movement toward freer trade has just achieved its most dramatic manifestation in the successful conclusion of the Kennedy Round of comprehensive and significant trade concessions among the major trading nations.

There is a powerful economic rationale for this trend and for its continuation. But the decisive considerations of policy can no longer be seen from the vantage point of international trade itself or in terms of the familiar arguments which since Adam Smith's day have rationalized the cause of freer trade as a means of reaping the harvest of the international division of labor.

The fact is that international trade is now itself incidental to the broader phenomenon of international production. This term international production is here used to describe the deliveries which one nation makes in the markets of another via the direct expedient of producing there locally, as distinguished from exporting to that market, the product of facilities located at home.

As will be shown, the producing stake of the United States and other countries probably now accounts for sales upward of some $150 billion, as against U.S. exports of about one-fifth as much. As this tremendous producing establishment has developed, American subsidiaries abroad have come to occupy a very substantial role among our foreign customers. And the free movement of goods, in favor of which our forebears could argue the relative luxury of the gains available from specialized trade, is now more in the nature of a structural imperative of the method of production itself—much in the same way one might urge the structural importance of the interstate commerce clause in the U.S. economic constitution. Moreover, when international trade —especially in the case of the United States—is seen in proper relation to production abroad, very serious doubt is cast upon the workability of any trade-policy initiative, such as export expansion, unless taken in compatible relation to policy initiatives pertaining to the entire range of our foreign production—here namely the encouragement of investment in production abroad.

International investment is transforming the character of the world economy; for one thing, it is no longer whimsical to speak of a world economy. The output associated with U.S. production in other nation's markets is large in relation to the national GNPs of the industrialized world. While the history of international investment goes back almost as far as the history of international trade, only recently has it emerged as the most important fact of international economic life. The implications of this fact are only beginning to be understood. Here an effort will be made to sketch the basic picture and suggest some of the implications for questions of trade policy.

THE SCOPE OF U.S. DELIVERIES TO FOREIGN MARKETS

The most important trade concept, and one that is essentially new in the structure of world trade, as fundamentally altered by international investment, is that of total deliveries to a market, in contrast to the traditional concept, now secondary in importance, of deliveries (exports) that happen to cross international borders. The aggregate world GNP, excluding Communist countries, for which compatible market statistics are not available, is in the order of magnitude of $1,600 billion, about half accounted for by the United States. Of this, a rapidly growing portion—perhaps $250 billion, but not definitely estimatable—is product associated with internationally owned and operated plants. U.S. statistics on investment abroad and associated production permit a firmer rough estimate of $150 billion as its share of this international production. U.S. total deliveries to foreign markets are some $180 billion. Of these, about a fifth—$30 billion—are exports; the rest emanating from U.S. production facilities located abroad.

PRODUCTION ABROAD AND EXPORTS GROW TOGETHER

The concept of total foreign sales properly brings together U.S. deliveries in response to foreign demands, whether involving products made here or there. Basically the two sources of supply are complementary, and, in fact, they have grown in a parallel and vigorous manner. The fact of their parallel growth, when coupled to the fact of the overriding quantitative importance which the high level of U.S. investment since World War II has given to production from facilities located abroad, constitutes a fact of utmost importance for United States foreign economic policy. For example, as against our present tendency to discourage investment and encourage exports in the thought that this realignment of delivery methods will have a beneficial effect on our net foreign exchange position, there stands the powerful inference from export and production trends that investment is a major stimulant to exports. Furthermore, detailed work with both national and company statistics suggests that the defense and extension of a sales position achieved through exports will require continuing investment.

Balance-of-payments accounting is trade oriented and largely neglects the economic impact of our foreign investment as the major channel through which U.S. producers operate in foreign markets. Investment may be limited to so-called direct investment; this is investment in which U.S. business has, by definition, at least a 10-percent equity, and has, in actual fact, outright control in the great majority of instances. The growth in investment includes new dollar capital outflow, which appears in the balance of payments, and retained earnings—which do not, but which are followed and published by the Department of Commerce. In the typical instance of investment, these two sources of financing are of roughly equal importance. But more important in evaluating the local impact of investment is a quantification of the value of product to be associated with the expanded productive facilities. From data now available on, for example, the value of sales by U.S. manufacturing subsidiaries abroad, a reasonable rule of thumb ratio of 2 to 1 can be derived for output to book value. From this, the implication of these figures is that gains in U.S.-initiated output abroad for, say, Europe grew from $6 billion in 1950—against U.S. exports of roughly half that amount—to some $32 billion in 1966—against exports of $10 billion, or less than a third. Moreover, at this level of local output from U.S. investment, a substantial tendency for an increase in local imports—perhaps $1½ billion—may reasonably be inferred as the import share of the increase in local income, and supplementary to imports directly associated with the capital increase, notably capital equipment. In the case of the less-developed countries, this tendency to import more as income rises contributes to the chronic foreign exchange shortages with which most of them grapple, and is curtailed by familiar import and exchange restrictions.

The basic income-import relationships have been more fully explored in the National Industrial Conference Board's report, *U.S. Production Abroad and the Balance of Payments* (1966). The recapitulation here is intended to show the extent to which local production abroad has outdistanced exports as a means of delivering goods to foreign markets, and how the gains in local production, so vital to the basic process of development, have been compatible with regular growth in traditional deliveries via exports.

DOES PRODUCTION ABROAD DISPLACE EXPORTS?

The answer to this question appears to be clearly "Yes" for specific products, but for total exports, clearly "No," and for products in the same general industrial classification, probably "No."

It is a commonplace of policy in less-developed countries (LDCs) to interdict imports in favor of programs of local production. The Mexican industrialization program is a nearby familiar example. A familiar response of U.S. companies to such programs has been to set up local production facilities, where cost-profit-risk factors warrant. In such cases, the alternative export of equipment, raw materials, and even other related finished products more than offsets the loss of the original product export.

In other cases, relative cost considerations lead to production abroad. In still other cases, and these are the most frequent, the marketing advantages obtainable only through the maintenance of a local foreign establishment prompt the decision. The many motivations of foreign investment, and the primacy of marketing considerations among them, have been widely studied elsewhere and need no recital here. It is important, however, to note emphatically that intensive case study rarely turns up a situation in which the producer abroad could have continued to export as an alternative to producing locally abroad.

Moreover, an important fact often forgotten in discussions of what impels companies to produce abroad as against supplying foreign markets through exports is that there are no acceptable substitutes produced in the United States for much of U.S. production abroad. This is the case even in manufacturing, but is particularly clear in the case of the extractive industries which establish facilities abroad so as to gain sources of supply rather than new market, and applies also to trading companies, utilities, and other service enterprises that are limited to foreign sites by the nature of their operations. These nonmanufacturing instances have especially close relevance to the LDC's. Even in consumer goods, versions developed for the U.S. market are keyed to income levels and social positions more advanced than those prevailing in the LDC's.

As for new U.S. exports induced by investment abroad, it seems likely that the relationship between exports and local production is close, and is probably particularly strong in the case of LDC's. In 1964, for example, the ratio of U.S. exports shipped to Latin American manufacturing affiliates to sales revenues of these affiliates was 11 percent. The comparable ratio for Europe: 6 percent. The difference is some indication of how much more producers in LDC's must look abroad for their supplies than is the case for those in more developed countries. Comparably competitive sources of supplies and equipment are simply not at hand for the LDC producers, and this relative inflexibility in source has a widespread impact.

In the case of capital goods, for example, the technology necessary to produce the machines for making other machines, as well as machines for making final products, is not readily available in the LDC's. Thus in 1964 Latin America imported $126 million of capital equipment from the United States; Europe imported only $65 million, despite the much more rapid pace of U.S. investment in Europe—six times the rate in Latin America. Available figures also permit a corroborating examination of capital-equipment sources for foreign manufacturing subsidiaries. Latin American subsidiaries obtained half of the materials used in their manufacturing operations from the United States, European subsidiaries about a tenth.

Investment-induced exports appear generally more impressive than those hypothetically displaced, although the latter concededly raise an imponderable question. What might have been the level of U.S. product exports had there been no production abroad cannot be determined. But the question is largely idle; producers did not have the choice in the first place.

The often expressed anxiety that U.S. production abroad displaces exports on balance is not persuasive. For one thing, U.S. foreign direct investment alone now (mid-1967) totals more than $55 billion, and accounts for possibly as much as $115 billion in product deliveries. It is not credible that foreign countries would permit or could finance these deliveries as supplemental exports from U.S. facilities. Moreover, as noted already, this productive activity within foreign markets has in fact been accompanied by a vigorous growth of U.S. exports (7 percent annual average, 1950–66), the more vigorous in areas where investment activity has been more intense. The directness of the relationship between investment activity and export growth is now further supported by various statistical and case-study surveys of the transactions of U.S. affiliates abroad. While so far the United States imports relatively little from foreign affiliates, its exports to them are substantial (about one-quarter) and growing—U.S.' own foreign affiliates already have emerged as a major customer of the United States abroad. Less direct but also significant for U.S. exports is the increase in foreign imports as a result of income gains associated with U.S. local (foreign) production. The increase in foreign imports (including, of course, U.S. exports) from the higher income is now a substantial figure.

It is perfectly compatible with this interpretation of the favorable effect of U.S. investment abroad on U.S. exports to acknowledge the uniqueness of exports as foreign-exchange earners and the importance of increasing exports, especially in periods like the present when dollars tend to accumulate in foreign hands, with the all-too-well-grounded likelihood that they will be presented for conversion into gold rather than spent on U.S. exports or invested here.

THE UNITED STATES AS A PEDDLER

The charm of exports from a balance-of-payments point of view is that they yield foreign exchange to the country equivalent to their sales value, not just their profit margin. In contrast, production abroad on the basis of U.S. investment, returns foreign exchange equivalent only to the remitted portion of the producers' profits—typically now about 5 percent of the sales revenue (in the case of manufacturing, for which sufficient figures are available to permit a fair estimate). Thus, from the narrow and short-run perspective of the transactions entering balance-of-payments accounting, the proceeds of commercial exports of goods and services constitute the No. 1 foreign-exchange earnings of the country. Even were the export transactions conducted at a commercial loss, there would be a foreign exchange gain.

The fact that the U.S.' primary role in the world economy is that of an investor and producer is plainly adventitious for its role as seller of U.S. products wherever made. In contrast, the point is now frequently heard that U.S. producers tend to overconcentrate on the investment/production approach to foreign markets. Those concerned with whatever element of truth there is in this contention argue that the salesmen of our main advanced-country competitors (Europe, Japan—and possibly Hong King?) have not forgotten how to hustle and do not disdain individually small (but cumulatively large) sales. Nor do they find that their selling requires a costly investment establishment.

It is not possible to quantify how extensive such presumably drummed-up sales by others may be—and therefore for a more competitive United States *might* be. Nor is it possible to quantify for comparison and by way of offset the volume of U.S. sales that could fairly be attributed to the competitively superior marketing position achieved through the U.S. producing establishment abroad. On the former—the success of sellers from competitive countries—American producers abroad frequently recite offhand instances of the effectiveness of other industrialized countries' salesmen operating without the benefit of an entrenched local marketing establishment, but with the benefit of readily available help from their governments. There is also some corroborative evidence of their effectiveness in foreign balance-of-payments figures of these countries, showing, for example, European surpluses achieved in third areas, say, Latin America. The comparability of available figures is open to question; the various nonuniform balance-of-payments accounts do not yield clear evidence on the geographic sources of export earnings.

Nonetheless, an arresting case can be made out inferentially that major U.S. competitors are earning their trade surpluses—and ultimately their net dollars and their gold—not with this country but with "third countries." No doubt there are real possibilities for improving our commercial competitive position, including increased exports to the LDC's. But whatever may be the export gains to be achieved temporarily, a real and sustainable improvement in LDC purchases from abroad, including the United States, depends on the further development of basic LDC income (production), with accompanying growth of LDC earning capacity (LDC exports).

TRADE POLICY IS PRODUCTION POLICY

The U.S. delivery system to foreign markets—based on advancing production, marketing, and above all, organization techniques —has now evolved into an essentially foreign-base plant system of supply. Although this development has carried exports to an ever rising level and at a rate of growth (7 percent) about halfway between that of domestic U.S. production (say 5 percent) and our production abroad (a steady 10 percent), U.S. companies' total deliveries to foreign markets are some six times larger than "conventional" exports alone.

This does not mean that the United States has a diminishing interest in good international trade policy. The freer international movement of goods and money—capital goods and capital funds as well as current goods and current funds—is now for us internationally as well as nationally an essential condition of production itself, not just of peripheral trading benefits. Production since the not entirely fictitious Robinson Crusoe has meant specialization and money. The effect of our intensively developed international producing position is a reminder that trade is an integral part of production, internationally as well as nationally. The sweep of international investment since World War II has removed any overtone of whimsy from the concept of a world economy rather than just an international one. From elaborated interproduction among nations, world production is emerging, and from international trade, world trade.

The policy implications of this shift away from the mere swapping of national products and toward world production cannot be fully anticipated. We are at a beginning here, and it is most appropriate, in my opinion, that we pause at this juncture to study, beginning our study with the responsible deliberations of this joint congressional committee.

Some major shortcomings of present policy can be sensed when reviewed against any sober effort to assess the irreversible requirements of our worldwide producing position:

1. We should squarely face the possibility that our present general policy of discouraging the normal growth of our producing establishment abroad by putting restraints and restrictions on investment is misconceived. This approach adopted as a "temporary" (now in its fifth year) bit of pragmatism thought to be required by the exigencies of the balance of payments and thought to be productive of balance-of-payments relief, is pursued at the direct expense of our economic position in the world and is likely to have been and to be prejudicial to our earning position in the world.

2. The current emphasis on encouraging exports, though highly desirable insofar as it pertains to goods produced at competitive cost, cannot operate as a substitute for our investment and pro-

duction abroad. An effective export effort in our stage of development can, for the most part, be maintained only on the basis of appropriate investment backstopping in foreign markets. Consistent with this, however, is any step that facilitates exports and thereby reduces the time lag between financial commitments we make abroad and the transfer of real resources (exports) to implement them.

3. Problems of improving the terms of credit available for international projects frequently arise in the context of specific export projects, particularly in the capital goods field. Almost certainly the importance of this range of problems, already high, will grow. The adequacy of international credit, of international financing institutions, and of foreign governmental policies to accommodate freer movement of capital and current funds is directly and vitally relevant to the viability of our tremendous position in worldwide production.

4. To a very real extent, international production—unlike national production—must take place on the basis of a very sketchy "legal infrastructure." National laws contain many conflicting policies, many of them simply for lack of occasion or motivation to harmonize them internationally. Among these are regulations already mentioned affecting the transfer of funds; company laws affecting the initiation and terms of operation of companies, often to the disadvantage of international companies; fiscal policies, especially unresolved problems of tax jurisdiction over international operations; antitrust and other laws affecting the permissible methods of operation in different countries.

5. The production context is especially vital to realism in considering any aspect of commercial policy affecting the less-developed countries. By definition, their position of underdevelopment means "underproduction" and "underinvestment"—investment being literally and precisely the process of committing resources to production. The question of their trade is, by the same token, a question of markets for more effectively organized production. Special measures of encouragement and accommodation for their exports may well be in order, but lacking appropriate investment support are almost certain to fall short of maintainable gains in production.

The foregoing are only a few general areas of policy requirement in the new world of international production. They are in a sense the real "nontariff" barriers that embarrass international economic development, and far outweigh the usually specified nontariff barriers such as awkwardnesses of customs procedure.

The real objective of trade policy today is to facilitate international production, and the cost of policies not appropriately responsive to this objective will from now on be measurable in terms of the adequacy of world economic development.

The American Challenge

GENE BRADLEY

This summary of The American Challenge (Le Défi Americain), *an important book by the French analyst Jean-Jacques Servan-Schreiber on the penetration of American capital in Western Europe, was prepared for the* Atlantic Community Quarterly *(Winter 1967–68) by Gene Bradley of the General Electric Company. Mr. Bradley is a member of the Board of Directors of the Atlantic Council.*

In *The American Challenge,* Jean-Jacques Servan Schreiber forcefully advances the thesis that Europe has been "invaded" and is engaged in a "war;" that the United States is a force creating substantial changes in the political, social, and economic structures of Europe; that should present trends continue, "in 15 years the third industrial power, after the U.S. and the USSR, could well be not Europe but American industry in Europe." The author then proceeds to identify positive responses for meeting the challenge, stating that prime responsibility for this task must fall to the Europeans themselves.

To meet the challenge, Servan-Schreiber believes, "we must change. We must change our educational system, our tax system, our whole intellectual outlook."

PART I—THE INVASION OF EUROPE

"In 15 years"—the author submits—"the third industrial power, after the U.S. and the USSR, could well be not Europe but American industry in Europe. Today, in the ninth year of the Common Market, the organization of the European market is essentially American."

Why have Americans succeeded better in Europe than Europeans? It is, in Servan-Schreiber's opinion, not a question of money—rather a question of adaptability. The American industrialist has taken advantage of the establishment of the Common

Market and, whereas the members of the Common Market are still in the process of looking for a statute which will permit the creation of large European enterprises, it is the American concerns which have become, in effect, the first truly European-wide enterprises.

The author notes that American investment in Europe is directed mainly toward the technologically advanced industries. He has compiled an impressive list of sectors where U.S. enterprises control production in Europe. According to the author, "Europe and the Common Market have become for American businessmen a new 'Far West,' and their investments take the form less of a transfer of funds than of the taking control of the European economy." He warns that a country which must import its essential electronic equipment will be in a situation of inferiority analogous to that of those nations which were not capable of mastering the mechanization of work. "If the failure of Europe in the electronics sector should be confirmed, Europe would risk, from this simple fact, and in one generation, to cease to be a zone of advanced civilization."

After discussing the methods by which American investment in Europe is financed, the author concludes that nine-tenths of American investment in Europe is financed out of European resources. "We are paying them, one might say, in order that they buy us."

He outlines the fears which the American penetration of Europe engenders on the part of European businessmen: (1) that the borrowing by American enterprises on the European capital market is having a detrimental effect on the financing possibilities of European enterprises; (2) that, although American enterprises have contributed to the creation of employment, the demand for manpower resulting from American investment provokes a rise in salaries because of the substantial increases offered by Americans to the candidates they recruit; (3) that American enterprises lower prices.

What should Europe do to combat American penetration? The author is firmly convinced that all defensive or restrictive measures directed against American investment would be fruitless and would even aggravate the present situation. He states that American investment has important beneficial aspects and, without doubt, is even irreplaceable. "If Europe should deprive itself of the talent for organization, the innovation and audacity which characterize large American enterprises, Europe's lag will only be maintained and aggravated."

Foreign Investor Is An Aid · Servan-Schreiber continues this line of thought by noting that "nothing would be more absurd than to treat American investment as 'guilty' and to conceive our reform along restrictive lines. As resolute as we must be to insure that Europe remains the master of its destiny, we should recall the remark made by Hamilton in 1791 apropos of investment in the United States: 'Rather than be treated as a rival, the foreign investor should be treated as a particularly precious auxiliary for he permits us to increase the quantity of productive work in efficient enterprises.'"

Thus Europe is faced with a dilemma: "If we accept the free entry of American investment under the present conditions we dedicate European industry—in any case those sectors which are technologically and scientifically advanced—to the role of subcontractor and Europe itself to the situation of a satellite. If we adopt restrictive measures we will perforce have to buy from abroad those products which we need and will condemn ourselves more surely still to underdevelopment."

The author remarks that European leaders faced with this situation are not able to develop a coherent line of action. "The public, badly informed by their leaders' contradictory statements and unexplained reversals, does not know whether American investment is good or bad. It is both at the same time: the stimulation of competition and the bringing of new methods and advanced technologies are without doubt good for Europe but the cumulative underdevelopment which threatens to transform support into influence is bad."

According to Servan-Schreiber, the "bad" does not reside in American capacity but in European incapacity and the vacuum that results therefrom. That is why restrictions do not answer the question or only resolve a small part of it. "The suppression of American investment will not fill the vacuum, just the opposite."

The author asks why Europe should be alarmed since the European standard of living is rising and will continue to rise. He seeks the answer to this question by taking a look at the future.

In a chapter entitled "The Post-Industrial Society," Servan-Schreiber draws heavily on a report by Herman Kahn of the Hudson Institute on what the year 2000 will be like. The Hudson Institute forecasts that, given present trends, those societies which by the year 2000 will be "post-industrial" are the U.S., Japan, Canada, and Scandinavia. Western European countries will be in that stage which the Hudson Institute characterizes as "advanced industrial societies." From this forecast, the author concludes that within the space of a generation there no longer will be only a difference of degree between the situation in the U.S. and Western Europe but rather a difference of nature: "Europe will be part of another world; a world half way between the civilization of the technologically-advanced nations and that of the backward countries."

Concerning the question of comparative advantage and the proposition that it is better from an economic standpoint to permit American industry and management to direct certain key sectors of European industry, the author is firmly convinced that the only course for Europe is that of complete economic independence. If Europe wants to remain a world power and maintain its economic independence, it must continue to have original innovating capabilities in all of the technologically advanced sectors, since only those societies which have original innovating capabilities will continue to remain in the fore of industrial advancement. Although American investment in the advanced industrial sectors results in a short-term advantage for Europe since it dispenses with the need for very costly research efforts, in the long term this investment deprives Europe of an independent, competitive capacity in the technologically advanced sectors which are the sources of future rapid economic expansion.

PART II—THE REAR BASES OF AMERICA

To illustrate his point that creative imagination and organizational talent are the basis for American success in Europe—and prerequisite for a successful European response to the American challenge—the author examines the "techno-structure" of the U.S. He emphasizes the significant economic growth achieved by the U.S. in the sixties and the giant size of U.S. corporations.

Servan-Schreiber compares the high degree of self-financing

in large U.S. corporations (due essentially to high profits) with the weak financial condition which exists in most European firms. He concludes that the weakness of the financial structure of European industry and the significant degree to which the resources available on European capital markets are preempted by the public sector and American investors, results in a shortage of the capital necessary for productive investment. Furthermore, this financial weakness has facilitated the takeover of many European firms by U.S. firms. He concludes that American enterprises are highly competitive because they have strong financial positions, devote a large proportion of their profits to technological research, and receive massive support from the Federal Government in their research efforts.

According to the author, a vigorous cumulative process characterizes the new America: (1) large-scale activity permits the establishment of a forward-looking scientific potential; (2) this potential leads to the development of new technology and places the enterprise at the forefront of progress; (3) this situation in turn makes it possible for the enterprise to undertake large government projects and thus procures for it important assistance from the public sector; (4) this aid in turn reinforces the enterprise's profit-making capacity and therefore its growth . . . and the cycle repeats itself again and again.

It is Servan-Schreiber's belief that the technological advances made by American industry are the result of a talent in management which stems from the overwhelming progress America has made in the field of education. "America is at this moment receiving a massive benefit from the most profitable of investments —the training of men."

Servan-Schreiber devotes an entire chapter to an analysis of the book by Edward Denison, *Why Growth Rates Differ*. From this, the author concludes that the most important factors contributing to economic expansion are education and technological innovation. He compares the efforts made in the field of higher education by the Americans and the Europeans and concludes that "the famous 'technological gap' which is growing between Europe and America is due first of all to the poorness of European higher education, to its relative weakness in the fields of research and science and to the apparent incapacity on the part of the Europeans to apply vigorously the modern methods of management."

In seeking further support for this thesis, Servan-Schreiber cites remarks made by Secretary McNamara at a seminar in Jackson, Mississippi in 1967, "The technological gap is the major problem of our time; but even the word is not completely accurate. It is not merely a technological gap but rather a management gap and if intellectuals immigrate to the United States it is not essentially because we (the Americans) are more advanced technologically but rather because we have more modern and efficient methods of working by team, i.e., management. . . . This technological gap, this management gap, can only be attacked at the roots, education. . . . Europe is weak, very weak, in education; this weakness is in the process of cutting down her development. . . . If Europe wants to reduce the technological gap which separates it from the American world, it must before anything else improve its general education both in quality and quantity."

PART III—EUROPE WITHOUT STRATEGY

The author begins by enunciating what he considers are the fundamental problems Europe faces: "1) The American challenge is not essentially industrial or financial. Above all else, it puts into question our industrial creativity and our ability to transform ideals into reality; 2) America today, although about 15 years ahead of Europe, still resembles Europe and belongs to the same system and concept of industrial society. However, in 1980 the United States will be in another world. If Western Europe is, as the USSR already has been, distanced and disqualified, the United States will find itself isolated in the world of the *avant-garde*—a situation which is unacceptable for Europe, deadly for America and disastrous for the world."

Of the possible strategies open to European industry, the author urges that the best course consists in choosing to be competitive, particularly in those sectors characterized as "big science." "However, to be competitive in the field of electronics, information, space research and atomic energy will require massive aid." The question is how is this aid to be coordinated. He concludes that only a European approach will permit Europe to confront the challenge in these essential areas. However, not just any type of European grouping will do; international "cooperation" is only a "hollow formula" which cannot lead to effective results. "There exists only one solution to European industrial problems —a federal type of organization."

The most urgent problem requiring a federal type of solution is in the area of calculators. It is the author's opinion that it is in this sector that the technological gap is most evident and, in fact, the point of no return might come at any moment. "It is in the field of computers where we will see if Europe is still living." He proposes that the only logical European policy would consist in devoting all possible resources in a united effort since "no other industrial sectors will remain independent if Europe loses the battle of the computers."

The author states that France and other countries of Western Europe are looking in three directions and progressing in none: the strictly national way which is no longer possible; the indistinct way of "cooperation" which leads nowhere; and the community way, which has been blocked. What should Europe do?

PART IV—THE WAYS OF COUNTEROFFENSIVE

Servan-Schreiber sets out what he believes are the means for a successful counteroffensive: (1) the formation of large industrial units capable, not only by their size but also by their management, of competing with the American "giants"; (2) the choice of "large-scale operations" in the technologically advanced sectors which will preserve an independent future for Europe; (3) a minimum of federal power which can be the promoter and director of community enterprises; (4) a transformation of the methods of association among industry, university, and government; (5) an extensive general education for the young and retraining for the adult; (6) finally, and "everything else depends upon it," a revolution in the techniques of organization, to free energies kept captive by outdated social structures. He notes that this is an ambitious program: the aim of his book is to outline in what form and under what conditions this program can be accomplished.

The first action required on the part of Europe is to achieve an economic union, to accelerate the establishment of large industrial groups capable of a worldwide strategy, and to integrate the European capital markets. The author states that in the accomplishment of these tasks "England *inside* the Common Market would be the best possible ally for France."

There will also have to be a massive intervention on the part of the state, and this state, according to Servan-Schreiber, can only be federal. This European federal state must have independent power in relation to the national states and its own financial resources: "Neither Europe nor France will accomplish those decisive acts which will permit them to escape from American 'colonization' so long as there is not a change in political thinking in favor of a federal European authority. . . ."

The author bitterly attacks the present European establishment which he characterizes as being totally unadapted to the new society which is coming into existence. "Today's European societies are closed and stratified; the evolution toward a society of mass consumption escapes the understanding of the European establishment which is incapable, for the moment, of mobilizing the resources necessary for a truly European development."

PART V—THE POLITICAL QUESTION

After enumerating once more the danger Europe faces and the need that the world has for an independent and competitive Europe, the author expresses his opinion that it is in the Left of the political spectrum where the leadership and qualities necessary to meet the American challenge will be found.

PART VI—THE LAYERS OF POWER

In this section, Servan-Schreiber attempts to substantiate his claim that the Left is the wellspring for a rejuvenation of the European spirit: "It is the Left which will break the stratified system which has refused for so long to place confidence in man." According to the author, the present political leaders have not understood that social justice in a growth-oriented economy is the condition precedent to industrial dynamism. Plans directed at changing the conditions of work and social life always will be met with passive resistance or sabotage if they are conceived without the consultation of the interested parties who must be informed and convinced of the justice of the change requested.

CONCLUSION

The author concludes his work by stating that the American challenge is not brutal as were those Europe knew in its history, but it is perhaps more dramatic. "The weapons are the employment and the systematic refinement of all the instruments of reason, not only in science but also in the domain of organization and management where the Europeans are accustomed to the reign of the irrational."

An Answer to *The American Challenge*

FORTUNE

In a note intended as a partial answer to Servan-Schreiber, the Editors of Fortune indicate that foreign direct investment is a two-way road: in addition to U.S. investments in Western Europe, there is also a reverse flow of capital to the United States.

U.S. INVESTMENT in foreign economies has stirred up passions abroad and resistance here from the guardians of the balance of payments. Meanwhile, much less attention has been given to foreign investment in the U.S., which is getting to be more significant than most people suspect.

The only official measure of the foreign stake in U.S. business is Department of Commerce figures for the end of each calendar year; those for 1967 will not be out until late October. At the end of 1966, the figure for foreign *direct* investment came to $9.1 billion, about one-sixth of the comparable American stake abroad. But the $9.1 billion understates the situation, since it is based on book value rather than current market value, and it encompasses only those U.S. corporations in which a foreign stockholder owns at least 25 percent of the common voting stock. Investments of less than 25 percent are toted up in a separate estimate of *portfolio* holdings; at the end of 1966, the total foreign portfolio of U.S. stocks, bonds, and government bonds was $14.7 billion. This figure is also somewhat misleading, since portfolio investments are highly volatile. In recent years, foreigners have been doing a lot of buying and selling on Wall Street, and at times have influenced the market.

According to the Commerce breakdowns, the bulk of the direct investment originated in a handful of European countries. In 1966, as it has been for many years, Britain was the biggest single source, with $2.9 billion. Much of the British money was in financial and insurance companies. Canada was next, with $2.4 billion; Canadians ranked first as owners of foreign-controlled

U.S. manufacturing companies. The Dutch were third with $1.4 billion, but ranked first in growth; as recently as 1950, they had only $334 million invested directly. The Swiss came fourth with $949 million.

Some $3.8 billion of foreign money was in manufacturing companies, a rise of 233 percent since 1950. About $2 billion was in insurance and finance, and $1.7 billion was invested in the oil industry.

Better clues to the real scope of foreign influence can be found by close scrutiny of *Fortune*'s lists of the 500 largest U.S. industrial corporations and the 200 leading foreign industrials. Eight corporations on the 500 list are either owned outright or controlled by seven corporations on the 200 list. Shell Oil (No. 14) is 69 percent owned by companies in the Royal Dutch–Shell Group (No. 1 on the 200); American Petrofina (No. 382) is 64 percent owned by Petrofina (No. 70 on the 200); American Enka (No. 380) is 55 percent owned by AKU (No. 72 on the 200); Lever Brothers (No. 195) and Thomas J. Lipton (No. 343) are owned by Unilever (No. 2 on the 200); Joseph E. Seagram & Sons (No. 201) is owned by Distillers Corp.–Seagrams of Canada ;No. 110 on the 200); and Olivetti Underwood (No. 435) is a wholly owned subsidiary of Olivetti (No. 99 on the 200). Also, 36 percent of the shares in Libby, McNeill & Libby (No. 245) are owned by Nestlé (No. 11 on the 200 list). Last year, all together, those eight foreign-controlled U.S. corporations had sales of $5,018,808,000, net income of $363,361,000, and assets of $5,115,066,000.

The eight companies are unusually generous with details of their finances, and their foreign ownership is visible and easy to measure. But they are only the tip of the iceberg. In most cases, foreign-owned U.S. subsidiaries publish no figures at all, and among the controlling companies abroad, disclosure practices vary widely. For example, Massey-Ferguson, a Canadian company (No. 59 on the 200) that has eight plants in the U.S., makes public its valuation of its assets on this side of the border: $300 million. It even publishes U.S. sales figures: $263,162,500 in 1967, or 31 percent of Massey-Ferguson's world total. The company does balk, though, at publishing separate profit figures for the U.S.

On the other hand, George Weston, a Canadian holding company reveals as little as possible about its U.S. operations. But these are known to include a 57 percent holding in National Tea, which ranked No. 14 on *Fortune*'s list of the fifty largest U.S. merchandisers. National Tea had sales of $1,147,221,000 in 1967, income of $10,774,000, and assets of $204,740,000. Among the companies that resolutely refuse to break out the statistics of their U.S. investment is Bowater Paper (No. 97), which has paper mills in Tennessee and South Carolina and is building a newsprint plant with the Newhouse Newspaper Group as its 49 percent partner. Bowater keeps its U.S. figures to itself.

Schlumberger, which makes electronic equipment and provides oil-field services, poses further problems of identification and accounting. It appears on the 200 list (No. 148 this year) because it is incorporated in the Netherlands Antilles, but it has its main office in New York, sixteen plants in the U.S., and does more than half its business here.

A great deal of recent foreign investment that does not show up in public accounting is involved with the opening up of new sales markets here. As their exports to the U.S. grow, more overseas corporations are establishing permanent bases for production and distribution. West German companies now have about 125 subsidiaries in the U.S., and Japanese businessmen are constantly investigating possibilities here. One recent development: a Japanese-owned textile plant in South Carolina, built by Tsuzuki Spinning to demonstrate a new weaving technique.

And Britain's Beecham Group (No. 179) has shown that foreigners can survive and prosper in the hectic, hard-sell U.S. pharmaceuticals and toiletries market. Its U.S. subsidiary, Beecham Inc., has two plants in New Jersey, and in fiscal 1968 had sales of $67 million and profits of $5 million. This June, Beecham marketed 10 percent of the equity of the subsidiary. U.S. investors showed their confidence in Beecham's future by snapping up the whole issue, worth a total of $10,600,000.

Economic Sovereignty at Bay

RAYMOND VERNON

This essay by Raymond Vernon, a Professor of International Trade and Investment at Harvard University, first appeared in the October 1968 issue of Foreign Affairs. *It considers the implications of the emergence of the multinational corporation for the nation states.*

THIRTY-SIX YEARS AGO, the President of the United States observed that the U.S. tariff was "solely a domestic question," a subject inappropriate for international bargaining. This view, archaic as it now may seem, stirred no public outcry, no editorial protest in the nation's leading dailies.

But that was another era.

Today, the commitments among the principal non-Communist countries of the world cover the subject of tariffs, import and export licenses, and subsidies; the level of foreign exchange rates and the price of gold; the price and quality of international air service; the price of coffee, wheat, sugar, and tin; safety-at-sea standards, deep-sea fishing, and whaling rights; and the international use of the ether waves. There is a pooling of foreign-aid funds through the World Bank and various regional banking institutions; a pooling of international technical assistance efforts through numerous U.N. agencies. More important still, through institutions such as the International Monetary Fund and the Organization for Economic Coöperation and Development (OECD), there are well-entrenched habits of international consultation and international persuasion on "domestic" subjects of the most sensitive sort: on internal interest rates, on budgetary and fiscal policy, and on employment and incomes policy. And within the European Economic Community and the European Free Trade Association both the commitments and the consultations go deeper still. A decent respect for the opinions of mankind now seems to require a willingness on the part of sovereigns to expose many critical national economic policies to the collective scrutiny of a jury of peers.

To be sure, the millennium is still far distant. Nations still take it for granted that "the vital interests" of any sovereign, as the sovereign perceives them, will take precedence over any international obligation. The fifty or sixty new countries that have erupted out of their colonial status into national independence over the past twenty years especially treasure their sovereign rights to independent action. Still, as far as the advanced countries are concerned, the generalization holds: the pattern of coördination, consultation, and commitment has evolved to such a point that freedom of economic action on the part of those nations is materially qualified.

How far will this trend go? As one looks back at the history of international economic relations, there is some basis for the view that the trend has been with us for a long time, pushed almost inexorably by advances in the technology of transport and communication, from the ocean-going windjammer to the airborne jet. But history suggests also that the responses of nations to the near-inexorable pressures for increased contact have been punctuated at times by subtle resistance or savage reaction, enough to throw the process back on its heels for protracted periods. All the elements of both the integrative process and the resistant counter-reaction are present today.

II

The persistence of man in reaching out beyond his national boundaries to exploit the economic opportunities in other lands is amply documented by history, from the Phoenicians' investments in the tin mines of Cornwall to Fiat's commitments in the Soviet Union. For many decades before World War I, international economic ties were critical to the economies that today are thought of as "advanced." Migration was high; capital was flowing across international boundaries at impressive rates; and there were considerable movements of goods among these countries.

From World War I to World War II, the technology of international transportation and communication steadily advanced. But with the characteristic perverseness that punctuates the history of human institutions, the advanced nations demonstrated that they were not the passive pawns of technological change and were quite capable of resisting the implications of such change for a decade or two. While world production went up something like

40 percent in the interwar period, nations managed to suppress the growth of world trade so that it increased by only half the production rate. International investment also was restricted; after an ebullient period of growth in the 1920s, the flow of investment was curbed and reversed in the 1930s.

In general, the interwar period was an era of early Keynesian experimentation, an interval in which many nations turned inward to learn if a proper mix of autarchic national policies could generate full employment and reasonable rates of growth. As part of the disposition for each nation to try to fend for itself, there was a rash of competitive devaluations and export subsidies, coupled with national policies aimed at propping up internal demand and floating national economies off the shoals. To implement these policies, it was necessary for governments to restrict trade and control capital movements, irrespective to the integrating pressures created by the advances in transport and communication.

The restrictive initiatives of governments between the two great wars were abetted by equally restrictive undertakings on the part of international business. By World War I, leading national firms in different countries had already begun to have painful encounters with one another in international markets. Part of the contact was by way of competition in international trade, especially for new products in the fields of chemicals, transportation, electrical equipment, and machinery. But part of the contact took place by even more intrusive means. A few scores of U.S. enterprises invested in overseas manufacturing subsidiaries, locating them in many instances within the markets of their principal international competitors; a smaller number of European firms did the same. Somehow, as many businessmen of the era saw it, the bruising contacts between business interests from different countries had to be arrested and contained. Accordingly, wherever a few large firms or a few strong producer associations controlled national industries, the industries concerned set about creating agreements that divided world markets on national lines or shared them pro rata among the producers from different nations, thereby limiting the flow of international trade and investment.

While governments and enterprises were busily attempting to clamp down the flow of international transactions, the objective conditions for the growth of those activities perversely continued to improve. World War II accelerated the trend spectacularly. It shrank the Atlantic crossing from four days to seven hours. It turned transatlantic tourism from a rich man's indulgence into a middleclass need. It opened up the possibility for international consultations on a day-to-day basis not only between the officials of governments but also between the engineers, controllers, salesmen, and strategists of private firms.

In the years immediately following World War II, before the prewar international cartels could effectively regroup, American businessmen rediscovered Europe; at the same time, Europeans began to rediscover one another and the American market. This time, however, the contacts were not confined to a few hundred firms on each side of the Atlantic, but were spread over some thousands of enterprises.

The full force of the acceleration in international contacts did not emerge, however, until the early 1960s. By that time, the improvements in transportation and communication had been assisted by a wholesale dismantling of governmental restrictions on trade, payments, and capital movements among the countries of the advanced world. It was then that the magnitude of the explosion in the international exchange of goods, money, people, and ideas really began to be evident. From 1953 to 1965, the volume of international trade in manufactured goods among the advanced countries almost tripled, outrunning the expansion of production by a very considerable margin. Symptomatic of one of the factors behind the increase was the spectacular growth in international air freight, which rose steadily by 20 percent or so per year (in ton-miles). The arrivals and departures of international travelers in North America and Europe grew about 10 percent annually. And direct investment by U.S. interests in the other advanced countries rose annually by about the same percentage.

It was not merely the quantum jump in international contacts that mattered; it was a change in the quality of those contacts as well. The development of a Eurodollar market abroad is illustrative of that qualitative change. Here is a market in which the sale of several billion dollars' worth of paper, denominated in U.S. currency, is being transacted annually between principals who have no ties of residence or nationality to the United States. Commercial banks throughout Europe use Eurodollars with aplomb, often for purely local purposes. Sometimes, for instance, these instruments are used by banks to lay off the surplus funds of their local economies, sometimes to acquire needed funds for local loans.

The quality of the interpenetration and interdependence of the advanced countries is suggested by many other indices, some quite subtle in character. Young Europeans feel detached from the concept of the nation-state: "We are all German Jews," chorused the French student militants as they marched on the National Assembly. There is a willingness to place on the agenda of the OECD and other international organizations such sensitive domestic issues as the monetary and fiscal policies of member governments. And there is a proliferation of private organizations, such as the multinational enterprises, with structures that take only casual account of the way in which sovereign states have drawn their national boundaries.

III

The multinational enterprise provides a striking illustration of the extent to which modern means of communication permit an integrated organization to link resources in different national economies in order to serve a common set of organizational aims. The term "multinational enterprise" is sometimes confusing and always imprecise; but what I have in mind here is simply a cluster of corporations of diverse nationality joined together by ties of common ownership and responsive to a common management strategy. That kind of definition serves well enough to characterize Ford or Nestlé, IBM or Philips.

Nothing is altogether without precedent in human institution-building; but the multinational enterprise, as I use the term here, comes very close to lacking a relevant precedent.

It was not until the latter part of the nineteenth century that nations began to allow businessmen, as a routine matter of right, to create corporations without limit of life or size of function. And it has only been six or seven decades since most jurisdictions permitted corporations to own other corporations. Because businessmen were not slow to exercise their new prerogatives, it rapidly became commonplace to find clusters of corporations linked together by a common parent, sharing a common pool of resources, and adhering to a common strategy.

Already before World War I, there were a few international clusters of corporations containing entities of diverse nationalities within a common organizational structure. Two dozen oil and mining companies, several scores of manufacturing companies, and a few banks and insurance companies made up most of the list. Not all of these, however, pretended to administer their far-flung subsidiaries in accordance with a common strategy. As long as the time-cost of face-to-face consultation among corporate affiliates in different countries was so high, there was neither much need nor much opportunity to develop a tight, continuous and integral strategy among them. Accordingly, the subsidiaries remote from the parents that had created them often fell under the effective control of local strong men.

By 1950, over 400 U.S. companies had assets of $1 million or more in foreign direct investments. But even at that late date, it is doubtful that many saw their foreign investments as much more than peripheral to the corporate structure. The domestic U.S. market was still the serious business of most of these enterprises. The requirements of that market usually determined the mix and design of the firm's products, the direction of its technological curiosity, and the nature of its preferred production process. The dollar was thought of as the riskless medium of exchange, while all other currencies were thought of as involving special risk. The Americans in the enterprise were the "natives" of the microcosm, while others in the enterprise were the "foreigners."

In the late 1950s, there were major signs of change, and in the ten years that followed the change went very deep. Two tendencies in particular became evident. One strong tendency, especially apparent in the corporate clusters headed by U.S. parents, was toward the reorganization of the control and command mechanism. The "international vice president" or his equivalent, brought into being by the first burst of overseas interest, is rapidly being eliminated. This change is not a sign of the downgrading of the organization's interest in foreign markets, but the very opposite. It is a sign of the elevation and absorption of the business done "abroad" into the mainstream of corporate strategy. In some cases it is more; it is the beginning of the obliteration of the invidious distinction inside the corporation between "home business" and "foreign business." It is the emergence of the strategic view that business should find the best markets, employ the best technology, finance through the best channels, irrespective of geography. It would be pushing history more than a little to say that the U.S. parent firms of multinational enterprises have reached the point at which their affinity to the dollar is no greater than to the franc, or that their identification with Italian markets is as close as with American, or even that their executive recruiting system is as partial to Bavarians as to Hoosiers. But that is the direction of the movement.

The second visible tendency in the structure of U.S. parent firms, closely related to the first, has been the ingathering of foreign subsidiaries, wherever they may be, under the discipline and framework of a common global strategy and a common global control. The headquarters planning of many of these enterprises is more "global" today than it has ever been. It is capable of scanning the world for sales opportunities or production sites or capital supplies or technical skills with greater ease and sophistication than ten years ago. International procurement, cross-hauling, and distribution are becoming a commonplace.

One ought not draw the inference from this description that the corporate officers of the subsidiaries are mere puppets of the center, yanked about by computers operating from a distant common post. Many have the discretion to tailor the commands from the center to their local needs. But their conditioning and their objectives are designed to contribute to a common organizational strategy of some sort; otherwise, there would be no reason for the existence of the multinational enterprise.

In appraising the possibilities of a reaction to the trend, one has to be aware that the nation-state has sometimes felt threatened by the trend in rather sensitive areas of its existence. So far, multinational enterprises have been concentrated largely in a few industries—in oil and mining, drugs and chemicals, machinery, transportation equipment, and food and tobacco. A few of these industries, as it happens, embrace national activities in which nation-states feel a special vulnerability and insecurity; some of these industries, for instance, relate to the national defense or to irreplaceable national resources or to technological leadership.

To add to the tension, nation-states have come to give credence to some of the more uninhibited projections of the future which picture the multinational enterprise as the overwhelmingly dominant vehicle of the world's business. This kind of projection, one ought to note, is not based on very solid evidence. On the contrary, various studies indicate that with every passing decade, as the world's markets grow, the basic standardized industries, such as aluminum, steel, and oil, contain a growing number of firms, not a declining number. More generally, as the technology of any line becomes well and widely known and as the markets for an established product enlarge, additional producers find the barriers to entry less formidable and manage to gain a foothold. It is not foreordained, therefore, that mankind will be swallowed up by the International Colossus Corporation. None the less, that fear exists.

Still another source of the tension created by multinational enterprises arises out of the fact that about four out of five such enterprises are headed by U.S. parents, and that the activity of these enterprises is usually thought of by other nations as an extension of the American hegemony. The notion that the General Motors subsidiary in France in some sense represents an extension of U.S. economic domination to the soil of France may seem a trifle farfetched to most Americans. The interests of General Motors and those of the United States are usually carefully differentiated and sometimes sharply distinguished by the American political process. To Europeans, however, the distinction is not readily evident.

Basing their reaction on an amalgam of fact, fear, and fancy, therefore, many governments view the multinational enterprise with a sense of acute discomfort. Few governments would be able to say precisely how and when they expect the global interests of the enterprise to conflict with the national interests of the economy; many of the illustrations that are used to document the fear are patently exceptional or farfetched. But as long as the multinational enterprise has the power, difficult or improbable though its use may sometimes be, to dry up technology or export technicians or drain off capital or reduce production or shift profits or alter prices or allocate export markets, there is a latent or active tension associated with its presence. As long as they are predominantly headed by U.S. firms, there is also a fear that they may be the instruments of U.S. policy. For some governments the tension can be tolerated perfectly well, but for others the sense of loss of control has been much more difficult to abide.

IV

Although it is unlikely that the business of the advanced world will be dominated by a few large firms, it is more than probable that the economic links between the national economies of the advanced world will become even deeper and more intimate. The increasing intimacy of these ties presents challenges of a new order to the individual nation-state.

Picture the economy of any of the advanced countries of North America or Europe as I have sketched it. It is an economy that draws a considerable part of its technology from outside its boundaries, even while it exports a continuous flow of information to others; it relies upon the plants of other nations to provide a flow of critical products, while relying also upon their markets to absorb substantial proportions of the products it generates; it draws on the savings of nationals in other countries for some purposes, while exporting quantities of its own savings to satisfy the needs of others; it offers sanctuary to enterprises which frame their strategy in global terms, while expecting some of its own nationals to establish themselves in other countries in pursuit of a global strategy.

One cannot easily trace out all the consequences of this pattern of interpenetration. Some of those consequences, however, are reasonably clear. When the rediscount rate is hiked in New York, the cost of money rises in Brussels; when the United States runs a large budgetary deficit, inflationary pressures build up in Europe; more generally, when Italy has an earthquake, dishes rattle in Holland.

From the point of view of national governments, such a degree of openness on the part of national economies is disconcerting enough. Whatever happens in any economy becomes the pressing business of all the others: a general strike in France; a fall of government in Britain. Regardless of the complex political jockeying that may be going on at a moment of economic crisis, there are compelling pressures on each country to help douse the other's fires. The French disdain of British economic management before their own May fiasco did not altogether exempt them from the need to assist the pound sterling in crisis. The wry American satisfaction at De Gaulle's discomfiture did not permit the U.S. Government to disregard the need to support the franc.

The interdependence of the advanced nations has made them especially vulnerable to the consequences when one of them decides to place a block in the system. When the United States began imposing restrictions on the export of its capital, the Government of Canada felt threatened. The remedy for Canada's problems was in some sense even more disconcerting for the nation-state concept than the original threat had been; in order to continue receiving the necessary flow of capital from the United States, Canada undertook to restrain the re-export of capital to third countries.

Those same United States restrictions led to largely unanticipated consequences for European capital markets. The subsidiaries of U.S. enterprises, eager to continue building their European business, searched the European economies for idle cash with which to finance their expansion. To help them in the search, American investment bankers made complex partnerships with European financial interests. Coupling American mass selling expertise with European savoir faire, these transatlantic syndicates sold some billions of dollars of bonds on the European market, thus changing rather dramatically both the channels and the instruments to which European savings were being drawn.

There is still another implication of the close ties among the economies of the advanced nations, one which in the end may prove the most disconcerting of all. A considerable part of the international flow of money, goods, and services among these economies can no longer be thought of as arm's-length transactions. Many of these transactions take place between the sister affiliates of multinational entities. For instance, close to one-third of U.S. exports of nonmilitary manufactured goods, about $6 billion annually, is shipped to the overseas affiliates of U.S. parent firms, while over $5 billion are returned annually to the United States by such affiliates in the form of dividends, interest, and royalties.

Apart from the international transactions that take place under the mantle of multinational enterprise, there are also the transactions that take place among the members of more informal international alliances. For instance, the commercial banking and investment banking systems of the advanced countries are now so intimately intertwined that it would be distorting reality to think of many of their transactions as representing arm's-length exchanges.

When international transactions are effected between parties whose relationships are long-term and organic in character, the regulatory capabilities of an intervening state inevitably decline. As a result, any state which senses an inadequacy in its capacity to impose effective restrictions at the border has ample reason for harboring that feeling. For brief periods of time, perhaps, regulatory controls may have a real impact; for longer periods, the illusion of such impact may persist simply because the specific channel that had been blocked by a particular set of controls was responding in line with governmental expectations. But, given the complexity of multinational institutions and the presence of so many alternative channels for the legitimate international movement of funds and other resources, the regulating sovereign seems increasingly at a disadvantage.

v

The advanced world, carried ebulliently on the crest of a technological revolution in transportation and communication, has absentmindedly set up a virile system of international institutions and relationships that sit alongside the system of nation-states. The system of nation-states has its built-in machinery of political process and public accountability, while the international system wields its power and garners its support by less well-defined means.

In part, the two systems are complementary; in part, they are at odds. The international system, when operating benignly, stands for all the good things that can be achieved by open boundaries: more trade, more capital flows, more movement of ideas and people, more growth. The system of nation-states, at its best, stands for all the good things that national policy can hope to provide: more economic security, more social equality, more identification and a sense of belonging. An economic determinist, if asked to project the outcome of the clash between the systems, would probably lean toward the assumption that the international order will prevail. The shrinkage of international distances will continue; the flow of international ideas will accelerate; the opportunities and the requirements of large-scale human endeavor will increase.

But such a prediction, if it were made, would be far too facile, especially for the three or four decades ahead that represent the planning horizon of most of us. There is a stubborn life and purpose in the system of nation-states, and there is a tenacious capacity on the part of mankind indefinitely to disregard the seemingly inevitable. It is perfectly possible, therefore, to picture a sequence of events in which the increasing openness of national boundaries leads to a reaction of disconcerting force. Restrictions on the flow of capital, goods, and people could conceivably be the first response to the difficulties and uncertainties that have been generated by the relatively open boundaries of the past decade or two. In classic Hegelian fashion, the world may experience a period of revulsion from the international order before it is prepared to move on to a new international synthesis.

Some kinds of problems are less likely to touch off a spasm of revulsion and withdrawal than are others. I would worry only a little, for instance, about the problems that arise over the conflicting jurisdictional reach of nation-states, such as the efforts of one nation to influence the actions of the nationals of another. Conflicts of this sort, which appear from time to time in fields such as antitrust or trading with the enemy or securities regulation, can be handled reasonably well as nations grow more sensitive to the problem. A tolerable state of affairs can be created partly by the nation-states' application of self-imposed constraints and partly by their negotiation of common standards.

There are some problems, however, whose solution is not amenable to modest measures of that sort. Some demand consciously coördinated action among sovereigns on issues that are fairly sensitive in terms of domestic politics. The balance-of-payments issue, for instance, when it involves agreements among governments to create Special Drawing Rights (SDRs) or "paper gold," begins to move into sensitive territory. The existence of agreements of this sort may be unnoticed by the politicians for a period of time, provided they are sufficiently technical and obscure. But when they begin to demand coördinated economic action tending to restrict the freedom of states to frame independent domestic policies, one can expect to see the beginnings of major difficulty. When this interrelation becomes widely apparent, coördinated action may be resisted by all the principal actors involved: by the governments which would have to share their power with others; and by the enterprises whose transactions would be the subject of the coördinated governmental control.

If governments were obliged to coördinate their monetary, fiscal, and other economic policies on any intimate and continuous basis, the consequences would presumably affect all business, whether oriented to the domestic market or to the international market. But multinational enterprises would have an especially heavy stake in such a trend. In some respects, the trend could increase the freedom of multinational enterprises; but the opposite might also be true. Intergovernmental coördination might, for instance, reduce the number of situations in which the rights afforded by some governments were thwarted by the regulations imposed by others. On the other hand, since there are some things that governments can do together which they cannot do separately, intergovernmental coördination could have the effect of increasing the effectiveness of regulations by the public sector in many fields, including taxation and monetary regulation.

In general, multinational enterprises as a group have exhibited no great enthusiasm for a coördinated approach by sovereign states to the problems that the states addressed individually in the past. Such a reserved reaction is readily understandable. The largest and most seasoned of such enterprises can point with justifiable pride to the fact that, despite the pitfalls and dangers that uncoördinated sovereign action may theoretically offer to multinational enterprises, few of them have fallen victim to the dangers of six or seven decades of war, depression, and tension. As far as such enterprises are concerned, a heavy presumption exists that they would continue to survive even in an uncoördinated world.

Instead of subjecting themselves to the uncertain consequences of multinational coördination, most such enterprises are quite ready to commit themselves to a "code of good behavior" toward the economies in which their affiliates are established. These enterprises are aware that their "conduct" has generally been quite reasonable and acceptable when viewed by any normal standards. Accordingly, most of them have been willing to commit themselves on paper to the continuation of such conduct. They are usually prepared to agree to train local nationals, observe local customs, obey local laws, and perform all the other acts expected of decent local citizens. But "conduct"—at least "conduct" defined in these terms—is not very relevant to the underlying issue. With varying degrees of intensity, nation-states have a sense that the locus of their power is challenged by an open international system in general and by multinational enterprises in particular. What some are searching for is the means of checking their sense of ebbing control and of retaining a tolerable amount of that power.

It may be that, in the end, sovereign states will learn to live with a decline in their perceived economic power. But one marvels at the tenacity with which man seeks to retain a sense of differentiation and identity, a feeling of control, even when the apparent cost of the identity and the control seems out of all proportion to its value. One cannot disregard the possibility that one of the advanced countries, imperiled by a sense of ebbing control and declining identity, may strike out blindly against the others.

The role of statesmen in a situation of this kind is to find the means for accommodating the tension before it grows intolerable. In this case, the accommodation will be painful and complex. On the part of governments, it will involve agreements that demand the conscious sharing of prerogatives that once were independently exercised. On the part of business, it may demand a tolerance for more coördinated and more effective measures of public control. Whether the advanced world has the resiliency and farsightedness to take the needed steps remains an open question.

PART THREE: Interdependence of
National Economic Policies

National Economic Policy in an Interdependent World Economy

RICHARD N. COOPER

Richard N. Cooper is Professor of Economics at Yale University. In this essay, originally published in the June 1967 issue of the Yale Law Journal, *Mr. Cooper considers the implications of increased economic interdependence for policymaking in the industrial nations.*

DURING THE PAST DECADE, there has been a strong trend toward economic interdependence among the industrial countries. This growing interdependence makes the successful pursuit of national economic objectives much more difficult. Broadly speaking, increasing interdependence complicates the pursuit of national objectives in three ways. First, it increases the number and magnitude of the disturbances to which each country's balance of payments is subjected, and this in turn diverts policy attention and instruments of policy to the restoration of external balance. Second, it slows down the process by which national authorities, each acting on its own, are able to reach their domestic objectives. Third, the response to greater integration can involve the community of nations in counteracting motions which leave all countries worse off than they need be. These difficulties are in turn complicated by the fact that the objective of greater economic integration involves international agreements which reduce the number of policy instruments available to national authorities for pursuit of their economic objectives. This article touches on all of these facets of higher economic interdependence among industrial nations, both as a fact and as an objective, but its principal focus is on the third complication—the process of mutually damaging competition among national policies.

There can be little doubt about the great growth in international economic interdependence over the last two decades. Import quotas in industrial countries have been virtually abolished on trade in manufactured products, tariffs have been reduced, and transportation costs have fallen relative to the value of goods. At the same time, the accumulation of capital and the spread of technology have made national economies more similar in their basic characteristics of production; comparative cost differences have apparently narrowed, suggesting that imports can be replaced by domestic production with less loss in national income than heretofore. Whether a country imports a particular good or exports it thus becomes less dependent on the basic characteristics of the economy, more dependent on historical development and on relatively accidental and transitory features of recent investment decisions at home and abroad. An invention in one country may lead to production there for export, but the new product will relatively quickly be produced abroad—or supplanted by a still newer product—and possibly even exported to the original innovating country.

Monetary disturbances, too, are likely to be much more quickly translated into changes in the volume of exports and imports than they were formerly. Under fixed exchange rates, greater than average monetary inflation in one country will invite a more rapid deterioration in the balance on goods and services than was true in the past.

Enlargement of the decision-making domain of the world's great producing firms results in the rapid movement of capital and technical knowledge across national frontiers, thereby contributing to the narrowing of comparative cost differences; but their activity will also quicken the speed with which trade adjusts to new sales opportunities because they have direct knowledge of foreign markets and access to distribution channels.

Finally, as financial markets become more closely integrated, relatively small differences in yields on securities will induce large flows of funds between countries. Banks will increasingly number "foreign" firms among their prime customers; the advantages of inexpensive credit to firms in countries with ample savings and well-functioning financial markets, such as the

United States, will be shared increasingly with firms elsewhere.

All of these changes in the characteristics of the international economy during the past decade—and it should be emphasized that economic integration is still far from complete—are crucial to the functioning of the international payments system and the autonomy which it permits to national economic policy formation. These changes mean that in normal periods prospective imbalances in international payments—imbalances which would arise if countries did not respond to reduce them or did not adjust policy measures to forestall them—are likely to be more frequent and of larger amplitude than they have been in the past. "Disturbances" arising from new innovations, from generous wage settlements leading to price increases, and from excess or deficient domestic demand will affect the balance of payments more peceptibly. Whether or not imbalances also last longer depends upon the relationship among the "disturbances"; if they are well distributed among countries and tend equally toward deficit or surplus, the duration of prospective imbalances may well be less than in the past; otherwise it may be longer.

These changes suggest that balance of payments difficulties are likely to be more common in the future, and that they will worsen as the structural changes continue in their recent trend. By the same token, however, correction of imbalances in international payments should be easier in the future. Trade flows will respond more sharply to given small "disturbances"; but they should also respond more quickly to policy measures designed to influence them. If a small relative increase in the price level will lead a national economy into greater balance of payments difficulties than heretofore, a relatively small decrease should undo the difficulties. Similarly, international capital flows will respond more rapidly to small differences in national credit conditions; but small differences in national credit conditions directed to correcting the imbalance can induce equilibrating flows of capital. Thus if the national authorities can recognize disturbances early, are willing to use some of the tools at their disposal for correcting imbalances in international payments, and act reasonably quickly in doing so, then the increased sensitivity of international payments to various disturbances need cause no undue difficulty—provided that policy instruments are properly chosen and adequately coordinated among countries.

ECONOMIC OBJECTIVES AND POLICY INSTRUMENTS

A well-known proposition in the theory of economic policy requires that the number of policy instruments be at least as great as the number of objectives (target variables) if all objectives are to be achieved. If the number of instruments is fewer than the number of targets, it will not be possible to reach all of the targets; in that case, at least some targets must be given up, and the authorities must choose among them.

A simple example can illustrate the need to have at least as many instruments as targets. Suppose the government of an isolated country has two economic objectives: it would like to assure full employment of its labor force at all times, and it would like its national product to grow at a specified rate each year. It can vary the overall size of the budget deficit or surplus (fiscal policy) to assure full employment. But full employment of resources can be met with a variety of combination of investment, consumption, and government expenditure. Without some other instrument, the desired growth rate cannot be assured. If, however, investment leads to more growth, then monetary policy and fiscal policy together can be manipulated to achieve the two objectives. The higher the growth rate desired, the lower should be the rate of interest. Fiscal policy can then be adjusted to assure full employment. This very simple model apparently influenced thinking in the early years of the Kennedy Administration.

Viewing economic policy as a problem in specifying targets and finding sufficient instruments to reach them helps to illuminate many policy problems confronting national authorities. The objective of greater economic integration has led many officials to reject both flexible exchange rates and frequent variations in fixed exchange rates as instruments for maintaining balance of payments equilibrium. A number of other instruments of policy have been ruled out by international agreement on the same grounds, or to avoid a round of retaliation and counter-retaliation that would leave all countries worse off than they were at the outset. Most types of export subsidies, tariff discrimination among countries, increases in tariffs, and discriminatory exchange regulations fall into this category. A number of provisions of the General Agreement on Tariffs and Trade

(GATT) are devoted to these exclusions and prohibitions; with specified exceptions, such as the formation of customs unions or free trade areas, trade discrimination is proscribed. So are many types of export subsidies and discrimination in domestic taxation between home and foreign goods. The Articles of Agreement of the International Monetary Fund (IMF) make similar prohibitions with respect to currency arrangements. The extensive use of these measures in the past, especially in the 1930's, led to widespread retaliation and mutual recriminations, and they acquired a bad name among outward-looking officials. But the price of international rules of good behavior as set forth in the GATT and the IMF Articles has been a reduction in the range of instruments available to national policy-makers.

Some usable policy instruments may be used, as a practical matter, only within a limited range. In the United States, changes in the discount rate of the Federal Reserve System and (since 1962) deliberate deficits or surpluses in the government budget are both regarded as legitimate tools of economic policy; but in normal times, the public is not likely to countenance a discount rate of 20 per cent or a budget deficit of $50 billion. These exceed the range of acceptability; policy instruments have "boundary conditions." In the abnormal situations when such limits become operative, they withdrew an instrument from use. Sometimes these limits are not fully known until they are tested; then we discover that we have more targets (or fewer instruments) than were previously apparent.

It goes without saying that to be attainable, economic objectives must be consistent. If they are not consistent, no number of policy instruments will be sufficient. One illustration in the forefront of discussion in most industrial countries involves the relationship between employment and price stability. Given the institution of private collective bargaining, is the target of "full employment" (4 per cent unemployment in the United States, under 2 per cent in the United Kingdom, each by its own standards and definitions) consistent with "price stability," defined, say, as stability in the consumer price index? Many economists would find a conflict.

This kind of inconsistency can perhaps be overcome by developing new policy instruments.[1] Another kind of inconsistency,

1. These new instruments would involve shifting the trade-off between unemployment and price inflation—called the Phillips Curve—enough to

especially important to national economies linked through international trade and capital movements, cannot be eliminated through the development of new instruments. Examples are objectives regarding the balance of payments or the trade balance. Since one country's trade surplus is another country's trade deficit, it is impossible for all countries to succeed in running trade surpluses. The same is true for balance of payments, taking into account capital movements. If there are n countries, only $n-1$ of them can succeed in achieving their independent balance of payments targets; at least one must accept defeat or else fail to target values for its trade position and its balance of payments position, thereby acting as an international residual. It has been suggested that the United States played this role until the late 1950's, by taking a relatively passive position toward its payments position after the termination of Marshall Plan aid.

The requirement of consistency is not merely theoretical. In 1962, for instance, all of the major industrial countries wanted simultaneously to improve their payments positions on current account. While mutual success was not logically impossible in this case, it did imply a correspondingly sharp deterioration in the current account position of the less developed countries taken together, which in turn would require ample financing from the industrial countries in the form of grants or loans. No such increase in capital movements was targeted. Thus national targets were inconsistent.

THE SPEED OF ADJUSTMENT

In summary, successful economic policy requires an adequate number of policy instruments for the number of economic objectives, and it requires that these objectives be consistent with one another. If either of these conditions fails, policymakers are bound to be frustrated in their efforts. Before turning to how these frustrations become manifest, however, one other point should be made: growing interdependence can slow down greatly the process by which independently acting national authorities reach their economic objectives, even when all the targets are consistent and there are sufficient policy instruments at hand to

---

make simultaneous attainment of the two objectives feasible. This is the thrust of "incomes policies."

reach them. Thus in practice nations may find themselves further from their objectives than would be true with less interdependence.

High interdependence slows the speed of adjustment to disturbances if national policymakers do not take the interdependence into account. This is because the economic authorities in different countries may be working at cross-purposes. An investment boom in one country may raise interest rates both at home and, by attracting internationally mobile funds, in neighboring countries. The first country may temporarily welcome the high interest rates to help curb the boom and may also tighten fiscal policy to keep inflationary pressures in check. But the other countries may fear that higher interest rates will deter investment at home and take steps to lower interest rates. Unless this monetary relaxation is taken into account in framing fiscal policy in the first country, its authorities will find that fiscal policy has not been sufficiently contractionary. But more contractionary fiscal policy will tend to hold up interest rates, so that the monetary authorities in the neighboring countries will find they have only been partially successful in lowering their rates. Even if in the end the whole process settles to a point where the various national authorities are satisfied, it will have taken longer than if there had been close coordination between the authorities in the several countries involved. The greater the interactions between the countries, the longer convergence will take if countries act on their own.

Sometimes, of course, actions in a neighboring country can reinforce those taken at home. If in the above example the domestic investment boom transmitted inflationary pressures to a neighboring country through enlarged imports, then contractionary fiscal policy there would complement contractionary fiscal policy at home. But in this case failure to take into account the interactions between the two countries may lead to *over*-correction and excessive unemployment. This will arise if the authorities in each country decide how much they have to act when acting alone to restore equilibrium; then when both groups act, the total effect will be excessive.

If policy decisions are truly decentralized among nations, in the sense that the authorities in each nation pursue only their own objectives with their own instruments without taking into account the interactions with other countries, then the more interdependent the international economy is, the less successful countries are likely to be in reaching and maintaining their economic objectives. This is due to the greater impact of domestic measures on foreign economies, calling forth correspondingly greater offsetting responses which in turn affect the first country. Under these circumstances, countries must either reconcile themselves to prolonged delays in reaching their objectives or they must coordinate their policies more closely with those of other nations.

It has of course long been true that small countries must watch closely economic developments and policies in their larger neighbors, and they would take these developments into account. For the Netherlands, forecasting German GNP and German economic policies is a critical component to forecasting Dutch GNP. But as economies grow more interdependent, the importance of *two-way* interactions increases, so that economically large countries such as Britain, Germany, and even the United States must increasingly take into account developments and policies abroad.

INTERNATIONAL COMPETITION IN ECONOMIC POLICY

In an interdependent economy, governments do not have full control over the instrument variables needed to influence the trade balance or the balance of payments. Each government can affect the domestic interest rate in an attempt to influence international capital movements or can set tariffs on imports and subsidies on exports to influence the trade balance. But success in influencing capital movements or trade flows depends on what other countries are doing. It is interest rate *differentials*, not the absolute level of interest rates, which induce the movement of capital. And it is domestic tariffs *less* foreign subsidies which influence the level of imports. There are many instruments of economic policy for which relative differences affect international transactions, but where the absolute value may continue to exert a strong influence on purely domestic decisions. This is true, for example, not only of short- and long-term interest rates, but also of liberal tax benefits to investment, generous depreciation allowances, lax regulation of corporate activities, and a host of other measures designed to influence corporate location. It is also true of foreign trade: generous credit arrangements or credit-risk guarantees for exports may encourage total exports without improving the trade balance if other countries are pursuing similar measures.

This feature of policy instruments—that the absolute level of the instrument may have important effects domestically, but that only the level relative to that in other countries influences the balance of trade or payments—raises the question: Where do the values of these instruments finally settle? International capital movements between two otherwise isolated countries will presumably be roughly the same whether interest rates are at 7 per cent in one and 5 per cent in the other or at 4 per cent in the first country and 2 per cent in the second. In each case, the differential is two percentage points. But what determines whether "community" interest rates settle at the higher level or the lower one? The effects on other objectives may be very different. Economic growth will be inhibited more in the first case than in the second.

This would be of secondary importance if all countries had many policy instruments at their disposal. Each country could compensate for any deleterious effects on domestic objectives arising from the value of instruments determined predominantly by the community as a whole. But, as we already noted, the number of instruments and the range of values they can assume are often sharply limited by tradition or law. Indeed, it is highly likely that at any point in time a country will have at its disposal *only* the minimum number of policy instruments that it needs to satisfy important domestic political demands. Policy instruments affect the welfare of particular members of the community as well as national economic objectives, so their use will be resisted. Public expectation is that certain measures, while theoretically conceivable, will in practice not be used. Any attempt to invoke them therefore meets stiff resistance.

The values which policy instruments take on in the community of nations, and the process by which those values are reached, are therefore of strong interest to the individual nations. They may not have sufficient domestic flexibility to offset the damaging effects of policy instruments which are forced to an inappropriate level by international competition among governments. As a result, greater international integration can force choices among national objectives which otherwise would all be attainable.

There are occasions in which most or even all members of the international community will find themselves worse off. The competitive devaluations and tariff wars of the interwar period offer the most striking examples; many of the proscriptions in the GATT and the IMF Articles of Agreement are designed to avoid a repetition of those events.

But competition among policies was not thereby banished on all fronts. For example, interest rates shot upward in 1965 and 1966 to levels one to two percentage points higher than those which had prevailed in most countries in 1964. Some of the increases were designed to curb domestic demand; others were defensive, to limit capital outflow. Even after domestic economies had cooled down, it took a dramatic meeting of finance ministers at Checquers, England, in early 1967, to reverse the process. Four other types of policy instruments having these characteristics have been used in the effort to strengthen the balance of payments of various countries: restrictions on government procurement, government-sponsored export promotion, tax incentives to domestic investment, and changes in domestic tax structure. The United States, faced with large payments deficits during the early sixties, made or considered moves in all of these areas; but in each case there was ample precedent abroad for doing so.

Government purchases for government use are specifically excluded from coverage by the GATT rules governing international trade. The result is that a conspicuously small proportion of government purchases, by any government, is from foreign suppliers who compete with domestic producers. In the United States, the Buy American provision—which since 1954 officially gives preferential treatment of 6 to 12 per cent (in addition to tariffs) to domestic over foreign competitors for the Government's custom—has existed since the 1930's. But in 1962 a number of government agencies, including most importantly the Department of Defense, raised the preference accorded to domestic suppliers as high as 50 per cent. Foreign aid expenditures by the American government are even more restricted. Starting with development loans in 1959, such expenditures were tied increasingly to purchases in the United States, until by 1965 only a limited class of expenditures was not so tied, regardless of the price advantages offered by foreign suppliers.

The government procurement practices of other countries are more difficult to document, since most governments do not require open bidding on government purchases with well-publicized preferences for domestic producers, such as those found in the Buy American provisions. Many countries follow the practice of tying foreign assistance, either by law or by skillful selection of projects and recipient countries, to purchases from the donor country. This is as true for those donors with fully employed economies as for those with excess capacity and unemployment —even though tying is far less effective in the former case, and merely stimulates additional imports—and it is as true for donor countries in balance of payments surplus as for those in deficit. Canada, Japan, and the United Kingdom tie the bulk of their foreign assistance, and France ties some expenditures. France and the Netherlands give virtually all of their foreign assistance to colonial or former colonial areas, where de facto aid-tying takes place through long-established trading firms. German aid often originates with requests from prospective exporters who have found projects in recipient countries eligible for foreign assistance by German criteria.

Many of these practices, of course, arise not only from balance of payments considerations but also from protectionist sentiment. Domestic producers apply strong political pressures on their governments to buy at home—the more so when the goods are to be "given away." But weakness in the balance of payments often strengthens their arguments and increases public acceptability of such restrictive measures.

Government activities are not solely restrictive of trade. On the contrary, a second range of practices involves all kinds of schemes, except direct subsidies proscribed by GATT, to promote exports of goods and services. Governments sponsor trade fairs, product exhibitions, and other advertisements for the products of their exporters; they insure commercial and so-called noncommercial risks involved in exporting; and they often help to finance exports directly. No major industrial trading nation can be found without a government or government-sponsored agency for insuring and/or extending credit for exports. Some countries, such as France and Italy, give especially favorable treatment to export paper in their banking systems or at their central banks. And export credit is often exempt from general credit limitations to restrict domestic demand. All of these measures really subsidize exports, although it is often impossible to identify the amount of the subsidy to any particular sale.

The United States established the U.S. Travel Service in 1961 to attract foreign tourists to the United States. European governments have been aiding tourism much longer, and each year spend substantial amounts for the purpose of attracting foreign tourists. Moreover, expenditure for tourist promotion has been growing rapidly, doubling every two to four years. In addition to straightforward publicity, most European countries subsidize the hotel industry either through preferential tax treatment or through low-interest or government-guaranteed loans. In most countries, these programs date from the late fifties or the early sixties.

Subsidies to domestic investment is the third area in which governments have moved to improve their international payments positions. Investment subsidies for manufacturing and agriculture improve the competitiveness of a country's products in world markets. Some countries give direct tax incentives to new investment in plant and equipment, such as the investment tax credit of 7 per cent adopted by the United States in 1962 and the 30 per cent investment allowance in the United Kingdom (in early 1966, the latter was also converted into a direct grant of 20 per cent of expenditures on new plant and equipment). Japan permits greatly accelerated depreciation of assets. . . .

Under a regime of fixed exhange rates, government subsidy for domestic investment is similar to a devaluation of the currency in that it improves the cost competitiveness both of the country's export products and of its products which compete with imports.

Subsidies to investment are obviously motivated by considerations extending well beyond the balance of payments; economic growth has become a target of economic policy in its own right, partly for political and strategic reasons (arising in part from the "economic race" with the Soviet Bloc), partly because rising standards of living are universally desired. But balance of payments considerations do play an important role in the decision to inaugurate investment incentives. Britain for years has emphasized the need to enlarge and improve its capital stock to compete more effectively in world markets. And former U.S. Secretary of the Treasury Dillon, testifying on behalf of the U.S. investment tax credit in 1962, argued that the measure was required "if U.S. business firms are to be placed on substantially equal footing with their foreign competitors in this respect. It is essential," he said, "to our competitive position in markets both here at home and abroad, that American industry be put on the same basis as foreign industry. Unless this is done, increased imports and decreased exports will unnecessarily add to the burden of our balance of payments deficit." [2]

Changes in the structure of domestic taxation, and in particular the "mix" between direct and indirect taxes, constitute a fourth area in which governments have moved, or have been tempted to move, to improve their national trade positions. GATT rules prohibiting export subsidies have been interpreted to preclude remission of direct taxes on exports but to permit remission of indirect taxes. Thus taxes on the corporate profits arising from export cannot be rebated, but manufacturers' excise taxes or turnover taxes can. Similarly, countries are permitted to levy indirect taxes, but not direct taxes, on imports. Because of this asymmetry in border tax adjustment, it is possible under fixed exchange rates for a country to stimulate exports and impede imports by shifting its tax structure from direct taxes to indirect taxes, provided that direct taxes affect prices.

The GATT rule is based on the classical economic assumption that indirect taxes are shifted entirely to the purchaser, while direct taxes are not shifted at all, being absorbed entirely (in the case of the corporate profits tax) by the firm. Recent work in the field of public finance suggests, however, that there may be much less difference in the price effects of, say, corporate profits taxes and manufacturers' excise taxes than was once thought to be the case.[3] To the extent that indirect taxes are partially absorbed by the producer, or that profits taxes are partially shifted forward to the consumer, the GATT rules regarding border treatment of national taxes allow some "subsidy" to exports and a country can improve its trade position by switching from cor-

2. *Hearings on H.R. 10650 Before the Senate Comm. on Finance,* 87th Cong., 2nd Sess., pt. 1, at 83 (1962).
3. M. Krzyzaniak & R. Musgrave, *The Incidence of the Corporation Income Tax* chs. 6, 8 (1963); Stockfish, *On the Obsolescence of Incidence,* 14 *Public Finance* 125–48 (1959).

porate profits taxes to excise or turnover taxes.

Some countries have made tax changes in this direction, and others have been urged to do so. Sweden reduced its income tax and imposed a general sales tax in 1960; in mid-1964, Italy reduced payroll taxes (which are not rebatable) and, to recoup the revenue, increased turnover taxes (which are rebatable). The German government in 1967 approved a change from a turnover to a value-added tax which will improve the export competitiveness of German products;[4] and Britain has been periodically urged to increase its indirect taxes and lower the direct corporate taxes, although a special committee set up to examine the matter rejected the proposed change.[5] Similar changes have been proposed for the United States.

Once again, many considerations have influenced these proposals; in some cases, there may be powerful arguments for making the change regardless of the effects on the balance of payments. But it is interesting to note that these proposals have come alive only since the late 1950's, as international competition has stiffened, and that improvement in the trade balance is often mentioned explicitly as an important reason for making the change. The Committee for Economic Development has stated, for example, that "a major advantage of a general excise tax [over a corporate profits tax] is that it would tend to improve the ability of the United States to compete with others in world markets," and it goes on to argue that the United States must "equalize" its tax structure with that of the Common Market as tariffs between the two trading areas are reduced.[6]

All of these policy measures have a common characteristic. Taken by one country alone, each represents a concealed devaluation of the currency, at least with respect to a selected class of transactions. But, like devaluation, these measures are effective only if other countries do not respond in kind. To each country, tying foreign aid and giving preference to domestic

---

4. Because rebates under the turnover tax, due to complications in calculating the exact burden of the tax on each commodity, are lower than the values of rebates—and import levies—that would be permissible under the GATT rules.

5. *Report of the Committee on Turnover Taxation,* Cmnd. No. 2300 (1964).

6. Committee for Economic Development, *Reducing Tax Rates for Production and Growth* 39–40 (1962).

producers in government procurement may appear to offer a means to improve the balance of payments; and, indeed, in the short run it may do so. But if all countries follow the same practices, the benefit to each is much reduced and some countries will have their payments positions worsened as a result. In the meantime, the total real value of foreign aid has been reduced by reliance on high cost suppliers, and inefficient production has been fostered.

The same thing is true of the other measures discussed. General adoption of export promotion schemes and government-sponsored tourist publicity will surely have a much greater effect on the total level of world exports and tourism than on the payments position of any one country, since the measures will largely cancel one another and leave only residual effects on the balance of payments. Similarly, if all countries adopt special tax incentives for domestic investment, the net improvement in competitiveness—which depends as much on incentives abroad as on those at home—will be haphazard and unpredictable. The principal effect may well be not on any one country's balance of payments position but on the total investment and the rate of growth in the world economy at large—so long as these effects are not nullified by a competitive rise in long-term interest rates! Finally, an effort to raise exports and impede imports through changes in domestic tax structure may have little overall effect on foreign trade and leave countries with tax structures which many would prefer not to have.

At any point in time there are often cogent and persuasive arguments for introducing one or more of these measures to improve the balance of payments. If other countries did not respond in kind, the desired improvement would be forthcoming. But if other countries act likewise, the measures largely cancel out. Not only is the purpose of the move nullified, but all countries may find themselves worse off in terms of their other objectives. As a rule, individual countries cannot act unilaterally without inviting reaction. If they are successful, they are quickly emulated by their neighbors, so that the initial gains are transitory at best. Countries often must act in self-defense, in response to the behavior of their trading partners. This is particularly so when measures to reduce one country's deficit do not reduce the surpluses of the surplus countries but increase the deficit of another deficit country or move countries in balance into deficit. These third countries then feel compelled to respond defensively and their actions in turn increase the deficit of the initial country. Moreover, many of the measures thus taken are difficult to reverse —countries do not readily contract export credit programs or lengthen the periods of depreciation allowable for tax purposes.

Today there is little blatant competition among policies, such as the round of tariff increases in the late twenties and the competitive depreciations of the early thirties. But more subtle and sophisticated methods can substitute, albeit imperfectly, for currency depreciation. Taken in sequence by different countries, these measures produce a kind of ratchet effect. We then have a series of competitive depreciations in disguise.

In this case it is balance of payments difficulties, actual or feared, which give rise to the undesirable competition in policies. Competition for the location of industry can also weaken economic policy in the area of regulation and taxation, due to the mobility of business. To attract new firms or to keep the firms they have, local authorities may eschew tax or regulatory measures which in the view of the authorities would benefit the community as a whole, but for the possibility of driving away investment.

National governments have not yet engaged in a scramble to adjust their policies to be most attractive to foreign-owned business firms; on the contrary, a number of countries are concerned about the amount of foreign control already present. Differences in taxation and other measures relating to business activity do, however, affect international corporate location, and some beginnings of national competition for this location can be seen. Luxembourg liberalized its depreciation allowances and offered an investment allowance in 1962 in what appeared to be a deliberate move to attract foreign investment for operations throughout the European Common Market. Belgium and the Swiss cantons have also adopted tax and other features designed to attract foreign enterprise.[7]

---

7. Furthermore, the relaxation in France's tough policy on foreign investment may have been dictated in large measure by the prospect of losing investment to other members of the European Economic Community which would nonetheless have free access to the French market.

IN SUMMARY

In a highly integrated economic area which surpasses in size the jurisdiction of governments, each group of policymakers is subject to such strong interactions with the surrounding area that the constraints on its actions become very severe. Indeed, in the hypothetically limiting case, these constraints determine entirely the course of action each jurisdiction must take. The region—or the nation—in a highly integrated economy becomes analogous to the perfect competitor—or at best the oligopolist—in a market economy. The range of choice it has, consistent with economic survival, is very small; for the most part, it simply adapts its behavior to stimuli from outside. Awareness of the high interactions will eventually inhibit action.

A. C. Pigou and John Maynard Keynes pointed out long ago that the sum of individual decisions by consumers and producers may not always be optimal for society as a whole (and hence for its members), even though its members may be acting individually on entirely rational grounds.[8] Some kind of collective action is therefore required to produce an optimal outcome.

The same can be true among nations, or among regions within a nation, if the interactions among their decisions are sufficiently strong. One jurisdiction gropes for new instruments in an attempt to improve its position. If it succeeds, others follow and there is a competition in policies which defeats everyone's objectives and in fact can even lead all participants *away* from their national or local objectives, like the members of a crowd rising to their tiptoes to see a parade better but in the end merely standing uncomfortably on their tiptoes.

An invisible hand seems to be working in economic policy as well as in the market place. Competition in the market place is alleged to lead to the most efficient allocation of resources. Whatever the merits of this claim, we can be much less confident that competition among policies will be optimal. Governments seek many ends, not the efficient allocation of resources alone; and the process of policy competition can certainly thwart some of

---

8. A. Pigou, *The Economics of Welfare* (1932). This was also the central underlying message of J. Keynes, *General Theory of Employment, Interest, and Money* (1936).

those objectives.

Existing rules of international behavior as set forth in GATT and in the IMF Agreement do limit the use of direct and straightforward means of policy competition such as open export subsidies and multiple exchange rates, and they therefore slow the process of policy competition since the more subtle and sophisticated methods—loopholes in GATT and the IMF Agreement—usually involve strong domestic considerations which delay their implementation. But existing rules do not fully accomplish the aim of preventing self-defeating policy competition and of freeing domestic policy measures to pursue largely domestic objectives. Moreover, the pressures on domestic policy are likely to become greater as the world economy becomes more interdependent. Freedom of action in economic policy formation can be lost through the need for each country to compete in policies with its competitors in commerce.

To minimize adverse effects from this competition, countries can coordinate closely their national economic policies, attempting to define and reach an optimum combination of policies for the community as a whole. This route involves extensive "internationalization" of the process of economic policymaking, transferring this governmental function to the larger integrated area.

Alternatively, countries can attempt to remove the major source of pressure on their actions—deleterious effects on their international payments positions—by providing each country with ample liquidity to finance any deficit and allowing it to go its own way. Or this goal can be accomplished by reversing the process of economic integration, artificially breaking down or reducing the numerous economic links between countries. While some movement can be seen on all three of these fronts, actions in the United States and Europe in the mid-sixties seemed dangerously pointed toward the third alternative.

The International Monetary System and the Reconciliation of Policy Goals

J. MARCUS FLEMING

J. Marcus Fleming is Deputy Director of the Research Department of the International Monetary Fund. In this paper, written in a private capacity for a Symposium on Monetary Process and Policy, he surveys the development of the international monetary system since the time of the Bretton Woods Agreement and examines the causes of the present problems of this system.

INTRODUCTION

IN SPEAKING of the "international monetary system," I shall be concerned not merely with exchange rates, external reserves, the financing of balance of payments deficits, and so forth but rather with the whole complex of arrangements and practices, whether resting on law or custom, that condition the behavior of national authorities with respect to the balance of payments. In other words, I shall have in mind the real as well as the monetary side of the international economic mechanism. And I shall inquire into the extent to which this system hinders or permits a simultaneous realization of "domestic" policy objectives, like full employment, price stability, and economic growth, on the one hand, and "international" policy objectives, like freedom of trade and freedom of capital movements, on the other.

The possibility of conflict between domestic and international objectives arises mainly because of the inflexible or otherwise noncompetitive behavior of the prices of goods and services, and notably of labor, within each country. When Keynes first discussed this problem, the point he stressed was the downward inflexibility of wages, as a result of which any attempt at a domestic adjustment of the price level in a deficit country might lead to unemployment. Since then, the situation has been complicated by the appearance, or emergence to consciousness, of various "cost-push" mechanisms which sometimes carry prices farther from, instead of nearer to, equilibrium. These price rigidities and perverse spontaneities create difficulties in bringing about even long-term adjustments in relative national price levels and render impossible those short-term adjustments to temporary balance of payments factors which would occur in an ideal price system and which, in turn, would tend to evoke equilibrating capital flows.

THE SYSTEM AS ORIGINALLY ENVISAGED

The system of adjustment set up during and immediately after World War II in the Articles of Agreement of the International Monetary Fund (IMF) and in the General Agreement on Tariffs and Trade (GATT) contained various features designed to resolve any tension between domestic and international economic objectives—on the whole, in favor of the former.

Thus, one of the principal objects of the par value system of the Fund was to permit countries, through exchange rate adjustments, to correct long-term disequilibria in international price levels when these had accumulated to the point of being serious. (The other principal object was to prevent competitive devaluations.)

To cope with more temporary disturbances to the balance of payments, a number of different expedients were envisaged:

In the first place, there would be facilities for financing payments deficits through movements in national reserves, supplemented by recourse to international credit facilities, notably those provided by drawing rights in the IMF itself.

Second, countries would be *allowed* to control outward and inward capital movements, and indeed, in certain circumstances, *expected* to control the former.

Third, though this was the least preferred alternative, countries in balance of payments difficulties would be permitted, as a temporary measure, to apply quantitative restrictions to imports and, with the Fund's permission, to current account payments.

It will be seen that this system protected national autonomy with respect to domestic economic policies and objectives at the expense of at least temporary departures from international norms. This was particularly true with respect to capital movements, which seemed to be held in rather low esteem by the Founding

Fathers of the system. But it is true to some extent also of current transactions. For example, the provisions of GATT designed to insure the temporary character of quantitative restrictions on trade were decidedly weak.

What I have been describing is, of course, not the regime under which countries were expected to live in the immediate postwar period. That was governed by the very permissive arrangements of which almost all countries were allowed to avail themselves under Article XIV of the Fund Agreement. It represents, rather, the goal that countries were expected to reach after they had grown strong enough to throw away the crutch of these transitional arrangements. In practice, it was not until 1961 that most industrial countries felt able finally to accept the full obligations of the Articles of Agreement of the Fund, though for a good many years they had been gradually dropping first the bilateral and later the regional discriminatory practices which had been allowed them under Article XIV. As for the less developed countries, most of them are still "living in sin" with Article XIV, though in a world in which the main currencies are interconvertible, they have little incentive to discriminate over the greater part of their trade.

SUBSEQUENT DEVELOPMENT OF THE SYSTEM

As the industrial countries approached convertibility and full acceptance of the obligations of Article VIII, the international system on which they converged was one that differed in spirit and in practice, though not in law, from what had been envisaged at Bretton Woods.

In the first place, there was, and continues to be, a tendency, so far as industrial countries are concerned, to interpret the exchange stability envisaged in the par value system in the sense of fixity of exchange rates. Since the general readjustment of initial par values in 1949, there have been rather few adjustments of exchange rates on the part of industrial countries. The main exceptions are the French devaluations of 1957 and 1958, and the revaluations of the Deutsche mark and the guilder in 1961. Canada, which conducted an experiment in fluctuating rates from 1950, returned to the fixed rate fold in 1962.

Second, there was, until recently, a tendency to consider that the architects of the Fund and GATT had set their sights too low, from the standpoint of liberal internationalism, in allowing such easy, even if temporary, access to trade restrictions and such unhampered access to capital restrictions in defense of the balance of payments. As the industrial countries, under the impetus of the liberalization program of the OEEC, gradually discarded their import restrictions—with certain exceptions in the agricultural sphere—they tended to abjure their use for good and all, even in the event of payments difficulties. As such countries adopted the obligations of Article VIII, it was the intention that they should not, save in dire emergencies, be allowed by the Fund to have recourse to exchange restrictions on current account. A similar change in attitude, though less strong and less universal, occurred with respect to capital restrictions. For a time, at least, it became fashionable to advocate what was called "Swiss convertibility," namely the notion that countries should be deemed to have fallen short of their duty in the matter of restoring convertibility if they stopped short at converting balances of their currencies acquired by nonresidents and did not extend the privilege to domestic residents who wanted to exchange domestic for foreign currency for the purpose of acquiring assets abroad.

The third departure, at least in emphasis, from the Bretton Woods system was with respect to the role of national financial policy and, in particular, monetary policy. The implication of the IMF Articles—and this was made fairly clear by an interpretation elicited by the United Kingdom in 1946—was that domestic monetary policy should, or at least could, be directed exclusively toward domestic goals—full employment, growth, or what not—while the responsibility for preserving external equilibrium was left to other instruments of policy. By the time most industrial countries became legally convertible, however, the orthodox view was that monetary policy should, to a considerable extent, be directed toward the objective of preserving or restoring balance of payments equilibrium. This was particularly true so far as deficit countries were concerned. Surplus countries were inclined to feel, with some justice, that in the generally buoyant state of world demand it was up to the others to restore balance by abstaining from inflation for a while.

REASONS FOR THESE DEVELOPMENTS

There were a number of reasons for this somewhat surprising reversion to the gold standard ideal of a liberal international system with fixed exchange rates. Trade and exchange restrictions were found in practice to be extremely irksome and hampering to enterprise, and their removal correspondingly favorable to expansion. Moreover, the experience that neither import restrictions nor currency devaluations afforded more than a temporary fillip to the balance of payments, unless accompanied by a contraction of monetary demand, encouraged countries to rely primarily on the latter instrument. Again, the fact that it proved so difficult to control capital movements and that such movements could be very disruptive if motivated by exchange anticipations made countries reluctant to contemplate, and even more reluctant to admit that they contemplated, alterations of exchange rates. On the other hand, the belief that with fixed rates, and suitable monetary policies, capital movements could play a useful equilibrating role was an argument for removing capital controls.

Perhaps the most important reason why countries felt able to do without restrictions or exchange rate adjustments, however, was that they found it possible to defend their balances of payments by means of demand policies alone, with effects on employment and economic growth that were slight and, in most cases, temporary. This—from a Keynesian standpoint—unexpected outcome can, however, be largely accounted for by the special circumstances of the time.

In the first place, the rapid reconstruction and modernization of the economy in Europe and Japan, in conjunction with the substantial and widespread adjustment of exchange rates which took place in 1949 (with subsequent devaluations in France), brought about a state of general balance of payments ease in which the countries that entered on the postwar period with low reserves and payments restrictions enjoyed payments surpluses, while the corresponding deficits were largely confined to the United States, which not only had enormous reserves to start with, but also was able to finance the major portion of its deficit through an accumulation of short-term liabilities. In such an environment, widespread abandonment of restrictions and discriminations was relatively easy, though the European countries deserve credit for the cooperative effort by which this liberalization was speeded up.

The second, and even more important, factor was the generally high pressure of monetary demand which prevailed and, with slight interruption, persisted in most industrial countries. This was attributable partly to such "autonomous" factors as the reconstruction needs, the increase in population growth, and the capital-intensive technological developments of the postwar period; partly to full-employment policies and national planning efforts that checked any flagging of demand, and partly to the situation of high international liquidity and balance of payments ease which has just been described. In such a situation, it seemed possible for such fundamental disequilibria as might develop, either owing to differential rates of inflation or to differential rates of productivity growth, to be corrected by a relatively mild and short period of disinflation on the part of the deficit country. This was true largely, though not completely, even for the United Kingdom, where the trends of competitiveness were least favorable.

Even in the halcyon period of fixed exchange rates and financial corrective techniques, however, exceptions to the rule occurred. For example, France had to devalue. Germany and Holland preferred to revalue rather than endure the price increases that would otherwise have been the necessary result of, and remedy for, their payments surpluses. And Canada preferred, for about a decade, to maintain a fluctuating rate rather than to absorb in price movements the disturbing effects of variations in the massive influx of U.S. capital.

It might be said with some justification that in the 1950s and early 1960s international liquidity was excessive and that had there been less of it, there would have been less inflationary pressure. From the standpoint of real income, or even of income distribution, however, this bias, in the degree to which it applied, was probably an error on the right side.

DIFFICULTIES OF RECENT YEARS

In the last few years, a number of developments have occurred, largely growing out of the situation just described, which have tended to complicate the task of reconciling domestic and international objectives.

In the first place, the adoption of convertibility and the abandonment of various restrictions in Europe and Japan have greatly enhanced the international mobility of capital and thereby increased the potentialities for disequilibrium in international payments. In particular, it has become attractive and profitable for short- and long-term funds to flow on a large scale from America to other industrial countries, in many of which output has been growing faster than in the United States and in some of which new opportunities for large-scale industry have been opening up owing to the widening of the market. This has naturally tended to raise the equilibrium level of prices in other industrial countries relative to the United States. Owing to the very high level of demand pressure and employment that has prevailed until very recently in Europe, relative price levels have in fact been moving somewhat in the required direction. Nevertheless, the United States has not been able to avoid considerable strain in its balance of payments.

In the second place, the problem of cost inflation has in recent years become more pressing, or at least more prominent in people's minds. In many countries—though this is perhaps not true of the United States—money wages have in recent years tended to rise faster for any given level of employment and productivity growth than in the 1950s. How far this is a delayed consequence of long-continued demand pressure is difficult to say. In several of the continental countries, for example, the Netherlands and Germany, this is less a matter of wage-push than of the dwindling of wage-restraint—not so much an intensification of the overpricing as a diminution of the underpricing of labor. However that may be, the result is to make it more difficult than formerly to reconcile the domestic objectives of price stability and full employment. These cost-inflationary factors are sometimes active causes of balance of payments disequilibria. In addition, they make it very difficult for governments in surplus countries to give weight to balance of payments considerations in determining their domestic demand policies, and in this way probably have a systematic tendency to impede the process of adjustment to disequilibria that arise from other causes. As was pointed out in the Fund's *Annual Report* for 1964,

Countries that are tending to fall into persistent payments deficits should be willing to pursue less expansionary policies than they would otherwise prefer, though they should not be expected to endure situations of high or prolonged unemployment of resources or economic stagnation. Again, countries that are tending to run into persistent surpluses should be willing to pursue, within limits, a more expansionary policy than they would have been inclined to adopt for purely domestic reasons.

But in the last year or so, important surplus countries have felt that, with costs in any case tending to rise faster than desired, they could not be expected to maintain demand at a higher level than purely domestic considerations made inevitable.

It might be thought that the growing attention being paid to incomes policies in many countries is an item favorable to the adjustment process. To some extent this is no doubt true. Countries in payments difficulty have a greater incentive than those in payments surplus to take the political risks involved in measures tending to hold back increases in wages and prices. On the other hand, the instruments available for the purpose are so extremely feeble at the moment in most countries that little assistance in the cause of international equilibrium is to be looked for from this source in the foreseeable future. Moreover, governments often think it more convenient, in the present embryonic stage of incomes policies, to aim at a very simple target, namely, price stability, than to adapt their targets to the state of the balance of payments.

The third important development casting a pall over the balance of payments situation has, of course, been the growing precariousness of the structure of international liquidity and, since 1964, the decline in the rate of growth of national reserves. Both of the countries whose currencies are held as reserves by the monetary authorities of other countries have in recent years encountered balance of payments difficulties. The United Kingdom has for most of the postwar period struggled on with low reserves and a low rate of productivity growth. Any attempt to force the pace of growth has tended to evoke a payments deficit. The U.S. deficit, which has been much larger in amount, has, until recent years, been an engine of world prosperity and growth. After about 1958, however, it gradually began to undermine the strength of the United States' own reserve position and to impair confidence in the dollar. As a result, many countries have become increasingly uneasy about their holdings of reserve currencies, and anxious, if not to reduce their holdings of foreign exchange, at least to increase, where decently possible, the ratio of gold to currency in their reserves.

If the situation just described spelled growing illiquidity and balance of payments difficulty for the reserve centers themselves, the measures which these centers, and particularly the United States, have taken to put a stop to their deficits are likely to give rise sooner or later to liquidity shortage in the rest of the world. As has been shown by many writers and in the *Annual Report* of the Fund for 1964, the rate of growth of monetary gold stocks, even in the absence of gold hoarding, is unlikely to keep pace with the rising world need for reserves unless it is supplemented by a more than proportionate increase in the currency holdings of monetary authorities. Such an increase is, of course, very unlikely to occur, save in the unusual circumstances that prevailed in the 1950s, namely, a combination of substantial payments deficit in the main reserve country with the maintenance of full confidence in the gold value of its currency.

In the first half of this year, world reserves, other than those created by the IMF, declined substantially for the first time since before the war.[1] This is probably a temporary and transitional situation. Though the payments deficits of the principal reserve centers have been checked, they have not yet been eliminated and confidence has not yet been fully restored, gold hoarding has been very severe, and the proportion of currencies to gold in national reserves has fallen. But even when confidence is restored, the growth of reserves will probably be slow. Such a slowing down would not be likely to have any significant effect on the stock of reserves, or on the ratio of reserves to international transactions, for some years to come. It might nevertheless have a very speedy effect on the demand for, and hence the scarcity of, reserves. Countries whose reserves are declining anticipate to a greater or lesser extent the continuance of this decline, and a given stock of reserves will seem to them much less adequate

---

1. The decline in world reserves, other than reserve positions in the Fund and gold sold by the Fund, amounted to some $2 billion, or 3 percent. This was offset in part by a rise in reserve positions in the Fund and a sale of gold by the Fund, together totaling some $1.5 billion. These were largely accounted for by a U.K. drawing of $1.4 billion in the second quarter.

than if their reserves were increasing. Any sharp deterioration in the rate of growth of reserves is, therefore, likely to stimulate the same kind of defensive actions with respect to the balance of payments as would a sharp once-for-all drop in the stock of reserves.

POLICY REACTIONS TO RECENT DIFFICULTIES

How have countries reacted to the intensified balance of payments strains that have resulted from, or been aggravated by, the various factors I have mentioned? To put the answer in a nutshell, countries have neither been willing nor, as yet, compelled to sacrifice internal financial stability to balance of payments adjustment. Nor have they been shaken in their adherence to fixed exchange rates. Deficit countries have sought to expand their access to balance of payments financing, but have been forced increasingly to restrict external expenditures both on capital and on current account.

I have already indicated that, owing to cost-inflationary tendencies, countries in surplus have become increasingly reluctant in the last year or two to pay much regard to balance of payments considerations in their overall demand policies, though within the framework of these policies they have made some efforts to keep interest rates down in order to avoid attracting foreign funds. More surprisingly, most deficit countries too have managed to avoid adopting financial policies significantly more restrictive than might reasonably have been adopted for purely domestic purposes—that is, to relieve undue pressure of demand on resources. This has been true, thus far, even of the measures adopted in 1965 by the United Kingdom, though perhaps less so of those adopted in 1963–64 by Italy, which in the end turned out to be more severe than was strictly necessary, even for balance of payments reasons. In the United States, it seemed several years ago that the government was willing, partly for balance of payments reasons, to tolerate the perpetuation of a level of employment and use of capacity which, by international standards, was decidedly low. In recent years, however, the degree of utilization of resources has risen steadily, though more slowly than in neighboring Canada.

The payments strains of recent years have not led to any

weakening in the tendency of the main industrial countries to interpret the par value system in terms of fixity of exchange rates. The last exchange rate devaluation by an industrial country, that of Canada in 1962, was accompanied by a return from a flexible rate to a fixed exchange rate system. No doubt the refusal to contemplate exchange rate adjustments is partly due to the fact that the principal countries that have been in payments difficulties have been reserve centers where the case against devaluation is particularly strong, and partly, also, to a belief on the part of members of the European Economic Community that an exchange rate adjustment by any of their members would create difficulties for their agricultural price maintenance system and other measures of economic integration within the Community. However, there has also been a widespread realization, especially since the revaluations of 1961, that the system under which exchange rates are regarded as movable, but only by substantial amounts at lengthy intervals, is one that requires very large amounts of balance of payments financing to offset the speculative capital movements to which anticipation of exchange rate alteration gives rise. The desire to avoid speculative capital movements is a primary reason why the par value system tends to be interpreted as a rigidly fixed exchange rate system.

In view of the reduced responsiveness of relative national price levels and exchange rates, it was predictable that increased reliance would have to be put either on international official financing or on interference with the liberty of private international transactions. In fact, both tendencies have been in evidence.

FINANCING VERSUS ADJUSTMENT

Naturally enough, it has been the countries in deficit, notably the reserve center countries, that have been keenest on increasing their access to balance of payments financing in order to maintain domestic prosperity without interfering with international transactions. The surplus countries, notably on the continent of Europe, have in general gone along with the provision of such financing, but have been increasingly anxious that its form should be such as to provide the creditors with safeguards against exchange risk and to give them more collective control over the amount provided. Their main object in seeking such control has been to insure that the deficit countries paid due regard to the need for adjustment processes that would limit their requirements for official financing, both in amount and in time.

These features can be seen in the various measures that have been adopted to provide balance of payments financing in recent years. The General Arrangements to Borrow (GAB) of 1962 were principally designed to insure that the IMF had sufficient access to borrowed resources to enable the reserve center countries, if necessary, to exercise to the full their drawing rights with that institution. Since, however, voting arrangements in the Fund give a very considerable influence to reserve center countries, because of their large quotas—whether or not they are in credit with the Fund—the GAB provided for the exercise, by participants, of a substantial degree of control over the use made of the arrangements and hence over any drawing which might require that use.

The network of bilateral swap arrangements which the United States began to build up in 1962 and which has now reached a total magnitude of nearly $2,500 million, was designed to facilitate short-term interventions on the exchange markets that might obviate unnecessary conversions of official dollar holdings into gold. Like the placing of Roosa bonds [2] with monetary authorities, which also began in 1962, they were a practical answer to the increasing restiveness of some continental central banks about holding on to the dollar balances which, as a result of U.S. deficits, came into their hands. The creditor claims arising out of the use of these arrangements, like those arising out of the more *ad hoc* operations undertaken by various monetary authorities in support of sterling in 1961, 1963, 1964, and 1965, enjoy an exchange guarantee. They do not, however, provide for any collective supervision or control by the creditors, and dissatisfaction with this feature was largely responsible for the decision of the Group of Ten in 1964 to set up a system of "multilateral surveillance" over the financing of payments disequilibria among their own members. This system comprises both provision through the Bank for

2. Medium-term obligations of the United States, denominated in the currency of the holding country, nonnegotiable, but, in most cases, convertible at short notice, into dollars.

International Settlements of statistical information relating to official and private financing and discussion in a working party of the Organization for Economic Cooperation and Development (OECD) of the steps being taken to finance and to correct payments disequilibria.

There are much firmer convictions among surplus countries about the desirability of speeding up adjustment processes than about the methods that deficit countries should use to attain this end. And yet this is the vital question, since some methods of adjustment produce economic distortion or misallocation of resources, and others, relatively speaking, do not. Indeed, to an economist, the important distinction is not between the financing and the correction of payments disequilibria, but between balance of payments policies, including excessive financing, that do and those that do not induce distortion.

MEASURES AFFECTING CAPITAL FLOWS

Few responsible officials in surplus countries would advocate the adoption by deficit countries of demand policies that would create substantial unemployment or would increase unemployment, where that is already substantial. Nor would the surplus countries in general welcome measures like devaluation or import restriction that act directly on the current balance of payments. Indeed, they are apt to think that their own current balance is not favorable enough. What they generally mean by adjustment measures are measures that will damp down the capital flow from deficit to surplus countries. And, of course, such measures have in fact been adopted in the last few years on a substantial scale. The United Kingdom has progressively tightened its exchange controls over capital movements to the nonsterling area. The United States introduced in 1963 and extended in 1965 a tax on the acquisition of long-term securities or indebtedness in developed countries, and on the second occasion introduced in addition a voluntary program for financial institutions and industrial firms operating abroad calculated to check or reverse the outflow of short-term funds, as well as to encourage foreign subsidiaries of U.S. firms to secure foreign financing. At the same time, not only have several continental countries made advance repayments of external public debt but the same or other countries have taken steps to discourage the inflow of short-term, and occasionally even long-term, private funds. Nothing in the field of balance of payments ideology has been more striking in recent years than the retreat from liberalism on the capital front. . . .

In addition to the various restrictions on capital transfers that I have mentioned, there have been a number of cases in recent years in which balance of payments difficulties have induced industrial countries to raise barriers to trade and other current transactions. Both Canada and the United Kingdom have recently had resort to temporary surcharges on imports; these, though greatly preferable in their economic effects to the quantitative restrictions on imports which the deficit countries in question would have been entitled to impose under GATT regulations, have aroused a degree of hostility that makes it doubtful whether they can be employed by major countries in the future. Again, the United States has introduced considerable distortions into its current account transactions, both public and private, by measures such as the application of substantial margins of preference for home suppliers in government contracts, the tying of aid and government expenditures abroad to U.S. export products, and possibly the curtailment of economic and military aid expenditures below what would otherwise have been desired.

It is a general principle of "the welfare economics of the second best" that if some departures from the criteria of optimization are inevitable, it is better that they be widely, though not evenly, spread. So the fact that there are distortions in international capital flows creates a presumption in favor of interfering with the current account items also. From a less academic standpoint, however, it is a pity to find a recrudescence of restrictions and interventions for balance of payments reasons in a field where such action is apt to provoke ill will and even retaliation.

Economic Progress and the International Monetary System

JAMES TOBIN

James Tobin is Sterling Professor of Economics at Yale University. In this paper, first presented at the spring, 1963, meeting of the Academy of Political Science, he discusses the need for increasing international reserves under a system of fixed exchange rates.

A GREAT teacher of mine, Professor Joseph Schumpeter, used to find puzzling irony in the fact that liberal devotees of the free market were unwilling to let the market determine the prices of foreign currencies, and that opponents of government support of the price of wheat were strongly committed to government support of the price of gold. Thanks to the Bretton Woods Agreement of 1944, the western world is committed to a system of fixed —or nearly fixed—rates of exchange among currencies and between currencies and gold. Market exchange rates are kept within one percent of official parities by governmental purchases and sales in the exchange markets. Since the major currencies of North America and Western Europe can now (for all practical purposes) be freely bought and sold, one for another, considerable official intervention may at times be necessary to prevent a currency in high demand from appreciating more than the allowed one percent, or to prevent a currency under selling pressure from depreciating beyond the permitted margin.

This is where international reserves come in. The international reserves of a country are essentially the resources it can quickly mobilize to buy its own currency and prevent it from depreciating. Clearly the need for international reserves is very largely a property of the system of fixed exchange rates. If countries were willing to entrust exchange rates entirely to private markets and to accept whatever gyrations in exchange rates might occur, they would have no use for international reserves. There would be, by definition, no imbalances in international payments and no need for international money to move from the country in "deficit" to the country in "surplus." Instead the exchange rate would move—in favor of the country which would otherwise be in surplus—enough to bring market supplies and demands for the currencies into balance.

I do not propose to discuss here the merits of a system of market-determined flexible exchange rates as compared to the Bretton Woods system of fixed rates to which we are now committed. I propose rather to discuss the workability of the system we have.

Its workability depends essentially on two things: (1) the availability of international reserves permitting deficit countries to defend their exchange rates, and (2) the efficacy and speed of those corrective mechanisms which arrest and reverse flows of reserves from country to country. If the corrective mechanisms are strong and fast, the system can operate with small total reserves. If they are weak and slow, the system requires large reserves.

I shall discuss below the principal mechanisms that might be used to correct imbalances in international payments today, and I shall consider the limitations on their effectiveness or acceptability. But before getting to the specific list, I would like to offer four general observations on the process of international financial adjustment.

CORRECTIVE MECHANISMS IN BALANCE OF PAYMENTS ADJUSTMENT

First, corrective mechanisms may be classified, in principle at least, into two groups: automatic and discretionary. Automatic mechanisms are economic processes that come into play as a result of imbalances in currency markets or as a by-product of the factors creating the imbalances. Discretionary mechanisms are policy actions taken by the governments concerned, designed to arrest or reverse outflows or inflows of reserves. The distinction is worth making, even though most of the automatic mechanisms are also discretionary, in the sense that government policy can moderate or suspend their operation.

Second, the mechanisms, automatic or discretionary, set into operation by payments deficits and surpluses are not necessarily or always corrective. They may aggravate, rather than correct, the initial disequilibrium. Economists are fond of self-correcting mechanisms. But we are far from having proved that a stable equilibrium in international payments exists, or that if it does exist it is speedily reached. We know, in fact, that some of the natural reactions of economics and of government policy-makers to disequilibrium may be destabilizing rather than stabilizing. I give a possible example below in discussing domestic deflation as a reaction to balance of payments deficits.

Third, pressures to take discretionary actions to correct imbalances are more keenly felt by deficit than by surplus countries. A country in deficit is forced to take action no later than when it exhausts its reserves and lines of credit. A country in surplus is under no similar compulsion. Indeed as a lender, a surplus country is in the driver's seat, able to exact adjustments by the deficit country as a condition of extending credit. Yet the appropriate corrections may involve adjustments at least as great in the economy and policy of the surplus country. One piece of financial ideology which obscures a dispassionate assessment of responsibilities for adjustment is the common facile assumption that balance of payment surpluses reflect financial virtue while deficits are the natural penalty for profligacy and sin. Often, no doubt, this judgment is justified. But sometimes the reverse is true. And most often, perhaps, serious imbalances of payments are the result of basic economic and political events and trends and reflect neither credit nor blame on either creditor or debtor.

The chief sanction inducing action by a surplus country is its awareness that balance of payments success is a transient glory, that some day it will sit in the debtor's chair. This reflection leads countries to grope collectively for some "rules of the game," which prescribe the behavior expected of good creditors as well as good debtors. The "rules of the game" are unwritten, informal, and uncertain. They are still in the process of development for the present monetary system of the West—evolving from gradual accumulation of precedents as well as from explicit consultation between governments and in the O.E.C.D., the Bank of International Settlements, and the International Monetary Fund.

The fourth point is the most fundamental. International monetary arrangements are not ends in themselves. They are means to more basic ends. Their ultimate purpose is to promote the economic progress of the free world, facilitating international commerce and the efficient use of the world's productive resources. In particular, the rationale of the Bretton Woods system is that stability of exchange rates eliminates a risk which would otherwise impede economically justified flows of goods and services and capital across national boundaries. It is essential not to lose sight of the basic objective and rationale of the system in appraising its various mechanisms of adjustment. The "rules of the game" should not force or even permit countries to defend their exchange rates by means which are inconsistent with the whole purpose of the system, i.e., by measures which retard world economic growth or restrict efficient movements of goods and services and capital.

In examining below the principal mechanisms of adjustment to imbalances in international payments, I shall ask in each case how effectively and speedily the mechanism can in today's world be expected to correct imbalances, and also how consistent the mechanism is with the essential objective and rationale of the system.

Changes in the Employment of Labor and Industrial Capacity
I refer here to short-run changes in real income and employment, and correspondingly in the utilization of industrial capacity. These changes result mainly from variations in aggregate demand. An increased trade deficit—say, from a fall in export sales—automatically lowers aggregate demand both directly and indirectly through its "multiplier" effects on domestic incomes and expenditures. A reduction in aggregate demand lowers imports and frees domestic capacity to compete for foreign orders. Thus a rise in the trade deficit is partially self-correcting. But it is only partially so. If the trade balance is to be restored by reduction of aggregate demand, government fiscal and monetary policy must be actively restrictive.

All advanced countries are committed, almost without regard to political party, to full employment. Our friends in Western Europe are even more committed than we of North America. Deliberate deflation of aggregate demand, creating unemployment and excess capacity, is not a method of adjustment consistent with these commitments. Indeed, we must count it as a serious defect of our present system that countries where resources are idle for lack of effective demand, where no inflationary price increases are occurring, should feel themselves under pressure to adopt deflationary measures or to refrain from expansionary measures. For after all, the purpose of our economies is production; the purpose of international monetary arrangements is to promote the efficient use of productive resources; and the wastes of unemployment and unused capacity are the greatest of inefficiencies. Canada, faced by an exchange crisis last year, felt it necessary to take deflationary fiscal and monetary measures at a time when the internal economic situation indicated the contrary. The United States has for several years felt itself compelled to follow monetary policies inappropriate to the need for domestic expansion.

The usefulness of this mechanism is, therefore, doubtful because of the priority of the objective of full employment and full production. But in any case it is far from clear that the mechanism always corrects, rather than aggravates, the imbalance which sets it in motion. No doubt it tends to correct the balance of trade. But in the process it may move the balance of capital movements in the opposite and perverse direction. This is because profit performance and prospects, so important in the geographical placement of direct corporate investment and purchases of equities, are very sensitive to the level of business activity and utilization of capacity. I personally suspect that the failure of the U.S. economy to achieve full employment and full use of capacity over the past five years has lost us more in direct and equity investment capital outflow than it has gained us in the balance of trade.

Changes in Price Levels · Price increases in surplus countries, and price declines in deficit countries, are of course the classic mechanism of adjustment of the trade balance. These price level adjustments are closely related to the movement of real economic activity just discussed; and they are set in motion by the same reactions of the economy and of government fiscal and monetary policy to external imbalance. However, this mechanism too has its serious limitations.

First, price deflation is simply not a realistic possibility in modern industrial economies, and has not been for several decades. For a number of reasons, wages and prices are not flexible downward. Deflationary stimuli, whether from the trade balance itself or from government policy, will be reflected in reduction of employment and output far more than in reduction of prices. For the reason suggested above, contraction of real economic activity may not be favorable to the balance of payments as a whole.

Second, our countries seek stability of their internal price levels as well as full employment. Surplus countries are certainly not willing to undergo rapid and drastic inflation in order to draw in imports and damage the competitive position of their export industries.

This does not mean, fortunately, that price levels can be or need to be absolutely frozen in every country. We know that European money wages and prices have been rising in recent years somewhat faster than employment costs and prices in North America. This divergence in price trends will in time contribute to the correction of European surpluses and American deficits. But the process does take time, because European governments will not tolerate more than a modest upward creep in their price levels. Governmental wage, price and "income" policies can encourage this type of adjustment if they are applied less severely in surplus countries than in deficit countries. But at present our countries differ widely in the ability and disposition of the government to enforce such policies, whether by law or by persuasion.

Changes in Monetary Policy and Interest Rates · Most national monetary systems, including our own, are geared to international reserves in such a way that domestic money is created to purchase inflowing gold and foreign currency, and destroyed when gold and foreign exchange are sold. If the authorities do not offset these transactions by other monetary measures, monetary conditions become easier and interest rates tend to fall in a surplus country, while the reverse is happening in a deficit country. The response of internationally mobile private funds to these changes in credit conditions and interest rates is a corrective mechanism, and sometimes a very powerful one. It is reinforced by the further effects of these monetary changes on domestic aggregate demand.

But this mechanism too has its limitations. First, the reallocation of private funds between national currencies is largely a one-time operation. The flow induced by a given interest rate differential will taper off. A country cannot expect to cover a basic deficit on current or long-term investment account indefinitely by attracting short-term money, unless it is prepared to jack its interest rates higher and higher.

Second, and more important, every country has domestic as well as external objectives for monetary policy. In many circumstances these will coincide, as when a country confronts simultaneously inflation at home and a deficit abroad. In other circumstances, like those of the United States today, the objectives diverge. Restrictive monetary policy would hold private funds here, but it would be generally deflationary. Correspondingly, a European surplus country could diminish its surplus by lower interest rates, but only at some risk of domestic inflation.

There are two ways in which the conflict between these objectives might be diminished. One is to dedicate monetary instruments to external balance, relying on fiscal measures for internal stabilization. Many Europeans have been urging the United States to tighten monetary policy, and to pursue a fiscal policy sufficiently expansionary to restore full employment even in the face of higher interest rates and tighter credit conditions. Correspondingly, European governments can be urged to combat whatever domestic inflationary problems they face by tighter budgets, while pursuing easier monetary policies in the interests of international balance.

The trouble is that there are in every country constraints, both economic and political, on the mixtures of monetary and fiscal medicine which can be administered. The proposed U.S. tax reduction looks to be about the largest dose of fiscal stimulant that is politically palatable in the Unites States. Moreover, domestic economic objectives going beyond full employment and counter-cyclical stabilization can limit the acceptable mixtures. For example, if we in this country place a high priority on private investment to promote long-run economic growth, we will not wish to suppress investment demand by tight money and high interest rates even if we could wholly compensate such restriction of demand by fiscal measures favoring consumption. Indeed we cannot even be sure that an "easy-budget tight-money mixture" will benefit the balance of payments in the long run. For improvement in our trade balance depends on an accelerated advance in productivity, difficult to achieve in a low-investment economy.

The other way of reconciling the conflicting uses of monetary policy is to devise and to employ techniques of monetary control which serve both masters at once. United States monetary authorities and debt managers have for the past two or three years sought to keep short-term interest rates relatively high while increasing bank reserves and credit availability, and so far as possible lowering long-term interest rates. The assumption of this policy is that short rates are relatively more important for international flows of funds, and bank reserves, credit availability, and long-term rates relatively more important for domestic expansion. The techniques used have been (a) to increase the supply to the public of Treasury bills and other Federal obligations of maturity less than one year, relative to other maturities of public debt, the Federal Reserve accordingly concentrating its open market purchases in securities of maturity longer than one year; (b) to reduce bank reserve requirements in order to supply banks with new free reserves without open market purchases; (c) to raise interest rates payable on commercial bank time and saving deposits, steering the bulk of the increase in bank deposits since the end of 1961 into this form rather than into demand accounts and giving the commercial banks an incentive to increase their holdings of mortgages, state and local bonds, and other long-term assets.

These policies have been moderately successful. In two years of recovery, short-term rates have risen by about three-quarters of a point. Rates on longer-term Federal obligations are virtually unchanged, and other long-term rates have fallen slightly. Conceivably this kind of policy could be pursued even more consistently and vigorously. For example, the Treasury appears to have acted counter to this policy in its successful efforts to place more of the Federal debt in maturities beyond ten years. And the Federal Reserve has not aggressivly sought long-term securities to buy, even in weeks when open market purchases were necessary to provide reserves.

Under the best of circumstances, however, these techniques can reduce somewhat but not wholly resolve the dilemma of the monetary and debt management authorities. Short and long-term interest rates are linked by a chain of substitution which limits the degree to which the differentials between them can be altered. Furthermore, short rates are of some importance to domestic expansion and long rates of considerable relevance to international capital flows. The policy we have been following is a good compromise, but it is at best a compromise.

We cannot escape the fact that in a regime of convertible currencies the money and capital markets of different countries are closely linked. This means that countries have less scope for independent monetary policies than in the past. But we cannot escape either the fact that national monetary policies must be adapted to domestic circumstances, needs, and objectives which differ widely from country to country. In my view the major monetary powers will have to concert their monetary policies, through international consultation and cooperation, more than they have done in the past. If interest rates need to be brought into closer alignment, at what level should the alignment occur? Do the countries with high interest rates need to come down, or the countries with low rates go up? This is the kind of problem which has to be laid on the table when government officials and central bankers meet at Paris or Basle or Washington. At the same time, I am convinced that our international monetary arrangements must leave room for divergences in national monetary policies and interest rates to accommodate differences in domestic requirements. In many cases it will be easier for the central banks and governments concerned to offset private capital flows by official movements in the other direction than to adjust national monetary policies so as to shut off these flows altogether.

Restrictions on Private Transactions in Foreign Exchange · An instinctive reaction of a government to a balance of payments deficit is to restrict private transactions leading to purchases of foreign currency. The devices are too numerous to catalogue—the spectrum ranges from higher tariffs to a complete battery of exchange controls and includes import quotas, controls of capital movements, and restrictions on foreign travel. Needless to say, these expedients undermine the central purpose of a system of fixed exchange rates, to facilitate the international exchange of goods and services and the efficient use of productive resources throughout the world. Moreover, the prospect that countries will resort to these devices in times of balance of payments stress imposes on foreign commerce and foreign investment risks comparable to the risks of exchange depreciation. Once again we have, therefore, a clear danger of inverting ends and means. Exchange parities may be defended, but by means which subvert the whole purpose of defending them.

From this standpoint, recent actions of countries facing exchange crises are not encouraging. Canada imposed in 1962 special import surcharges, which are only now being removed. The United Kingdom in 1961 tightened its controls over long-term capital exports. We ourselves cut down the duty-free import allowance for returning tourists.

Removal or liberalization of restrictions by surplus countries serves both to remedy imbalances in payments and to promote the basic objectives of the system. Indeed so long as this course is open to surplus countries, one is not disposed to sympathize with their complaint that the deficit countries are forcing inflation upon them. It is, of course, a great achievement that the tight network of quantitative controls and bilateral trade and clearing agreements which governed European commerce in the days of dollar shortage has now been largely dismantled. But some discrimination against U.S. goods remains, and the Common Market confronts us with new discriminations, especially in the important field of agriculture. Euorpean capital markets are, by and large, either controlled or poorly developed or both. Most governments other than the U.S. still regard control of private capital movements as a legitimate tool of balance of payments policy.

Government Transactions · Largely because of foreign aid, foreign lending, and defense, government outlays and receipts now play a large role in international payments. They are obvious candidates for adjustment whenever a government faces a problem of imbalance. The principal reaction of the U.S. to its persistent deficit has been to economize on the government account: tying foreign aid to purchases in the U.S., increasing the preference given to American suppliers in defense procurement, cutting back the outlays for and by U.S. troops stationed abroad, negotiating for greater participation by our NATO allies in expenditures for the common defense. To a much lesser degree—reflecting the characteristic asymmetry between surplus and deficit countries—European surpluses have led European governments to increase their defense expenditures and their assistance to underdeveloped countries.

In practice the balance of payments has doubtless been the occasion for some economies and readjustments of burdens which were overdue on other grounds. But in principle these methods of adjustment are as objectionable on grounds of economic efficiency as the imposition of discriminatory controls or taxes on private outlays in foreign currency. A dollar of government outlay in foreign currency should not have to pass a more, or less, severe test than a dollar spent domestically. Nor should a dollar of government outlay in foreign currency have to pass a test more severe than a dollar of private outlay in foreign currency. One of the paradoxes of our present balance of payments difficulties is that stringent economies and controls are placed on government outlays abroad serving national purposes of the highest priority, while private individuals and firms can buy foreign currencies freely for any purpose—recreational travel, competitive investment abroad, or even speculating against the dollar. Nationalistic restrictions on government outlays may be justified as a temporary expedient. But such measures as aid-tying and "buy American" preferences will build up vested interests and be difficult to reverse.

The relative "burdens" of defense and development assistance of the various advanced countries should be related to their basic capacities to bear these burdens—as reflected in national income and wealth. Participation in these programs should not vary with the vagaries of national currencies. We cannot turn these programs on and off as balances of payments change. The effectiveness of the programs will be greatest, for a given collective cost to the participating countries, if the goods and services needed to implement the programs are bought in the cheapest markets.

Changes of Economic Structure · Under favorable circumstances certain basic economic processes will work towards the restoration of international balance. Let me give several examples:

Specific industries challenged by foreign competition at home and abroad respond with better design, lower prices, or increased sales effort. The response of the American automobile industry to European imports is a case in point.

High profits attract capital overseas and contribute to payments deficits. But these profit rates decline as the most obvious technological and market opportunities are grasped and as labor shortages are encountered. At the same time, repatriated earnings on the initial surge of foreign investments eventually strengthen the balance of payments. The United States already appears to be enjoying some relief of this kind.

As comparative advantage shifts, a country suffers from new foreign competition in a particular industry, call it industry A. But as the surplus country shifts resources to industry A in order to exploit this opportunity, it leaves itself vulnerable to competition in other products. The deficit country can restore its overall payments position by shifting to these products the resources displaced by competition from industry A.

These fundamental adjustments depend on changes in relative prices and wages rather than on dramatic inflations or deflations of national price levels. They require changes in the composition of output rather than in aggregate production and employment. But they cannot be achieved without mobility of labor and other resources within each country. They are certainly neither easy nor quick.

Adjustment of Exchange Rates · Finally, the IMF agreement does not contemplate that exchange rates are eternally fixed. Rather the Bretton Woods system is a system of "adjustable pegs." A country can unilaterally alter its originally declared rate as much as 10 percent. Further adjustment is permitted in case of "fundamental disequilibrium," with approval of the IMF. In practice, advance consultation with the IMF is considered impossible because of the dangers of speculation, and the approval of the IMF is perfunctory ratification of a *fait accompli*. Although each exchange rate adjustment is a specific national policy decision, dominated by the circumstances and needs of the individual country at the time, the frequency of such adjustments is an important property of the system as a whole. For it determines with what confidence or suspicion the world looks on any existing structure of exchange rates.

Frequent alterations of exchange rates between convertible currencies rob the system of its principal advantage over a system of freely floating rates. The merit of fixed exchange rates in promoting international trade and investment is to remove from these transactions the risk of exchange loss. But this risk is not removed if exchange rates are only temporarily pegged. Needless to say, exchange rate stability is especially important for a currency, like the dollar, which is used as an international unit of account, medium of exchange, and store of value both by private individuals and businesses and by governments.

The possibilities of devaluation under the "adjustable peg" system inevitably lead to speculation, first against one currency, then against another. Any currency can be suspect, as we in the U.S. have been reminded several times during the past few years. The private resources available for such speculation in a regime of convertible currencies stagger the imagination. There is always a danger that speculative rumors and whims will be self-fulfilling. To guard against such danger, the central banks, governments, and international institutions which manage the "adjustable peg" system must command large counter-speculative resources.

This is the dilemma of exchange rate policy. If the pegs are adjusted from time to time, currency speculation will be a major factor aggravating or even originating imbalances in international payments. If the pegs are never changed, we deny ourselves the use of an important instrument of adjustment, in many ways the simplest, most powerful, and least costly instrument. This means that the burden of correcting imbalances has to be assumed by more far-reaching and time-consuming processes of adjustment. Whichever exchange rate policy is followed, large international reserves are necessary. In the one case, they are necessary to withstand the waves of speculation endemic to a system in which rates do in fact change from time to time. In the other case, they are necessary to permit a country to ride through a period of deficit which it must correct by slower and more difficult processes than devaluation.

Thus we can conclude that a system of fixed exchange rates does contain some effective and acceptable corrective mechanisms, but these certainly cannot be relied upon to operate quickly and powerfully. Major imbalances are likely to take years to eliminate, unless they are corrected by measures which hamper economic growth or restrict world commerce. Consequently, in my opinion, successful operation of the Bretton Woods system requires an adequate and growing stock of international liquidity, permitting countries to ride out prolonged periods of deficit.

In stating this conclusion, I run squarely into the debate between those who say the trouble with the international monetary system at present is lack of liquidity and those who say, on the contrary, that the trouble is simply the exsiting imbalances in payments. Certainly we have troubles on both counts. I want nothing I say to be interpreted to mean that any country, even the U.S., is able or should be able to run balance of payments deficits forever. No country can do so unless it possesses the printing press for creating international money, whether this takes the form of inexhaustible gold mines or some more rational and less costly equivalent. And no one country should possess such a printing press; this is a function which ought to be internationalized, for the same reasons that have led governments to nationalize the power of creating domestic money.

However, I do not find convincing the observation, so frequently repeated, that international liquidity would be ample if the system were only in balance of payments equilibrium. True enough, if we were always in equilibrium no reserves would be needed. But this is asking a great deal of the adjustment mechanisms. Every major imbalance may seem to be the last one—if we can only remedy this one, the system will have smooth sailing from now on. But the dollar shortage is succeeded by the dollar problem; Korea is followed by Suez, and Suez by Berlin and Cuba; the seemingly endless exchange troubles of France give way to an apparently chronic French surplus. The causes of imbalances are many—technological, economic, military, political. The only thing we can be sure of is that these causes will not all disappear, and that they will frequently represent and require deepseated structural changes. If we are to weather the readjustments they impose within a system of fixed exchange rates, we will need both a large supply of international money in the future and improved international procedures for regulating this supply.

The details of such procedures are not part of my present subject. Let me say only that the technical details are secondary in importance and in difficulty to an understanding of the problem and a concerted will to resolve it. No more important aspect of international economic cooperation confronts the governments of the major advanced countries. If they do not solve it successfully and soon, then the Bretton Woods system will be a barrier rather than an avenue to economic progress and will eventually give way.

PART FOUR: The International Role of the Dollar and the U.S. Balance of Payments

The Dollar and World Liquidity: A Minority View

EMILE DESPRES, CHARLES P. KINDLEBERGER,
and WALTER S. SALANT

Emile Despres is Professor of Economics at Stanford University, Charles P. Kindleberger is Professor of Economics at MIT, and Walter S. Salant is Senior Staff Member of the Brookings Institution. In this article, originally published in the February 6, 1966 issue of The Economist, *they argue that, rather than being a sign of disequilibrium, the measured deficit in the U.S. balance of payments is a manifestation of the role of the United States as a world banker.*

THE CONSENSUS in Europe and the United States on the United States balance of payments and world liquidity runs about like this:

1. Abundant liquidity has been provided since World War II less by newly mined gold than by the increase in liquid dollar assets generated by U.S. balance-of-payments deficits.

2. These deficits are no longer available as a generator of liquidity because the accumulation of dollars has gone so far that it has undermined confidence in the dollar.

3. To halt the present creeping decline in liquidity through central-bank conversions of dollars into gold, and to forestall headlong flight from the dollar, it is necessary above all else to correct the United States deficit.

4. When the deficit has been corrected, the growth of world

reserves may, or probably will, become inadequate. Hence there is a need for planning new means of adding to world reserves—along the lines suggested by Triffin, Bernstein, Roosa, Stamp, Giscard, and others.[1]

So much is widely agreed. There is a difference in tactics between those who would correct the U.S. balance of payments by raising interest rates—bankers on both sides of the ocean and European central bankers—and those in the United States who would correct it, if necessary, by capital restrictions, so that tight money in the United States may be avoided while labor and other resources are still idle. There is also a difference of emphasis between the Continentals, who urge adjustment (proposition 3 above), and the Anglo-Saxons, who stress the need for more liquidity (proposition 4). British voices urge more liquidity now, rather than in the future. But, with these exceptions, the lines of analysis converge.

FOUR COUNTER PROPOSITIONS

There is room, however, for a minority view which would oppose this agreement with a sharply differing analysis. In outline, it asserts the following counter propositions:

1. While the United States has provided the world with liquid dollar assets in the postwar period by capital outflow and aid exceeding its current account surplus, in most years this excess has not reflected a deficit in a sense representing disequilibrium. The outflow of U.S. capital and aid has filled not one but two needs. First, it has supplied goods and services to the rest of the world. But second, to the extent that its loans to foreigners are offset by foreigners putting their own money into liquid dollar assets, the U.S. has not overinvested but has supplied financial intermediary services. The "deficit" has reflected largely the second process, in which the United States has been lending, mostly at long and intermediate term, and borrowing short. This financial intermediation, in turn, performs two functions: it supplies loans and investment funds to foreign enterprises which

[1]. For one of many good discussions of the proposals by Triffin, Bernstein, and Stamp, as well as others not mentioned above, see *Plans for Reform of the International Monetary System* by Fritz Machlup, Special Paper in International Economics No. 3, revised March 1964 (International Finance Section, Department of Economics, Princeton University).

have to pay more domestically to borrow long-term money and which cannot get the amounts they want at any price; and it supplies liquidity to foreign asset-holders, who receive less for placing their short-term deposits at home. Essentially, this is a trade in liquidity, which is profitable to both sides. Differences in their liquidity preferences (that is, in their willingness to hold their financial assets in long-term rather than in quickly encashable forms and to have short-term rather than long-term liabilities outstanding against them) create differing margins between short-term and long-term interest rates. This in turn creates scope for trade in financial assets, just as differing comparative costs create the scope for mutually profitable trade in goods. This trade in financial assets has been an important ingredient of economic growth outside the United States.

2. Such lack of confidence in the dollar as now exists has been generated by the attitudes of government officials, central bankers, academic economists, and journalists, and reflects their failure to understand the implications of this intermediary function. Despite some contagion from these sources, the private market retains confidence in the dollar, as increases in private holdings of liquid dollar assets show. Private speculation in gold is simply the result of the known attitudes and actions of governmental officials and central bankers.

3. With capital markets unrestricted, attempts to correct the "deficit" by ordinary macro-economic weapons are likely to fail. It may be possible to expand the current account surplus at first by deflation of United States income and prices relative to those of Europe; but gross financial capital flows will still exceed real transfer of goods and services (that is, involve financial intermediation, lending long-term funds to Europe in exchange for short-term deposits) so long as capital formation remains high in Europe. A moderate rise of interest rates in the United States will have only a small effect on the net capital outflow. A drastic rise might cut the net outflow substantially, but only by tightening money in *Europe* enough to stop economic growth; and this would cut America's current account surplus. Correcting the United States deficit by taxes and other controls on capital, which is being attempted on both sides of the Atlantic, is likely either to fail, or to succeed by impeding international capital flows so much as to cut European investment and growth.

4. While it is desirable to supplement gold with an internationally created reserve asset, the conventional analysis leading to this remedy concentrates excessively on a country's external liquidity; it takes insufficient account of the demands of savers for internal liquidity and of borrowers in the same country for long-term funds. The international private capital market, properly understood, provides both external liquidity to a country, and the kinds of assets and liabilities that private savers and borrowers want and cannot get at home. Most plans to create an international reserve asset, however, are addressed only to external liquidity problems which in many cases, and especially in Europe today, are the less important issue.

With agreement between the United States and Europe—but without it if necessary—it would be possible to develop a monetary system which provided the external liquidity that is needed and also recognized the role of international financial intermediation in world economic growth.

EUROPE NEEDS DOLLARS

Analytical support and elaboration of this minority view is presented in numbered sections, conforming to the propositions advanced above as an alternative to the consensus.

1. The idea that the balance of payments of a country is in disequilibrium if it is in deficit on the liquidity (U.S. Department of Commerce) definition is not appropriate to a country with a large and open capital market that is performing the function of a financial intermediary. Banks and other financial intermediaries, unlike traders, are paid to give up liquidity. The United States is no more in deficit when it lends long and borrows short than is a bank when it makes a loan and enters a deposit on its books.

Financial intermediation is an important function in a monetary economy. Savers want liquid assets; borrowers investing in fixed capital expansion are happier with funded rather than quick liabilities. Insofar as the gap is not bridged, capital formation is held down. Europeans borrow from the United States, and Americans are willing to pay higher prices for European assets than European investors will, partly because capital is more readily available in the United States than in Europe, but mainly because liquidity preference in Europe is higher and because capital markets in Europe are much less well organized, more monopolistically controlled, and just plain smaller than in the United States. With unrestricted capital markets, the European savers who want cash and the borrowers who prefer to extend their liabilities into the future can both be satisfied when the United States capital market lends long and borrows short and when it accepts smaller margins between its rates for borrowing short and lending short. European borrowers of good credit standing will seek to borrow in New York (or in the Euro-dollar market, which is a mere extension of New York) when rates of interest are lower on dollar loans than on loans in European currencies, or when the amounts required are greater than their domestic capital markets can provide. But when interferences prevent foreign intermediaries from bridging the gap, and when domestic private intermediaries cannot bridge it while the public authorities will not, borrowing possibilities are cut, and investment and growth are cut with it.

The effects are not confined to Europe, or even to the advanced countries. Slower European growth means lower demand for primary products imported from the less developed countries. Preoccupation of the United States, Britain, and now Germany with their balances of payments dims the outlook for foreign aid and worsens the climate for trade liberalization. And the American capital controls are bound to reduce the access of less developed countries to private capital and bond loans in the United States—and indirectly in Europe.

2. It may be objected that no bank can keep lending if its depositors are unwilling to hold its liabilities. True. But savings can never be put to productive use if the owners of wealth are unwilling to hold financial assets and insist on what they consider a more "ultimate" means of payment. If the bank is sound, the trouble comes from the depositors' irrationality. The remedy is to have a lender of last resort to cope with the effects of their attitudes or, better, to educate them or, if neither is possible, to make the alternative asset (which, against the dollar, is gold) less attractive or less available. To prevent the bank from pursuing unsound policies—if it really tends to do so—it is not necessary to allow a run on it. The depositors can have their say in less destructive ways, for example, through participating in the

management of the bank of last resort or through agreement on the scale of the financial intermediation.

The nervousness of monetary authorities and academic economists is a consequence of the way they define a deficit and the connotations they attach to it. No bank could survive in such an analytical world. If financial authorities calculated a balance of payments for New York vis-à-vis the interior of the United States, they would find it in serious "deficit," since short-term claims of the rest of the country on New York mount each year. If they applied their present view of international finance, they would impose restrictions on New York's bank loans to the interior and on its purchases of new bond and stock issues. Similarly, the balance of payments of the U.S. financial sector consists almost entirely of above-the-line disbursements and therefore nearly equal "deficits." Between 1947 and 1964, the liquid liabilities (demand and time deposits) of member banks of the Federal Reserve System alone increased from $110 billion to $238 billion. This increase of $128 billion, or 116 percent, was not matched by an equal absolute or even proportionate increase in cash reserves. Indeed, these reserves increased only $1.6 billion, or 8 percent. Yet nobody regards this cumulated "deficit" of over $126 billion as cause for alarm.

The private market has not been alarmed about the international position of the dollar in relation to other currencies or the liquidity of the United States. Although there has been private speculation in gold against the dollar, it has been induced largely by reluctance of some central banks to accumulate dollars. The dollar is the world's standard of value; the Euro-dollar market dominates capital markets in Europe; and the foreign dollar bond market has easily outdistanced the unit-of-account bond and the European "parallel bond." As one looks at sterling and the major Continental currencies, it is hard to imagine any one of them stronger than the dollar today, five years from now, or twenty years hence. Admittedly, short-term destabilizing speculation against the dollar is possible, largely as a consequence of errors of official and speculative judgment. It can be contained, however, by gold outflows and support from other central banks, or by allowing the dollar to find its own level in world exchange markets, buttressed by the combination of high productivity and responsible fiscal and monetary policy in the United States. In the longer run, as now in the short, the dollar is strong, not weak.

3. Since the U.S. "deficit" is the result of liquidity exchanges or financial intermediation, it will persist as long as capital movement is free, European capital markets remain narrower and less competitive than that of the United States, liquidity preferences differ between the United States and Europe, and capital formation in Western Europe remains vigorous. In these circumstances, an effort to adjust the current account to the capital outflow is futile. The deficit can best be attacked by perfecting and eventually integrating European capital markets and moderating the European asset-holder's insistence on liquidity, understandable though the latter may be after half a century of wars, inflations, and capital levies.

An attempt to halt the capital outflow by raising interest rates in the United States either would have little effect over any prolonged period or else would cripple European growth. With European capital markets joined to New York by substantial movements of short-term funds and bonds, the rate structure in the world as a whole will be set by the major financial center, in this instance New York. Interest-rate changes in the outlying centers will have an impact on capital flows to them. Higher interest rates in New York will raise rates in the world as a whole.

The effort is now being made to "correct the deficit" by restricting capital movements. Success in this effort is dubious, however, for two reasons.

MONEY IS FUNGIBLE

In the first place, money is fungible. Costless to store and to transport, it is the easiest commodity to arbitrage in time and in space. Discriminating capital restrictions are only partly effective, as the United States is currently learning. Some funds that are prevented from going directly to Europe will reach there by way of the less-developed countries or via the favored few countries like Canada and Japan, which are accorded access to the New York financial market because they depend upon it for capital and for liquidity. These leaks in the dam will increase as time passes, and the present system of discriminatory controls will become unworkable in the long run. The United States will have to choose between abandoning the whole effort or plugging the leaks. Plugging the leaks, in turn, means that it must either get the countries in whose favor it discriminates to impose their own restrictions or withdraw the preferences it now gives them. Accordingly, the choices in the long run are between no restrictions, restrictions on all outflows, and establishment of what is in effect a dollar bloc, or a dollar-sterling bloc, within which funds move freely but which applies uniform controls against movements to all non-bloc countries.

In the second place, it is not enough to restrain the outflow of United States-owned capital. As Germany and Switzerland have found, to keep United States funds at home widens the spreads between short-term and long-term rates in Europe and also the spreads between the short-term rates at which European financial intermediaries borrow and lend, and so encourages repatriation of European capital already in the United States. For Europe, this effectively offsets restrictions on capital inflows. "Home is where they have to take you in." It would be possible for the United States to block the outflow of foreign capital—possible but contrary to tradition. If this door is left open, the $57 billion of foreign capital in the United States permit substantial net capital outflows, even without an outflow of U.S. capital. Although it would require powerful forces indeed to induce foreign holders to dispose of most of their American investments, they might dispose of enough to permit the "deficit" to continue for a long time.

4. Capital restrictions to correct the deficit, even if feasible, would still leave unanswered a fundamental question. Is it wise to destroy an efficient system of providing internal and external liquidity—the international capital market—and substitute for it one or another contrived device of limited flexibility for creating additions to international reserve assets alone? In the crisis of 1963, Italy borrowed $1.6 billion in the Euro-dollar market; under the Bernstein plan, it would have had access to less than one-tenth of the incremental created liquidity of say $1 billion a year, perhaps $75 million in one year—a derisible amount. It would be the stuff of tragedy for the world's authorities laboriously to obtain agreement on a planned method of providing international reserve assets if that method, through analytical error, unwittingly destroyed an important source of liquid funds for European savers and of loans for European borrowers, and a flexible instrument

for the international provision of liquidity. Moreover, agreement on a way of creating additional international reserve assets will not necessarily end the danger that foreigners, under the influence of conventional analysis, will want to convert dollars into gold whenever they see what they consider a "deficit."

But, it will be objected, the fears of the European authorities about the dollar are facts of life, and the United States must adjust to them. Several points may be made by way of comment.

EUROPE SQUEEZES ITSELF

In the first place, the European authorities must be learning how much international trade in financial claims means to their economies, now that it has been reduced. Europe has discovered that liquidity in the form of large international reserves bears no necessary relationship to ability to supply savers with liquid assets or industrial borrowers with long-term funds in countries where financial intermediation is inadequately performed and which are cut off from the world capital market. Financial authorities in Italy, France, and even Germany have lately been trying to moderate the high interest rates which reflect strong domestic liquidity preference and the wide margins between the rates at which their intermediaries borrow and lend, as well as (in the case of Germany) their own policies. Having scant success in getting households, banks, or private intermediaries to buy long-term securities, these authorities are increasingly entering the market themselves. Investment is declining: in Germany with long-term interest rates touching 8 percent for the best borrowers; in Italy despite Bank of Italy purchases of industrial securities; and in France where government bonds are issued to provide capital to a limited list of industrial investors. It is ironic that United States firms seem able to borrow in Europe more easily than European firms, as they continue investing in Europe while abiding by their Government's program of voluntary capital restraint. Given their liquid capital strength in the United States, they have no objection to borrowing short, and command a preferred status when they choose to borrow long. But their operations in Europe put pressure on European long-term rates and enhance the incentive of other European borrowers and United States lenders to evade the restrictions.

Europe's own capital markets cannot equal that of the United States in breadth, liquidity, and competitiveness in the foreseeable future. Europe must therefore choose between an open international capital market, using fiscal policy to impose any needed restraints, and use of monetary restraint with an insulated capital market. The second alternative involves serious dangers. Without substantial European government lending to industry, which is unlikely, the terms on which long-term money would be available may cause industrial stagnation.

The first choice is the more constructive one, but it can work only if its implications are understood in both Europe and the United States. The United States, too, has failed to appreciate the role of New York in the world monetary system and has acquiesced in the Continental view of the U.S. payments position. It must be recognized that trading in financial assets with the United States means a United States "deficit"; United States capital provides not only goods and services, but liquid assets to Europe, which means European acquisition of dollars. Moreover, the amount of dollars that private savers in Europe will want to acquire for transactions and as a partial offset to debts in dollars, and for other purposes, will increase. This increase in privately held dollars will involve a rising trend in the United States deficit on the Department of Commerce definition, though no deficit on the Bernstein Committee definition.

But that is not all. The new liquid saving in Europe which is matched by European borrowing in the United States is not likely to be held largely in dollars, and certainly will not be held entirely so. Savers typically want liquidity in their own currencies, and so do banks. If household and commercial banks want to hold liquid assets at home rather than securities or liquid assets in dollars, the counterpart of foreign borrowing by industry must be held by the central bank of their country in dollars, or converted into gold. This implies a deficit for the United States even on the Bernstein Committee definition.

Whether householders and banks want to hold dollars or their own national currencies, the effect is the same: both alternatives now frighten the United States as well as Europe. They should not. And they would not if it were recognized that financial intermediation implies a decline in the liquidity of the intermediary as much when the intermediation is being performed in another country as when it is being performed domestically. An annual growth in Europe's dollar-holdings averaging, perhaps, $1½ to $2 billion a year or perhaps more for a long time is normal expansion for a bank the size of the United States with a fast-growing world as its body of customers. To the extent that European capital markets achieve greater breadth, liquidity, and competitiveness, the rates of increase in these dollar holdings consistent with given rates of world economic growth would of course be lower than when these markets have their present deficiencies. But whatever rate of growth in these dollar holdings is needed, the point is that they not only provide external liquidity to other countries, but are a necessary counterpart of the intermediation which provides liquidity to Europe's savers and financial institutions. Recognition of this fact would end central bank conversions of dollars into gold, the resulting creeping decline of official reserves, and the disruption of capital flows to which it has led.

It must be admitted that free private capital markets are sometimes destabilizing. When they are, the correct response is determined governmental counter-action to support the currency that is under pressure until the crisis has been weathered. Walter Bagehot's dictum of 1870 still stands: In a crisis, discount freely. Owned reserves cannot provide for these eventualities, as International Monetary Fund (IMF) experience amply demonstrates. Amounts agreed in advance are almost certain to be too little, and they tip the hand of the authorities to the speculators. The rule is discount freely, and tidy up afterwards, transferring outstanding liabilities to the IMF, the General Arrangements to Borrow, or even into funded government-to-government debts such as were used to wind up the European Payments Union. Owned reserves or readily available discounting privileges on the scale needed to guard against these crises of confidence would be inflationary in periods of calm.

LET THE GOLD GO

Mutual recognition of the role of dollar holdings would provide the most desirable solution, but if, nevertheless, Europe unwisely chooses to convert dollars into gold, the United States could restore a reserve-currency system, even without European cooperation in reinterpreting deficits and lifting capital restrictions. The decision would call for cool heads in the United States. The real problem is to build a strong international monetary mechanism resting on credit, with gold occupying, at most, a subordinate position. Because the dollar is in a special position as a world currency, the United States can bring about this change through its own action. Several ways in which it can do so have been proposed, including widening the margin around parity at which it buys and sells gold, reducing the price at which it buys gold, and otherwise depriving gold of its present unlimited convertibility into dollars. The United States would have to allow its gold stock to run down as low as European monetary authorities chose to take it. If they took it all, which is unlikely, the United States would have no alternative but to allow the dollar to depreciate until the capital flow came to a halt, or, much more likely, until the European countries decided to stop the depreciation by holding the dollars they were unwilling to hold before. If this outcome constituted a serious possibility, it seems evident that European countries would cease conversion of dollars into gold well short of the last few billions.

This strategy has been characterized by *The Economist* as the "new nationalism" in the United States. It can reasonably be interpreted, however, as internationalism. It would enable the United States to preserve the international capital market and thereby protect the rate of world economic growth, even without European cooperation.

While United States–European cooperation in maintaining the international capital market is the preferable route, it requires recognizing that an effective, smoothly functioning international capital market is itself an instrument of world economic growth, not a nuisance which can be disposed of and the function of which can be transferred to new or extended intergovernmental institutions, and it requires abandoning on both sides of the Atlantic the view that a U.S. deficit, whether on the Department of Commerce or the Bernstein Committee definition, is not compatible with equilibrium. Abandonment of this view, in turn, requires facing up to the fact that the economic analysis of the textbooks—derived from the writing and the world of David Hume and modified only by trimmings—is no longer adequate in a world that is increasingly moving (apart from government interferences) toward an integrated capital and money market. In these circumstances, the main requirement of international monetary reform is to preserve and improve the efficiency of the private capital market while building protection against its performing in a destabilizing fashion.

The majority view has been gaining strength since 1958, when Triffin first asserted that the dollar and the world were in trouble. Between 1958 and 1965, world output and trade virtually doubled, the United States dollar recovered from a slight overvaluation, and the gold hoarders have foregone large earnings and capital gains. Having been wrong in 1958 on the near-term position, the consensus may be more wrong today, when its diagnosis and prognosis are being followed. But this time the generally accepted analysis can lead to a brake on European growth. Its error may be expensive, not only for Europe but for the whole world.

Does the United States Have a Payments Deficit?

EDWARD M. BERNSTEIN

Edward M. Bernstein is a former Research Director of the International Monetary Fund and President of EMB, Research Economists. In his statement to the Joint Economic Committee of the U.S. Congress, he addresses his remarks to one of the three authors of the previous selection, and submits that continuing deficits are bound to undermine confidence in the dollar.

THE CONCEPT OF A DEFICIT in the balance of payments is extremely complex and there is always considerable scope for reasonable differences of opinion on the amount of the deficit and, at times, whether there is a deficit. Unfortunately, it is not possible to say that the balance of payments of the United States is not in deficit at this time.

Professor Kindleberger emphasizes that the interpretation of the balance of payments cannot be the same for a country whose international transactions consist almost entirely of exports and imports of goods and services (a trader) and a country that not only engages in an enormous volume of trade but also is an enormous foreign investor and has large short-term foreign assets and foreign liabilities (a banker).

Banks [as distinguished from traders] are in the business of owing money. They have reserves, to be sure, generally of the order of 1 to 5 between their primary reserves and their demand liabilities. For the rest they are in the business of financial intermediation, or lending long and borrowing short. A definition which asserts that a bank is in disequilibrium every time its deposits rise without a parallel [equal?] rise in primary reserves would come as a shock to most bankers, although they do not protest when the Department of Commerce applies this definition to the United States.

When a trading nation buys more goods and services than it sells, it can meet the excess of its payments by drawing down its reserves (gold and foreign exchange), borrowing from the International Monetary Fund (IMF) or other central banks (reserve credit), or securing long-term or short-term credit from foreign financial centers. A trading country that meets its deficit on goods and services by borrowing long-term (through security issues) or short-term (through bank credit) is regarded as having a capital inflow. Its deficit on goods and services is offset by a surplus on capital account. The overall balance of payments is neither in surplus nor in deficit. On the other hand, when a trading country draws down its reserves or secures reserve credit, its overall balance of payments is in deficit.

The deficit of a banking nation is far more difficult to define acceptably. There are any number of definitions that may be used. The Commerce Department definition of the deficit (changes in reserves plus all changes in liquid liabilities to foreigners) is open to serious objection as being one-sided. As Kindleberger says: "All that count on the assets side are gold and convertible foreign exchange owned by the monetary authorities. All other assets are taken to be frozen, while all demand liabilities are regarded as just about to be presented for payment." The liquidity definition exaggerates the size of the deficit if that term is used as a measure of the payments problem.

There are other definitions of the deficit of a banking nation (reserve center) that are not open to this criticism, although they may be objectionable for other reasons. The reserve transactions deficit is measured by the decrease in reserve assets (gold, foreign exchange, and claims on the IMF) plus the increase in liabilities to foreign monetary authorities (reserve liabilities). In this definition, an increase in foreign short-term claims in the United States, other than those of foreign central banks, is treated as a capital inflow, just as an increase in U.S. banking and other claims on foreigners is treated as a capital outflow.

The pragmatic test of a deficit is whether the balance of payments could be continued indefinitely with the existing relationship of the accounts. Obviously, a deficit on the liquidity definition could be continued indefinitely. Foreigners do want to accumulate dollar assets. As Kindleberger has emphasized, they are attractive assets, denominated in a currency whose foreign exchange value is assured, earning a good return, and easily bought and sold (or deposited and withdrawn) in a broad financial market. Even the Commerce Department experts recognize that a deficit on the liquidity definition of an average of $500 million to $800 million a year could be continued indefinitely—it is an equilibrium position requiring no change.

On the other hand, a reserve transactions deficit either depletes the reserves of a country (and cannot be continued indefinitely) or increases its reserve liabilities and confronts it with the risk of a sudden drawing down of its reserves in the future by conversions of foreign official holdings of its currency. This is an uncertain risk, although the United Kingdom has been confronted by it from time to time, and even the United States has had such conversions in 1965 and 1966. Nevertheless, it could be argued that there is a normal growth in foreign exchange reserves in the form of dollars that other countries would find necessary and acceptable, and such an increase in the holdings of a reserve currency could be regarded as capital inflow. Even so, for a banking nation that is a reserve center, there is no escaping the definition of the deficit as a decline in its reserve assets (including short-term reserve credit), for it cannot continue indefinitely a balance of payments that depletes its reserves.

The Kindleberger thesis is replete with description and analysis of the role of the United States as a financial intermediary—that is, a banker. There is much that is enlightening in this discussion. He fails, however, in his attempt to draw an analogy between the position of a commercial banker and the position of the United States as a reserve center. Of course, commercial banks are very happy to increase their liabilities and their assets—that is how they make profits as bankers. But a commercial bank could not continue to make loans (capital outflow in the balance of payments analogy) if it were to find that as a consequence of increasing its income-earning assets it were confronted with an unfavorable balance with other banks at the clearing-house or withdrawals of cash over the counter (reduction of reserves in the balance of payments analogy). It might have no objection to borrowing from the Federal or buying Federal funds (incurring reserve liabilities), provided it could do so without assuming undue risk. But if the Federal is reluctant to let it borrow and it cannot buy Federal funds, it will have to curtail its acquisition of income-earning assets, however profitable its lending and investment operations may be.

That is the situation of the United States. We have acquired a large amount of very valuable income-earning assets abroad. Our earnings from net exports of goods and services, after U.S. aid, have not been sufficient to pay for our foreign investments. This is true even after allowing for the increase of foreign banking claims in this country. As a consequence, we have been drawing down our reserves, and this no country (and no banker) can do indefinitely. It is futile to say, as Kindleberger does, "that the dollar has no need for adjustment, if financial intermediation is properly understood." This would seem to imply that foreign countries would always want to acquire as many dollars as the United States would wish to invest abroad in excess of its balance on other transactions—a thesis of doubtful validity. So long as the United States continues to pay out reserves, it has a deficit in its balance of payments, however much we may rationalize our role as a banker. The proof that we have a deficit is that we cannot continue the present balance of payments without ultimately being confronted with an exchange crisis.

Unfinished Business

FRITZ MACHLUP

Fritz Machlup is Professor of Economics and Director of the International Finance Section at Princeton University. In this essay, taken from his book The Rio Agreement and Beyond, *published in 1968, Machlup examines the causes of the recurrent crises of confidence in the dollar and the remedies offered.*

THE PAYMENTS DEFICIT OF THE UNITED STATES

THE UNITED STATES has been running a deficit in its balance of payments since 1950, that is, for 18 years, except in 1957, the year following the Suez crisis. (Even for that year a deficit would be shown if "errors and omissions," carrying a positive sign at the time, were not included as receipts.) The computation of a deficit is, of course, a matter of statistical convention, and by the conventions of the 1950's one would still be speaking of American "surpluses," as was done when additional dollar balances were in heavy demand by almost all foreign nations. But by the definitions now most widely adopted,[1] the United States ran deficits in the 1950's as well as in the 1960's. The hard fact behind all statistical calculations is that the United States, between 1949 and 1967, has seen its monetary gold stock decline from $24.6 billion to $12 billion and its liquid liabilities to foreign monetary authorities increase from $3.2 billion to $15 billion. (By the middle of March 1968 the gold reserves were down to $10.5 billion and the official liabilities were up to nearly $16 billion.)

No one was worried about these deficits between 1950 and 1958. Indeed, most commentators were pleased about the redistribution of gold and about the increase in dollar reserves of the non-dollar countries during these years of "dollar shortage." Later,

1. At present, the United States calculates two official figures: the deficit on the "liquidity basis," and the deficit on the "official-settlement basis." Two other significant concepts are the deficit in the "basic balance" and the decline in "net foreign reserves." Although these four balances are drastically different, the deficit has persisted no matter which of the four concepts is used.

however, the appetite for official dollar reserves had been fully satisfied and misgivings about a "dollar glut," a supply of more dollars than were wanted, began to be voiced. As a matter of fact, the supply of dollars increased, instead of declining, and many of the unwanted dollars were returned to the United States for conversion into gold. From December 1957 to December 1961, the monetary gold stock of the United States fell from $22.9 billion to $16.9 billion.

Beginning in 1960, the United States adopted a series of measures designed to reduce or remove the payments deficit. These measures were of two kinds: (1) selective correctives, that is, measures supposed to operate on particular types of transactions and to improve selected items in the balance of payments, and (2) general adjustment policies, that is, policies to affect the general level of incomes and prices in ways that would through market forces improve the balance on goods and services.

The adjustment process seemed to work satisfactorily for a number of years, thanks chiefly to the fact that price levels were kept relatively stable in the United States but rose substantially in many other countries, especially in the large industrial countries of Europe. This allowed the American export balance of goods and services to increase from $2.2 billion in 1958 to $8.5 billion in 1964. However, a sharp increase in capital outflows canceled out much of the improvement of the current account: from 1959 to 1965, the outflow of private long-term capital increased from $1.6 billion to $4.4 billion. (One must not assume, however, that these changes are independent of one another; it is quite likely that the increase in capital outflow stimulated foreign demand and thus helped increase commodity exports from the United States.)

After 1964, the adjustment process came to a halt, probably because of an updrift of incomes and prices in the United States and a simultaneous attenuation of wage-and-price inflations in Europe.[2] The American export balance of goods and services began to decline: from the $8.5 billion in 1964, it fell to $5.1 billion in 1966.

To record that the adjustment process came to a halt is not to

---

2. Wholesale prices in the United States, which had been virtually unchanged for six years—from 1958 to 1964—rose from March 1965 to August 1966 at an annual rate of 3.8 per cent.

say that adjustment policies will not work. They will, if consistently pursued. Nor is it to condemn the United States for not pursuing them consistently. The government evidently believed that policies of restraining the increase in effective demand were too costly in terms of employment and national product. It was a conscious decision to give prime consideration to the objective of achieving greater employment through stepping up aggregate demand. An economist may have his own value judgments about which ought to be more important to the nation: more employment or a smaller payments deficit. But the decisions are made by governments. In any case, the expansion of aggregate demand in the United States halted and reversed the improvement in the current balance and did not prevent a drastic deterioration of the capital balance.

The corrective measures, recommended by those who believe that you can correct a deficit by picking particular items in the balance of payments and working on them by means of selective restrictions and controls, have had only the success expected by (allegedly "unrealistic") economic theorists: if a chosen item was improved and the dollar outflow reduced under that particular heading, trouble quickly arose for another item, leaving the overall payments deficit just about where it was. More will be said later on the question of "item-picking" and on the effectiveness of selective controls. One point, however, calls for reflection now. The deficit in the balance of payments has been between one and four billion dollars during the past 18 years. With a gross national product of over $800 billion at the end of 1967, and between $500 and $750 billion in the past seven years, why should it be so difficult to improve the balance of goods and services by just another two billion dollars? With all controls and restraints, the payments deficit has refused to budge and the balance of international transactions has not done us the favor of improving by as little as one-half of 1 per cent of the gross national product. This, I believe, is most impressive. It impresses me chiefly as an indication of the great strength of market forces and an indication of the humbling weakness of governmental controls.

The upshot of it all is that after 18 years the payments deficit of the United States is worse than ever and shows no signs of improvement.

In the past, the deficits have been financed partly by increases in liquid liabilities to foreign holders of dollars and partly by drains on the monetary gold stock. It now looks as if in the future our deficits may have to be financed increasingly, and perhaps mainly, by the surrender of gold. If so, the United States will have spent all its gold within four or five years—provided it has not surrendered it even earlier through conversions of dollars which foreign holders have accumulated in previous years.

THE DOLLAR OVERHANG FROM EARLIER YEARS

On September 30, 1967, the national monetary authorities of the noncommunist countries held a total of 14.4 billion of United States dollars; private foreign holdings of dollars totaled 15.1 billion. The combined total of $29.5 billion had been accumulated chiefly in the years between 1950 and 1965.

The division of foreign dollar holdings into official and private is significant on several grounds, although it is well known that central banks on occasion "place" some of their dollar holdings with commercial banks.[3] As a consequence, published figures do not tell the complete story in that they do not reveal how many private holdings are actually hidden monetary reserves of the central bank. But to the extent that the statistics tell the correct story, the division is important, especially because of the different motives for holding dollars.

Private foreign dollar balances are held almost entirely for transactions purposes. The "transactions demand" for dollar balances on the part of commercial banks and traders abroad is determined by daily, weekly, monthly, and seasonal variations in receipts and expenditures, by interest-rate differentials, by the cost of foreign-exchange operations, and by expected changes in exchange rates. Official dollar holdings, on the other hand, are determined largely by political considerations. The central banker of a large industrial country does not look in the first place at the alternative costs and earnings of his asset-mix, but rather on the

---

3. The central bank does this by way of swap or repurchase agreements that make it attractive for commercial banks to use their excess reserves for acquiring the dollar assets, which yield interest and a small gain in the resale price. The main purpose of the central bank is to syphon off some excessive lending capacity, or excess liquidity, of the banking system; in this fashion, dollar assets take the place of government securities in open-market operations.

advantages or necessities of international financial cooperation or noncooperation. These differences in motivation bear on the problem of the large liquid liabilities of the United States to foreign holders and of the danger that these dollar holdings may be drastically reduced.

Not all "asset switching" has the same effects. If there is a massive flight into gold, it need not be a flight from the dollar; and if there is a massive flight from the dollar, it need not be into gold. Private foreign holders of dollars who wish to get rid of their dollars may prefer to hold other currencies which they regard as safer. And foreign hoarders or speculators who wish to buy gold may intend to reduce their holdings, not of dollars, but of other currencies, especially their own. To equate an increase in the demand for gold hoards with a decrease in the demand for dollar balances may therefore be wrong. Of the non-dollar-holder's flight into gold, I shall talk later; let us first concentrate on the danger of a flight from the dollar, either into gold or into other currencies.

The decision of a private foreign holder of dollars to exchange them into gold can be regarded as exceptional. Ordinarily, he needs his working balance for day-to-day transactions and, if he can spare some of it, it will not be much and he will sacrifice his liquidity only in consideration of a large and immediate gain—say, if he expects that the price of gold will be raised over the week-end. A decision to exchange dollars into other currencies is much more likely, because the cost of in-and-out trading is much smaller and the liquidity of other currencies not much lower even if only dollars were usable for the regular foreign transactions of the particular firm or bank.

Yet, under the arrangements in effect until March 17, 1968, both kinds of switch affected the gold stocks of the United States in a rather similar way. This resulted from a combination of two practices: (1) The arrangements of the Gold Pool provided for sales of monetary gold to private buyers whenever the demand in the London gold market was not fully met by supplies from private stocks and new production; 59 per cent of the wanted gold was supplied by the United States, the other 41 per cent by Germany, Italy, Belgium, Netherlands, United Kingdom, and Switzerland. (2) Several of these countries had set upper limits to their holdings of dollars; as the proceeds of their sales of gold increased their dollar holdings, the collected dollars would sooner or later be presented to the authorities of the United States for conversion into gold.

Now, what effects can be expected if private dollar holders switch from dollars into francs, DM, lire, or other strong currencies? The central banks issuing these currencies and acquiring the dollars may again find their dollar holdings increased beyond the limit and may seek their conversion into gold. Thus it seems that in both cases of private foreigners reducing their dollar balances, whether they want to replace them with another currency or with gold, the end-effect would be a loss of gold by the United States.

In March 1968, the seven countries of the Gold Pool agreed on a new policy. They will no longer supply gold to the London market, even if the market price of gold should rise as a result. Moreover, the six countries may allow their dollar holdings to increase; that is, they will not present surplus dollars for prompt conversion into gold. There is probably no commitment to this effect and certainly there is nothing that would commit other countries to refrain from asking the United States to surrender gold for dollars. A brief review of the past behavior of foreign monetary authorities regarding their holdings of gold and foreign exchange may be helpful in an appraisal of official attitudes.

Taking all noncommunist countries together, their official holdings of dollars increased steadily until the end of 1965, when they reached a peak of $15.9 billion. The decline that followed was quite modest; to $14.4 billion in September 1967. Focusing, however, on the industrial countries of Europe, we notice that they began earlier to reduce the foreign-exchange portion of their monetary reserves: at the end of 1964 they held $9.2 billion, a year later only $7.5 billion. In the same year, they increased their gold holdings from $16.9 billion to $18.9 billion. France and Germany were leading in this switch of their monetary reserves. Germany had started a year ahead of all others, reducing her foreign-exchange holdings from $3.3 billion at the end of 1963 to $2.7 billion in 1964 and to $1.7 billion in March 1965, while increasing gold stocks from $3.8 billion to $4.4 billion in the same period. France reduced her foreign-exchange reserves from $1.4 billion at the end of 1964 to $0.8 billion in 1965 and $0.5 billion in 1966, building up her gold holdings from $3.7 billion at the end of 1964 to $4.7 billion a year later and $5.2 billion at the end of 1966. All these switches cut into the gold reserves of the United States, reducing them from $15.5 billion at the end of 1964 to $14.1 billion in 1965 and to $13.2 billion in 1966.

The reductions in dollar holdings by monetary authorities were halted when the situation became critical. Several countries, indeed, agreed to reverse the direction of change in the composition of their reserves. Leading among those that have increased their holdings of dollars are Germany and Italy. But this does not mean that the official holders of dollars have forever foresworn conversions into gold. One may assume that the authorities in practically all countries wish to avoid a crisis, the outcome of which cannot be predicted but is apt to be deleterious to most. Yet, if in some countries, in a moment of stress, the men in charge of international monetary affairs were to lose their heads, and a threat of a stampede for gold seemed imminent, official demands for conversions could become large enough for the United States to realize that the sale of gold cannot be continued.

In any case, the double threat of the "dollar overhang" accumulated over many years and of the current "dollar overflow" from continuing payments deficits of the United States makes it difficult to be sanguine about the ability of this country to satisfy all potential official requests for gold.

THE GOLD RUSH

Having talked about the dangers of gold hoarding by nervous dollar holders, I must now proceed to discuss private gold purchases by holders of other currencies.

Purchases of gold in the London market are paid in dollars. If those for whose accounts the gold is bought have no dollar balances, they first have to acquire dollars with whatever currencies they may have been holding—pounds, Swiss francs, rupees, kyats, bahts, wons, kips, piastres, or any other.[4] The results of an increased private demand for gold will differ according to whether it is met out of new production of gold; or is met out of monetary reserves under the arrangements of the Gold Pool (rescinded in March 1968); or results in a higher gold price in

4. The last five are the currencies of Burma, Thailand, Korea, Laos, and Vietnam.

the free market.

Assume that the final buyers are Thais, paying in bahts, and that the sellers are South Africans, who want their proceeds in rands, to pay for the production cost of gold. There will therefore be a supply of bahts in search of dollars, a payment of dollars for gold, and a supply of dollars in search of rands. If both the baht and the rand are pegged in terms of dollars and, hence, the authorities of Thailand and South Africa intervene in the foreign-exchange markets, the dollar holdings of Bangkok will decrease and those of Johannesburg increase. If the adjustment process works, the balances of goods and services of the two countries will eventually adjust and show larger exports from Thailand and larger imports (matching the exports of commercial gold) into South Africa. The dollar, having served in the process as transactions currency, will not be affected either way.

Let us now see what happens if the new demand for gold cannot be met out of new production but, under gold-pool arrangements designed to stabilize the gold price in the free market, is met out of official reserves sold by monetary authorities. Assume that the final buyers are Indians, paying in rupees, and the sellers are the monetary authorities participating in the Gold Pool. I shall not go into the delicate question whether the Reserve Bank of India will furnish dollars to the rupee owners (whose demand for foreign exchange may come in a disguise that appears quite legitimate) or in what other ways dollars become available to them. The relevant part of the process is the loss of monetary gold. Under the old arrangements, the seven countries joined in the Gold Pool had shared the loss. The European central banks in this case would not necessarily have acquired additional dollars in exchange for their gold, since the private demand for dollar balances had not declined: it was the demand for rupee holdings that declined. If the Indian authorities stayed out of the picture, the rupees may have been offered at a price attractive enough for some people to buy them with dollars or other currencies, either to make purchases in India or even to hold the rupees temporarily for speculative reasons. The central banks supplying the gold might find their note circulation or demand deposits reduced or their dollar holdings increased. And eventually they would return such dollars to New York for gold. Thus, at least in part, the Indians' gold hoarding would have encroached on American gold stocks.

If enough statistical information were at hand, we could establish to what extent major scrambles for gold were associated with reductions in private foreign holdings of dollars. It would be important to know whether the tidal wave of private gold purchases in December 1967, which took $900 million from the American gold stocks within four weeks, left private foreign dollar holdings more or less unchanged or reduced by a similar amount. There had been earlier gold rushes, besides the gradual increases in private hoards. Thus, in 1960, additions to private gold stocks jumped by $311 million, or 68 per cent of the 1959 purchases, and in 1965, by $449 million, or 67 per cent of the 1964 purchases.[5] But we do not know whether private dollar holdings in those years reflected any "movements out of dollars."

One conclusion of these reflections is that, under the old gold-pool arrangements, private gold purchases could encroach upon the gold reserves of the United States even if the purchases were made by foreigners not holding dollars but using their own currencies to pay for the gold. Regardless of whether the gold rushes between December 1967 and March 1968 were associated with reductions in the demand for dollar balances or were financed with other currencies, the depletion of American gold holdings was too rapid for the authorities to stand by inactively. More than $2.4 billion worth of gold was lost within the three months, reducing the stocks to $10.5 billion. The decision by the members of the Gold Pool, on March 17, 1968, to halt sales to private parties and no longer to intervene in the London gold market was a sensible reaction. But what will now be the effects of private excess demand for gold?

Assume that speculators want to acquire more gold than is available from new production after the requirements of industrial and artistic users and traditional hoarders are satisfied. Without any sales out of monetary stocks, the sole source of supply for bullish speculators is gold relinquished by less bullish speculators. That is to say, the eager buyers will bid up the market price to a point at which less eager holders are willing to part with enough

---

5. These large jumps clearly refute the hypothesis, advanced by official and unofficial experts, that the increase in private purchases of gold is a nonspeculative, "structural" development. Nothing but speculation can explain the sudden leaps in 1960, 1965, and 1967.

of their gold to meet the demand. Although dollars are used in the transactions, the position of the dollar in the exchange markets will not be affected if neither buyers nor sellers of the gold reduce or increase their dollar balances in the end. If the buyers have, at the outset, had currencies other than dollars, and had to buy dollars in order to buy gold, whereas the sellers, at the increased price of gold, hold on to the dollar proceeds, the dollar will be strengthened in the process and some central banks may have to sell dollars against their own currencies. Conversely, if the buyers have held dollars whereas the sellers want to hold their proceeds in other currencies, the dollar will be weakened and some central banks may have to acquire dollars under our system of fixed exchange rates.

It would be difficult to predict which of these three possibilities is the most likely to materialize—were it not for the continuing supply of additional dollars originating from the payments deficit of the United States. With this continuing deficit, one may expect that dollars, both from the current overflow and from the amassed overhang, will land in the hands of foreign monetary authorities and, through conversion, contribute to the further erosion of the gold position of the United States.

CHEAP ADVICE

If the predicament is due chiefly to the deficits in the balance of payments and to a lack of confidence in the United States dollar, it requires no great wisdom to conclude that all will be well if balance and confidence are restored. The cheapest advice is to say that restoring balance will restore confidence and that therefore no more is needed than to remove the continuous overspending, overlending, and overinvesting by the United States.

External balance does not guarantee confidence in the sense of maintenance of a given volume of foreign dollar holdings. The foreign demand for dollar balances depends chiefly on the volume of dollar transactions for which working balances are needed. Any measures or policies that reduce the volume of foreign trade and payments may well reduce the foreign demand for private dollar holdings, and thus lead to further conversions and to American gold losses, even if the payments deficit (on liquidity basis) is reduced or removed. Moreover, "overspending, overlending, and overinvesting" are relative magnitudes, and absolute reductions in foreign spending, lending, and investing need not reduce, and may even increase, the relative oversize of the particular items in the balance of payments.

What can really be done to achieve a cure of the chronic imbalance of payments and to safeguard against crises of confidence?

RESTORING BALANCE: DIRECT CONTROLS

There are several ways of dealing with a deficit in the balance of payments: to finance it, suppress it through restrictions, try to remove it through real or financial correctives, or restore balance through real adjustment.

After 18 years of financing the deficit, the time has come to end it. Picking some conspicuous deficit items in the balance of payments, the United States has decided to "take action" against these items, partly by means of direct controls and prohibitions. The government hopes the country will save at least $1 billion by a "mandatory program" to restrain direct investment abroad and to bring home larger portions of foreign earnings from past investments; another $500 million by a "tightened program" to restrain foreign lending by banks and other financial institutions; another $500 million by reducing "nonessential travel outside the Western Hemisphere"; and again another $500 million by reducing the foreign-exchange cost of keeping troops in Europe.

Even if the new program suceeded in improving the balance of payments by $2.5 billion, it would still not *restore balance*. It would only *suppress imbalance*, and probably only temporarily. When the controls and restrictions are lifted, the deficit is apt to reappear in its full size. At best, the reduction of the cost of keeping troops in Europe may turn out to be a continuing saving—either by bringing some of the troops home or by receiving compensatory payments from the NATO allies. All the other items, however, have to be regarded as regular flows, determined by underlying conditions such as levels of incomes and prices and rates of profit and capital formation. Such flows can be restricted or suppressed for a time but, if the underlying conditions are not altered, they will resume at the same or even increased strength as soon as the restrictions and prohibitions are taken off.

That the suppression of a deficit by use of police power does not restore "equilibrium" but merely conceals the symptoms of "disequilibrium," is relatively easy to grasp (though many manage to forget it). It is less easy to understand that the suppression of deficit items in amounts equal to the present deficit may yet fail to remove the deficit. The naive observer of the statistic of international transactions is inclined to assume that each reduction of a deficit item will be fully reflected in a reduction of the "over-all deficit." It takes hard intellectual work to comprehend the interdependence between the various items, to see, for example, why a reduction in the expenditures of American tourists abroad or a reduction in American direct investment abroad will to some extent result in increased imports and reduced exports of goods and services. These "feedbacks" may be large or small, but will rarely be zero. They can be zero only if the reduction in the flow of funds does not affect the use of funds either in the domestic or in the foreign market. Assume that an American, A, is prevented from lending his money to a foreigner, F; only if A then decides to sit on his money and not to spend, lend, or invest any part of it, and if F manages to disburse abroad exactly the same amount of money that he could have disbursed thanks to the receipt of A's funds, only then will imports and exports be unaffected by the financial corrective. In all probability, A will use some of his funds at home and F will have less to spend abroad, and the United States will have larger imports and smaller exports as a result.

RESTORING BALANCE: PARTIAL DEVALUATION

Besides direct controls, various measures have been introduced to alter the ratios between selected domestic and foreign values. These measures are designed, by changing the basis of economic calculation, to divert purchases from foreign to domestic markets. They can most conveniently be regarded as disguised, partial devaluations of the dollar.

First, the dollar used for military expenditures abroad was devalued when the official in charge were instructed to "buy American" whenever the cost was not more than 50 per cent above the cost in foreign currency calculated at the official exchange rate. Next came the concealed devaluation of the dollar used by recipients of foreign aid; they were forced to buy in the United States, even if they could have bought elsewhere at lower prices. As a result of the tied purchases, the worth of the aid-dollar was reduced by about 25 per cent. The third partial devaluation was that of the dollar used for purchases of foreign securities: the so-called interest-equalization tax was equivalent to an increase in the price of foreign currencies by 15 per cent. The proposals made early in 1968 include a devaluation of the tourist's dollar by means of special taxes on travel expenditures outside the Western Hemisphere.

All such selective correctives through partial devaluation are inequitable, discriminatory, and inefficient, although they are superior to direct controls in that they work by means of price incentives and disincentives and leave the market essentially free. They all invite substitution, evasion, and circumvention; they discriminate against some sectors and in favor of others, distort the structure of prices, and induce misallocation of productive resources. Usually, they are also incapable of effecting their purpose. For, while they improve particular items in the balance of payments, they worsen others, partly because of the substitution of purchases for which the dollar is not devalued, partly because of foreign and domestic repercussions from the reduction of purchases for which the value of the dollar is reduced.

If the disguised devaluations of the dollar were uniform—for example, by means of proportional taxes on all imports and subsidies on all exports of goods, services, and securities—they might work indiscriminately; but the administrative difficulties would be serious. While theoretically taxes and subsidies could be used in lieu of a uniform alteration of exchange rates, in practice they would amount to a system of multiple exchange rates with plenty of bureaucratic bungling and high rewards for cheating and bribing.

I conclude that selective measures to remove the deficit, whether they are real correctives (designed to affect the flow of goods and services) or financial correctives (operating on the flow of capital funds) are not likely to achieve sustainable balance. Only real adjustment is likely to accomplish that.

RESTORING BALANCE: REAL ADJUSTMENT

In the process of real adjustment, relative prices and incomes are changed in such a way that the allocation of real resources and the international flows of goods and services are altered sufficiently to improve the current account so as to make it match the balance on capital account and unilateral payments. I distinguish three approaches: aggregate-demand adjustment, cost-and-price adjustment, and exchange-rate adjustment. The first two are practically inseparable, because demand adjustment works largely through changes in costs and prices, and cost-and-price adjustments cannot, as a rule, be achieved without demand adjustment.

Aggregate-demand adjustment implies income deflation and less employment in the deficit country and/or income-and-price inflation in the surplus country. Since excessive expansion of demand in the deficit country has often contributed to the emergence or persistence of the payments deficit, stopping the inflation is, in such instances, the first and most urgent recommendation. But merely disinflationary policies cannot accomplish full adjustment when the surplus countries likewise desist from inflating aggregate demand. Only if these countries allowed their income and price levels to rise would the prevention of income-and-price inflation in the deficit country initiate a process of real adjustment, leading gradually to restoration of external balance as the "demand pull" in foreign countries washed their surpluses away.

While halting or containing the inflation in the deficit country is not yet a sufficient condition for real adjustment, it is a necessary condition for preventing the deficit from getting bigger. Thus, fiscal and monetary restraint—higher taxes, reduced expenditures, tighter credit—are imperative, simply to keep the imbalance of payments from getting worse. Yet, to prescribe the same orthodox medicine in doses large enough to induce full adjustment would mean to expose the country to great risks. Stopping an inflation is one thing; forcing a deflation is another. In the absence of inflation abroad, real adjustment of the existing imbalance would require net deflation in the deficit country, at a probably exorbitant social and economic cost, which no government is willing to impose on the country.

The third approach to real adjustment—exchange-rate adjustment—is also resisted by governments. The United States regards it as practically impossible, partly because of some past promises and commitments, partly because of the role of its currency in international affairs. The trading partners of the United States regard this kind of adjustment as undesirable, and perhaps intolerable, chiefly because it would weaken the competitive position of their industries. Exchange-rate adjustment may, nevertheless, prove to be the only practicable way out.

PART FIVE: Solutions to the International Monetary Problem

The Threat to the Dollar

ROBERT TRIFFIN

Robert Triffin is Pelatiah Perit Professor of Political Science at Yale University. In this article (published originally in 1961) and in his books Europe and the Money Muddle, Gold and the Dollar Crisis, *and* Our International Monetary System; Yesterday, Today, and Tomorrow, *he reviews the contemporary international monetary scene and provides suggestions for changes in the world monetary system.*

THERE ARE two ways to go broke: a slow one and a fast one. The slow way is to go on, year after year, spending more money than you earn. But if you are rich to begin with, you won't go broke very fast that way. You will pay for your overspending by depleting your bank balance and other assets and by getting loans from people who trust your capacity to repay them later.

A much faster way to go broke is to finance too much of your overspending by short-term borrowing. Even if you stop overspending, you may then still run into serious trouble if your IOU's are suddenly presented to you for repayment at a time when your bank balance has fallen too low to cover them. If you still have other, longer-term assets in sufficient amount, you will remain perfectly solvent, but you will be confronted, nevertheless, with what is called a liquidity crisis.

This, in a nutshell, is the United States' problem today and the reason why our dollar is facing a serious threat in the international exchange markets. We have, over the past decade, spent, lent, and given away about $20 billion more than we earned and covered the difference by cash payments in gold ($6 billion) and also by short-term IOU's ($14 billion), which foreign central banks, private banks, and individuals were, until recently, quite glad to invest in, since the dollar was regarded as safer than any other currency, and even, for the time being, as safe as gold itself.

The Eisenhower Administration woke up belatedly to the problem when gold prices suddenly flared up on the London free market last October and when U.S. gold losses shot up in the following weeks to a rate of between $400 million and $500 million per month. A wind of panic blew over Washington officialdom, and hurried steps were taken or planned "to restore overall balance in our foreign transactions."

Although the exact measures adopted may not have been the wisest ones, their objective was highly laudable. We should, of course, steer away from the slow road to bankruptcy. The trouble is that we have not given much evidence so far of any clear understanding of the liquidity, as opposed to solvency, crisis that constitutes the real and most urgent threat to the dollar and of the measures needed to combat this far greater danger.

We might well regain full equilibrium in our overall balance of payments—we are indeed far closer to that goal already than the Eisenhower Administration seemed to suspect—and yet be faced by massive demands for conversion into gold of the short-term debts inherited from our former deficits. Such massive liquidation by foreigners of their present dollar holdings would certainly become less likely as we gave evidence of our determination and ability to put a stop to our persistent deficits of the last decade. It would still exist, however, and might be triggered at any time by speculative rumors—justified or unjustified—or, more simply, by interest-rate differentials between New York and other financial centers, primarily in Western Europe. As long as such a threat is allowed to persist, we may find ourselves unable to manage our own credit and interest-rate policies, in the best interests of our economy, without running the risks of large gold outflows from our shores and, ultimately, of a totally unnecessary devaluation of the dollar, disastrous to us and to the rest of the world as well.

Even if we chose to close our eyes to this danger, another major crisis would in time develop from the very success of our efforts to redress our own balance-of-payments position. The elimination of our deficits would indeed dry up at the source two thirds of the annual supply of monetary reserves on which the rest of the world has come to depend for the maintenance of international currency convertibility in an expanding world economy.

The present crisis of the dollar is in fact inextricably bound up with the ill-fated attempt to dig up and dust off an international monetary system which collapsed nearly half a century ago, during World War I, and which must be thoroughly overhauled in order to adapt it to present-day needs and conditions.

This international monetary system is theoretically based on the old, pre-1914 gold standard. In the decade following World War I, the "world gold shortage" was a frequent subject for discussion among academic economists and the main topic on the agenda of a long series of international conferences which culminated in the marathon debates of the Gold Delegation of the defunct League of Nations. The "gold shortage" was temporarily solved in the meantime by the growing use of two national currencies, sterling and the dollar, as international world reserves, along with the gold, in short supply. This, however, could not be more than a makeshift. It ended, disastrously, in the early 1930s with the successive devaluations of both of these currencies and the consequent collapse of the world monetary system.

In the decade following World War II, the basic role played by gold in our international monetary system was all but forgotten. A new slogan came to dominate academic discussions and governmental policies: the slogan of the "world dollar shortage." These policies were eminently successful. They accelerated the reconstruction of war damage and the expansion of the underdeveloped economies, and stimulated a rate of growth in world trade and world production unprecedented in duration and magnitude in the history of the world.

Yet they, too, were built upon the same make-shifts as in the 1920s. They, too, threatened to end in the early 1960s in a new collapse of world trade and world currencies similar to that of the early 1930s.

This grim parallel has its roots in a common and age-old problem: the routine and inertia which tie man to his past and make him unable or unwilling to effect in time the adjustments necessary to the successful performance, and ultimate survival, of his economic, social, and political institutions in a fast-changing world.

A simple comparison may be helpful at this stage. We all know too well the need which we have to carry some amount of currency in our pockets and to keep a checking account at our bank in order to bridge the gap between paydays and to be able to pay for our groceries and other purchases. The amounts of currency and deposits which we have to hold for this purpose bear some obvious, even though fairly loose, relation to the level of our income and expenditures. In very much the same way, countries must hold, generally in their central bank, international reserves to bridge seasonal and other inevitable and unpredictable gaps between their receipts from and payments to other countries. The amounts of reserves required for this purpose also hold an obvious, although equally loose, relation to the turnover of trade and production.

Now, imagine how little trade and production could have grown in the United States over the last century if the only means of payment available to all of us, as a group, had been the number of gold coins that could be minted from the haphazard growth of gold mining in California and Colorado. This, fortunately, was never the case, either here or in any other country. Paper currency and bank deposits played, throughout, a large and growing role, alongside declining amounts of gold, silver, and other minor coin, in the national monetary system of every country. Even in the heyday of the gold standard, the total monetary gold stock of the United States, for instance—both in the form of gold coin and central gold reserves—fell from about 30 per cent of the overall means of payment of the country in 1860 to about 8 per cent in 1914. The provision of an adequate, but noninflationary, volume of money for our expanding economy already depended then, as it still does today, upon the soundness and resiliency of our banking institutions and credit policies, rather than on any blind enslavement to the much-vaunted automatic discipline of the so-called—or miscalled—gold standard.

The basic problems which deposit banking has long been able to solve within national borders, under the guidance of national monetary authorities, still remain largely unsolved, however, as far as international payments are concerned. Or, rather, since the world has to go on, they have been solved after a fashion, but only through a succession of makeshifts and at the cost of recurrent international crises manifesting themselves in the form of widespread deflation, currency devaluations, and trade and exchange restrictions.

Under the so-called full-fledged gold standard, prevalent in the last third of the nineteenth century and until World War I, gold was used exclusively, or nearly exclusively, by most central banks as international reserves and as the ultimate means of settlement for temporary imbalance in all major countries' international transactions. The enormous gold discoveries of the mid-nineteenth century had made possible for a while the adoption of such a system, but the maintenance of adequate gold reserves by central banks the world over was fed in addition, even then, by the gradual replacement of gold coin by currency and deposits in the countries' national monetary circulation. But this latter process was bound to come to an end and did with the world-wide demonetization of gold in the 1920s and early 1930s. The world gold shortage has been with us ever since, although its timing and acuity have also been vitally affected by the vast price disturbances arising from wartime and post-war inflation and from the Great Depression of the 1930s.

Over the whole period from 1914 through 1959, new gold production outside the Soviet bloc has fed considerably less than half of the average increase in the world's monetary reserves. In the fifteen years from 1914 through 1928, it accounted for only 38 per cent of reserve increases, another 30 per cent of which was derived from the withdrawal of gold coin from active circulation, and the remaining 32 per cent from the growing use of major *national* currencies—primarily sterling in those days—as *international* reserves by central banks, alongside gold itself. This custom had spread under the prodding of British currency experts and the spur of the interest that central banks could earn on such foreign exchange investments—but not, of course, on the gold kept in their vaults. Together with the flight of hot money from the war-torn and inflation-wrecked continent of Europe, it helped the British restore the pound to its pre-war parity in 1925, while Continental currencies sank excessively in value under the impact of speculative money flights from the Continent to London.

This soon proved a very mixed blessing for Britain. The overvaluation of sterling or the undervaluation of other European currencies handicapped British exporters in relation to their main competitors in world markets. Europe boomed while Britain suffered from economic stagnation and unemployment. Britain, moreover, felt impelled to tighten credit and interest rates in order to attract or retain foreign funds in London and avoid unsustainable gold losses. Such monetary policies were bound to aggravate the deflationary pressures already at work on the British economy. They became, in any case, powerless to stem the flow when the later stabilization of currency conditions on the Continent triggered a massive repatriation of the funds which had previously sought refuge in London.

Continental central banks reluctantly agreed to support sterling for a while by moderating their own conversions of sterling funds into gold. This merely postponed the day of reckoning. The collapse of a bank in Vienna unleashed a new wave of currency speculation which led to further withdrawals of funds from London. On a fateful day in September, 1931, Britain threw in the sponge. The collapse of the most powerful currency that the world had ever known spelled the collapse of the international gold exchange standard itself and ushered in a long period of exchange chaos in the world's monetary relations.

A grim parallel could easily be drawn between the rise and fall of the sterling exchange standard after World War I on the one hand, and on the other the rise of the dollar exchange standard after World War II and the difficulties which we are facing today. Foreign funds have, ever since 1931, sought a haven in New York rather than in London. These speculative movements played a role in the consolidation of exchange rates—mostly in 1949—at levels which appear now to have undervalued European currencies with respect to the dollar. Our economy has grown, for the last ten years, at a snail's pace in contrast to the rates of growth experienced by most European countries. The repatriation of European funds which had previously sought refuge here initiated a gold outflow of more than $2 billion in 1958.

This drain was slowed down to $1 billion in 1959 and to a mere trickle in the first half of 1960 under the impact of a drastic stiffening of interest rates in this country. It again assumed dramatic and even alarming proportions, however, in the second half of last year. This was primarily, at first, the result of the lower interest rates and the darkening Wall Street outlook brought about here by an incipient recession coupled with booming activity and a tightening of interest rates in Europe. Incredible bungling by some of our Treasury officials during the September meetings of the International Monetary Fund poured oil on the fire by allowing a flare-up of gold prices in the London market, which unleashed a wave of speculative gold buying by Americans as well as foreigners. Our gold losses jumped from an average of only $25 million a month during the first half of 1960 to more than $200 million a month in the third quarter, $300 million in October, and $500 million in November; that is, to an annual rate of nearly $6 billion a year, just about equal to the amount which antiquated and ill-conceived legislative provisions leave us as "free gold" reserves.

Fortunately, other countries have as great a stake as we have in helping the United States ward off a devaluation of the dollar, which would once more usher in a long period of chaos in exchange rates, such as followed the 1931 sterling devaluation, and benefit mostly the two largest gold-producing countries in the world, South Africa and the U.S.S.R. Time is running short, however, and we are each day living more and more dangerously on the edge of the precipice.

The most feasible and constructive way to ward off the international monetary breakdown which a dollar collapse would entail would be to enlarge and streamline the present methods of operation of the International Monetary Fund. This could be done in two stages.

All that the first stage would require would be a mere declaration by the Fund that it stands ready to accept reserve deposits from its member central banks, just as our Federal Reserve System accepts reserve deposits from commercial member banks in this country. Under the rules of the Fund, such deposits would carry a gold-exchange guarantee, making them extremely attractive to central banks. They would be as safe as gold itself and as usable for payments anywhere in the world. Their conversion into any currency needed for payment would be effected most simply, efficiently, and economically by drawing a check on the paying country's account and depositing it in the account of the country whose currency was purchased.

The Fund, moreover, would be in a position to pay interest on these deposits out of the earnings derived from investment of the assets transferred to it by members in exchange for such deposits. The advantages of interest-earning, gold-guaranteed deposits with the Fund over both sterile gold holdings and exchange-risky balances in national currencies should be sufficient to induce most countries to exchange voluntarily for Fund deposits the bulk of their present foreign exchange holdings and possibly even some portion of the reserves which they now retain in gold.

Countries other than the United States and the United Kingdom would constitute, initially, the bulk of their deposits with the Fund by transferring to it the dollar and sterling balances which they now hold as part of their monetary reserves. The United States and the United Kingdom would, as a consequence, owe these balances to the Fund rather than to several scores of foreign central banks. The Fund would hardly wish to liquidate precipitously its holdings of such balances at the risk of precipitating a monetary crisis in the United States or the United Kingdom, and should not, in any case, be allowed to do so. Its right to demand repayment should be limited to a pre-agreed annual ceiling and should, even then, be exercised only insofar as is useful for the conduct of its own operations. In view of the vast expansion of its resources which the proposed reform would entail, it could, on the contrary, be expected to seek to expand, for several years to come, its dollar and sterling investments, thus giving us a further and useful breathing spell to bring about, in as smooth a manner as possible, the needed readjustments in our overall balance of payments.

The United States and the United Kingdom would, in this manner, recoup the freedom of monetary management—particularly in relation to their interest-rate policies—which is now so severely handicapped by the fear of the gold losses that would accompany the liquidation of foreign-owned short-term dollar and sterling balances. As for the other countries, they should also welcome the opportunity of exchanging their over-bloated dollar and sterling balances for equivalent Fund deposits. They now hold large amounts of such balances in preference to gold because of the interest earnings which they carry. They do, however, expose themselves thereby to the exchange losses which would be entailed in a dollar or sterling devaluation, to say nothing of the risks of blocking or inconvertibility. Deposits with the Fund should offer them the same incentive of interest earnings—although at a slightly reduced rate—while giving them the full gold guarantees which automatically attach to all transactions with the International Monetary Fund.

The second stage of my plan would require a modification of the Fund's Charter, but a very simple and unobjectionable one. The present system of arbitrary and rigid quota subscriptions to the Fund's capital should be dropped and replaced by minimum deposit requirements with the Fund. That is to say, all countries would undertake to hold, in the form of deposits with the Fund, an agreed proportion of their total monetary reserves. They would remain free to convert into gold, if they wished, any amounts accruing to their Fund deposit over and above this agreed minimum.

Such an obligation would adjust automatically and continuously each country's actual lending to the Fund according to its contributive capacity and to the need of the Fund for the currency of the particular country. It would do away with a system under which the Fund is now flooded with national currency capital subscriptions in bahts, kyats, bolivianos, and other currencies for which it has no earthly use and under which 90 per cent of its lending has in fact been made in dollars, thus aggravating our reserve losses, rather than in the currencies of the countries which were actually accumulating large reserve surpluses in their international transactions.

These proposals have been amply scrutinized and discussed in recent months, here and abroad, by academic, financial, and government experts. They obviously raise a host of questions which cannot be fully examined in this brief article. The real obstacle to action does not lie in their technical details, which could easily be modified in the course of negotiations, but in their long-run political implications. There is no denying the fact that such a reform of the International Monetary Fund could be interpreted as a first step toward the setting up of a supranational monetary authority to which central banks and governments are understandably reluctant to yield any portion of their cherished national sovereignty and independence.

Whatever one's views are in relation to this broad issue, it should be obvious that none of the measures proposed here would restrict the present real sovereignty of any country any more than it is already restricted. These measures would substitute, in a limited area, collective, mutually debated, and agreed limitations on national monetary sovereignties for the much harsher, haphazard, and often disastrous limitations now imposed upon them by chance events and by the uncoordinated use of sovereignty by several scores of so-called independent countries, with little or no regard to their compatibility and their impact on others.

Clearly, the world cannot tolerate much longer an international monetary system which has become so utterly dependent for its functioning on such accidental sources of reserve supplies as these:

1. Gold digging in a country—South Africa—whose economic life might be paralyzed tomorrow by the eruption of racial warfare.

2. Mr. Khrushchev's policies about U.S.S.R. gold sales to the West, which were responsible for more than a third of monetary gold increases in both 1958 and 1959 and whose abrupt cessation in 1960 contributed, at least in part, to the recent explosion of gold prices in London.

3. The perpetuation of our balance of payments deficits and the continued acceptance of dollar IOU's as monetary reserves by other countries; such gold and dollar losses by us have accounted for about two thirds of foreign countries' reserve increases over the last ten years and cannot continue much longer without undermining confidence in the dollar and its acceptability as a reserve currency.

I have no doubt, therefore, that future events will push us inevitably toward a basic reform of our present international monetary system. The real question at issue is not whether the proposals outlined here, or other broadly similar ones, will be adopted in the end. It is whether political leadership in the United States and the other free countries will prove sufficiently enlightened and dynamic to adopt them in time or whether they will have to be forced upon us by new crises and upheavals such as we experienced thirty years ago, during the first years of the worst international depression that the world has ever known.

International Monetary Reserves and the Composite Gold Standard

EDWARD M. BERNSTEIN

To avoid speculative shifts between gold, dollar, and sterling, in this essay Edward M. Bernstein suggests the establishment of a Reserve Settlement Account with the International Monetary Fund, in which countries would hold their reserve assets. It was prepared for the Subcommittee on International Exchange and Payments of the Joint Economic Committee of the U.S. Congress in September 1968.

GOLD RESERVES IN THE POSTWAR PERIOD

GREAT WARS are inevitably destructive of the gold standard in its traditional form. The war and postwar inflation exhausts the money creating power of gold standard countries with fixed reserve requirements. The uneven inflation results in the overvaluation of currencies at the historic gold parities where inflation has been large relative to that in other countries. And the large rise in prices and costs inhibits the growth of reserves by discouraging gold production and diverting more of the gold output to private uses instead of monetary reserves. Under these conditions, the traditional gold standard could be restored and maintained after a great war only through a deep and prolonged deflation, such as that of the 1930's.

The Second World War is unique in having escaped a destructive postwar deflation, but only because the gold standard itself has been gradually freed from the rigorous restraints it imposed in the past. Countries no longer regard the amount of their gold reserves as an acceptable measure of the appropriate money supply. When gold reserves are not adequate to permit the growth of the money supply required by the economy, the reserve requirements are changed. Countries no longer regard the maintenance of the historical gold parities of their currencies as the primary objective of economic policy. When a country cannot correct its balance of payments at the existing parity, it no longer deflates the economy, it changes the parity with the approval of the International Monetary Fund (IMF). But gold still remains the most important form of international monetary reserves, and countries are only now beginning to make a rational adjustment to the effects of war on the growth of reserves.

The Second World War had the usual effect on gold production and gold reserves. In 1940, the gold production of all countries, excluding the Communist countries, was $1,283 million. Gold production fell sharply during the war, and although it recovered after 1945, the prewar level of output was not reached again until 1962. There was a modest increase of gold production between 1962 and 1965, when it was at a peak of $1,440 million, but production fell in the two following years, although it may rise slightly in 1968. Thus, gold production this year will be only 12 percent higher than it was 28 years ago. In every country except South Africa, production is substantially lower than it was before the war. In South Africa, production has increased because of the opening of new mines with high-grade ore. But operating costs are rising, and there is no assurance that gold production in South Africa will continue to increase. At best, the growth of gold production hereafter will be very slow and it may, in fact, stay on a plateau or possibly decline.

Furthermore, as gold became cheaper relative to goods, and as money incomes rose sharply, more of the newly mined gold was absorbed in industrial uses and private hoards instead of going into monetary reserves. In the 30 years since the end of 1938, the monetary gold stock of the world, excluding the Communist countries, increased from just under $26 billion to just over $40 billion, including the gold holdings of the IMF and other international monetary institutions. This is equivalent to an average annual increase of less than 1.5 per cent. Most important, the rate of increase has declined sharply. From 1938 to 1948, the monetary gold stock increased at an average rate of 3 per cent a year. From 1948 to 1958, it increased at an average rate of 1.4 per cent a year. In 1968, the monetary gold stock was virtually the same as at the end of 1958, although this was mainly because of the large sales by the monetary authorities of the gold pool countries to private holders in 1967 and 1968. In any case, as the members of the IMF will no longer sell monetary gold to the private market and as little or none of the newly mined gold will be sold to the monetary authorities in the future, the monetary gold stock may be expected to remain frozen at about the present level of $40 billion.

FOREIGN EXCHANGE RESERVES AND RESERVE CREDIT

A system of fixed parities, defined in terms of gold, cannot function satisfactorily unless there is an adequate growth of monetary reserves. In fact, international trade and payments have expanded at an unprecedented rate in the postwar period and the world economy has prospered, despite the very small increase in gold reserves. The international monetary system, although based on the gold standard, was able to adapt itself to a minimal growth of gold reserves because the need for additional monetary reserves was met in other ways—primarily through a steady increase of foreign exchange reserves and secondarily through the development of very large facilities for reserve credit.

Foreign Exchange · The enormous growth of foreign exchange reserves during and after the war was a once-for-all phenomenon that cannot be repeated. In 1938, the foreign exchange reserves held by all countries amounted to about $1.8 billion. During the war, the United Kingdom financed a considerable part of its overseas military expenditures by the sale of sterling for local currencies to the monetary authorities—mainly in the Far East and the Middle East, but also in Europe and other regions. After the devaluation of sterling in 1949, foreign exchange reserves in the form of sterling amounted to about $8 billion. Since 1950, the sterling reserves of the monetary authorities have declined. The recent rise in official holdings of sterling, as reported at the end of March 1968, is the counterpart of swap operations and should be regarded as reserve credit to the United Kingdom rather than true holdings of sterling reserves. There is no practical possibility of a further growth of sterling as reserves. The more urgent problem is to avoid a flight from sterling reserves by sterling area countries.

The growth of reserves since 1950 has been primarily in the form of dollars. In the past 19 years, the dollar reserves of foreign monetary authorities have increased from $3 billion at the beginning of 1950 to over $17 billion in mid-1968, including nonmarketable Treasury obligations. Without this steady rise in dollar reserves, it would not have been possible to provide for the reserve needs of the world economy. Since the beginning of 1950, the gold and foreign exchange reserves of all countries, excluding the Communist countries, have increased from just over $45 billion to about $67 billion. Excluding the recent increase in holdings of sterling acquired in swaps, the growth of gold and foreign exchange reserves since the beginning of 1950 has been at an average annual rate of less than 2 per cent. About four-fifths of the increase in reserves has been in the form of foreign exchange, and about 85 per cent of the foreign exchange has been in dollars.

This vast creation of foreign exchange reserves was the result of the U.S. balance of payments deficit, which has been particularly large since 1958. Obviously, it is not possible for the United States to continue a payments deficit, on a reserve transactions basis, on the scale of the past 10 years. There is an understandable reluctance on the part of some countries to underwrite a large and continuing U.S. payments deficit by acquiring all the dollars that would accrue to their monetary authorities. Under extreme conditions, this would mean that other countries would be severely limited in managing their own monetary policy. Nor is the creation of dollar reserves in indefinite amount in the interests of the United States, particularly if its gold reserves cannot increase. The steady building up of reserve liabilities to foreign monetary authorities exposes the United States to the danger of massive conversions of dollars into gold in a period of economic or political crisis.

Reserve Credit · The need for reserves in the postwar period has also been met by an enormous increase in reserve credit facilities. The IMF makes resources available to its members under prescribed conditions. The total quotas of the IMF, which are an indication although not a true measure of the resources it has for extending reserve credit, amounted to just over $9 billion at the end of 1958. The total exchange transactions of the IMF to the end of 1958, which is the gross reserve credit extended by the IMF in the first 12 years of its operations, amounted to $3.2 billion.

Since the end of 1958, the quotas of the IMF have been increased twice and now amount to over $21 billion. To assure the liquidity of the IMF—its capacity to extend reserve credit in the currencies of the surplus countries—it has entered into General Arrangements to Borrow up to an aggregate of $6 billion in the currencies of the 10 large industrial countries (the Group of Ten). In the past 10 years, the IMF has engaged in exchange transactions amounting to $11.5 billion. The access of its members to the resources of the IMF has made it possible to expand the use of other forms of reserve credit because of the assurance that such credits could be repaid by drawings from the IMF.

The other important form of reserve credit was the creation of a network of reciprocal currency arrangements among the large central banks and with the Bank for International Settlements (BIS). The United States, which is the center of these arrangements, has swap facilities amounting to $10 billion with 14 countries and the BIS. These swap facilities have been extensively used by the United States and other countries to meet sudden pressures in the exchange market. Apart from the reciprocal currency arrangements, reserve credits have been extended by central banks to each other, notably to the United Kingdom, on an *ad hoc* basis. As already noted, drawings on the IMF have been used from time to time to repay reserve credits extended through swaps and on an *ad hoc* basis.

The enormous use of reserve credit facilities in recent years is an indication of their importance to the international monetary system. Nevertheless, reserve credit can be only a limited substitute for reserves. The swaps are actually short-period credits, and although they can be renewed, their usefulness depends upon reversing them in a relatively short period, so that they may be available again when required. Drawings on the IMF are intermediate-term credits, as they must ordinarily be repaid (except super-gold-tranche drawings) in three years, with an outside limit of five years. Although the IMF has immense resources for extending reserve credit, very large drawings by a great trading country may be regarded as a sign of weakness. In any case, countries cannot become more and more dependent on larger and larger use of reserve credit, with an obligatory schedule of repayments, without losing the comparative freedom in policy making provided by their own reserves.

QUANTITATIVE AND QUALITATIVE RESERVE PROBLEMS

Although it has hitherto been possible to secure the necessary growth of monetary reserves through a steady increase in the dollar component of reserves, this method cannot be continued much longer. This is not entirely because of a lack of confidence in the dollar, although the continued U.S. payments deficit has been a disturbing element in the international monetary system in recent years. The fact is that no national currency, including the dollar, can provide for an adequate growth of reserves over an indefinite period. That is because at present only gold is a final reserve asset. The strength and stability of the international monetary system depends not only on having adequate reserves, but on having a large proportion of them in the form of final reserve assets.

The nature of the gold problem is evident in the steadily declining proportion of gold in aggregate monetary reserves. The ratio of gold to the gold and foreign exchange reserves of all countries, excluding the Communist countries, was 94 per cent in 1938, 71 per cent in 1948, and is about 57 per cent at present. The sharp decline in the ratio of gold to total monetary reserves reflects the relatively small increase of gold reserves and the very large increase of foreign exchange reserves. The reserve position of the United States has deteriorated with the decrease in U.S. gold reserves and the concomitant increase in U.S. reserve liabilities. Confidence in the dollar depends more on the underlying strength of the U.S. balance of payments than on the U.S. reserve position. Nevertheless, without the creation of new reserve assets, the reserve position of the United States cannot be improved except by raiding the gold and dollar reserves of other countries.

The ratification of the Amendment authorizing the establishment of the Special Drawing Account and the activation of the plan for SDRs will solve some of the reserve problems. Their issue at regular intervals in accordance with the trend need for reserves will assure a steady and adequate growth in reserves. Their allocation to all members of the IMF will enable them to increase their reserves without forcing a reduction in the reserves of other countries. The SDRs will be defined in terms of gold, and within the holding and use limitations they will be a final reserve asset.

They will not, however, deal with the gold aspect of the reserve problem. In brief, even after the activation of SDRs, the international monetary system will remain exposed to the disruptive effects of the preference that the monetary authorities have for gold relative to other reserve assets.

The preference for gold as a reserve asset did not arise from the burst of speculation that preceded and followed the devaluation of sterling. It has grown steadily with the declining growth of gold reserves and the rising growth of dollar reserves. The preference for gold is indicated by the fact that the proportion of the U.S. payments deficit settled in gold became progressively larger in the 1950's and 1960's. From 1950 to 1957, the U.S. deficit on a reserve transactions basis was about $7.6 billion. As the U.S. gold tranche position increased by $500 million in this period, the United States transferred $8.1 billion of reserves to other countries, of which $2.3 billion was gold and $5.8 billion was dollars. Thus, the gold settlements in this period were 32 per cent of U.S. reserve transfers to other countries.[1] From 1958 to 1965, the U.S. deficit was about $21.6 billion. As $1.4 billion was financed by drawing on the U.S. gold tranche, the United States transferred $20.2 billion of reserves to other countries, of which $9.4 billion was in gold and $10.8 billion was in dollars. Thus, the gold settlements in this period were 46 per cent of U.S. reserve transfers to other countries. The preference for gold was reflected in the larger proportion of gold to foreign exchange that nine continental European countries added to their reserves.[2] From the beginning of 1950 to the end of 1957, these nine countries increased their gold and foreign exchange reserves by about $7.8 billion, of which 53 per cent ($4.1 billion) was in gold. From 1958 to 1965, they increased their gold and foreign exchange reserves by about $14.0 billion of which 89 per cent ($12.4 billion) was in gold.

The creation of a two-tier gold market with a premium price in private transactions will dramatize and heighten the preference of the monetary authorities for gold. The premium may come

1. The gold transfers to other countries are calculated by the decline in U.S. gold reserves after adjustment for gold acquired from IMF investment in U.S. Treasury bills. The gold transfers are overstated to the extent that domestic consumption of gold exceeded gold production in the United States.

2. Austria, Belgium, France, Germany, Italy, Netherlands, Portugal, Spain, and Switzerland.

down in the short run as the private market adjusts to a steady flow of newly mined gold, as the speculative overhang is gradually liquidated, and, most important, if confidence in currencies is restored. In the long run, however, the supply and demand situation would seem to indicate that the price of gold in the private market will remain at a premium. The gold preference problem cannot be dealt with by driving down the premium. In fact, it is a mistake for the monetary authorities to stake the prestige of their currencies on the private price of gold. The monetary authorities cannot reduce the preference for gold; but they can cooperate to prevent it from disrupting the international monetary system.

A MONETARY SYSTEM WITH MULTIPLE RESERVE ASSETS

An international monetary system with multiple reserve assets consisting of gold, dollars, and other foreign exchange, and SDRs can function properly only if all of the reserve assets are used without distinction and discrimination in international settlements. Otherwise, the monetary authorities will hoard gold and make their settlements in foreign exchange and SDRs. If the preference for gold becomes too great, it will disrupt the international monetary system. Conceivably, the monetary authorities would use gold in international settlements only under extreme conditions, so that the mere transfer of gold by a country would be regarded as an indication of a monetary crisis. At best, the hoarded gold would become an inactive part of reserves, thus diminishing the amount of effective reserves. At worst, the preference for gold would lead to gradual conversion of foreign exchange holdings, so that the growth of aggregate reserves would be inhibited, despite the regular issue of SDRs.

The restoration of a U.S. payments surplus on a reserve transaction basis would moderate, but not end, the preference for gold. The fact is that the preference for gold is only in part due to the payments difficulties of the United States. The real basis for the preference is the diminishing proportion of gold in international monetary reserves. The more difficult it becomes for countries to add gold to their reserves—and that will now be impossible for any country without cannibalizing the gold reserves of other countries—the greater will be the urge to hoard gold reserves, regardless of the effect on the international monetary system. Unless positive steps are taken to prevent it, we may see a modern version of the rush from silver to gold in the 1870's that ended in the demonetization of silver and the 25-year scarcity of reserves. Alfred Marshall's description of what happened in the 1870's seems to be relevant today: "Each Government has thought first of the interests of the nation which it represents, and has endeavoured to secure for it a good supply of gold with but little reference to international interests." [3]

The international monetary system can function very well with a two-tier gold market, provided the monetary authorities cooperate to assure the appropriate use of gold and other reserve assets in international settlements. The best way to achieve this is through linking them together in a composite gold standard. In 1962, I proposed the creation of a reserve unit based on the currencies of the Group of Ten and Switzerland. Under my proposal, these countries would have been required to maintain the convertibility of their currencies in gold and reserve units in a fixed ratio of 60 per cent gold and 40 per cent reserve units. This would have been practical for a small group of countries holding over 80 per cent of total gold reserves and including the principal countries with a high preference for gold. With all of the 109 members of the IMF participating in the Special Drawing Account, and with many of these countries holding their reserves predominantly in dollars and sterling, a composite gold standard now would have to be based on gold, foreign exchange, and SDRs in a ratio different for each country. The two basic principles for operating a composite gold standard with multiple reserve assets held in different proportions can be summarized as follows:

1. Each deficit country should use its different reserve assets in settlement of its deficit in precisely the same ratios as it holds these reserves—gold, foreign exchange, and SDRs.

2. Each surplus country should acquire the different reserve assets in settlement of its surplus in the average ratios of gold, foreign exchange, and SDRs used by the deficit countries, so that all surplus countries would acquire the different reserve assets in precisely the same ratios.

These principles would have to be applied to cumulative

3. *Official Papers,* London, 1926, p. 24.

deficits and surpluses, otherwise a country might have to pay a high ratio of gold when it is in deficit and receive a small ratio of gold when it is in surplus. Even if a country had a balanced payments position over a period of years, the composition of its reserves could change. However, if settlements were made on a cumulative basis, the composition of a country's reserves would be unchanged, apart from new allocations of SDRs, whenever its previous surpluses equal its previous deficits. There is another practical difficulty in operating a composite gold standard with multiple reserve assets. It would be cumbersome for a deficit country to transfer to a surplus country a mixed bag of reserves consisting of X amount of gold, Y amount of dollars, Y' amount of other foreign exchange, and Z amount of SDRs. For convenience, a single bookkeeping entry should suffice to transfer the desired amount of reserves in the ratios required by the composite gold standard.

These difficulties could be obviated by establishing a Reserve Settlement Account as an independent administrative department of the IMF in which countries would hold their reserve assets—gold, foreign exchange, and SDRs—denominated in a composite reserve unit (CRU), defined as one gold dollar of the present weight and fineness, and consisting of the different reserve assets in appropriate ratios. A transfer of reserves from a deficit country to a surplus country would be recorded as a decrease of CRUs in the account of the former and an increase of CRUs in the account of the latter. At any given time, a country whose balance of CRUs is less than the total of the various reserve assets it placed in the Reserve Settlement Account would be in cumulative deficit, and it would have implicitly settled this deficit *pro rata* in the same ratios as the reserve assets it placed in the Reserve Settlement Account. A country whose balance of CRUs is more than the total of the various reserve assets it placed in the Reserve Settlement Account would be in cumulative surplus. This surplus would have been implicitly settled in the different reserve assets in the average ratios that all cumulative deficit countries placed such reserves in the Reserve Settlement Account. An actual transfer of gold, foreign exchange, and SDRs in connection with these implicit settlements, however, would be made only when a country withdraws from the Reserve Settlement Account.

ALTERNATIVES TO THE COMPOSITE GOLD STANDARD

The functioning of an international monetary system with multiple reserve assets depends on assuring the appropriate use of all reserve assets in international settlements. A preference by the monetary authorities for holding gold rather than dollars or sterling has already emerged, and this preference will become more marked in the future as the monetary gold stock becomes frozen at about its present level. The activation of the plan for issuing SDRs may make it more difficult to maintain the equivalence of all reserve assets. The addition of a new fiduciary reserve asset (SDRs) with characteristics of its own—particularly the gold value guarantee and interest on net acquisitions—may give countries a further inducement to alter the composition of their reserves. . . .

Some rules governing the use of reserves are necessary in an international monetary system with multiple reserve assets. It may be questioned, however, whether the rules set out in the Articles and Schedules in the Amendment authorizing the Special Drawing Account are the best way of achieving the appropriate use of all reserve assets. The limitation on the amount of SDRs that surplus countries are required to accept and hold (three times their cumulative allocations) and on the amount of SDRs that deficit countries may use (an average of 70 per cent of their average cumulative allocations over the preceding five years) indicates that participants are very much concerned with the reserve assets they transfer or that are transferred to them in balance of payments settlements.

A requirement for the balance used of all reserve assets cannot be dispensed with so long as countries have a preference for gold rather than other reserve assets. But the rules can be made simple and automatic, so that they will not require constant guidance, designation, specification, and reconstitution—a process which underlines the preference for different reserve assets and serves to intensify it. Most important, the rules in the Amendment to the Fund Agreement deal only with the preference for other reserve assets relative to SDRs, a minor problem in the international monetary system. They do not deal with the most disruptive preference of all, the preference for gold over foreign exchange, a preference that may become greater after the SDRs are activated.

The great advantage of a composite gold standard is that it can be applied automatically on a cumulative basis to all countries regardless of the composition of their reserves. There is no more equitable way of assuring the balanced use of reserves than to require countries to use all of their reserve assets in the same ratios in which they hold them. Moreover, once the composite gold standard is adopted, there is no need for any supervision of reserve transactions. The establishment of a Reserve Settlement Account with transfers of reserves made only in the form of CRUs would prevent constant maneuvering to change the composition of reserves. The final settlement on the withdrawal of a participating country from the Reserve Settlement Account could give effect to any agreed principles regarding the use of different reserve assets, including those in Schedules F and G of the Amendment to the Fund Agreement.

The adoption of a composite gold standard is a natural evolution of the gold standard. It is the only way to assure the continued use of gold as reserves, in distinction to its hoarding by the monetary authorities. The attempt to operate a gold standard without the use of gold reserves in international settlements, except in emergencies, could ultimately lead to the complete demonetization of gold. The adoption of the composite gold standard requires no new international machinery. The establishment of the Reserve Settlement Account requires no amendment to the Fund Agreement. It can be administered by the IMF as an independent department to carry out the provisions for the use of SDRs and other reserves. All that the IMF would have to do would be to require that implicit transfers through the Reserve Settlement Account should be in accordance with the present rules for designation and reconstitution as stated in the Amendment until new rules can be adopted under the authority of Article XXV, Sections 5(c) and 6(b).

The Case for Going Back to Gold

M. A. HEILPERIN

M. A. Heilperin is a European Editor of Fortune *and a former Professor of Economics at the Graduate Institute of International Studies in Geneva. In this essay, he argues the case for the reestablishment of the gold standard.*

THIS SUMMER the gathering doubts about the strength of the U.S. economy, reflected in the stock-market plunge and the flagging of business enthusiasm, were accompanied—and indeed reinforced —by renewed uneasiness about the strength of the dollar. To be sure, as Washington spokesmen have been emphasizing, the balance-of-payments deficit has been running at a lower rate than last year. But there is still a considerable deficit, and the cumulative effect of deficits in ten out of the last eleven years has given foreigners a $16.9-billion claim against U.S. gold reserves. And although the outflow of gold itself has somewhat abated, memories of the frightening 1960 run on gold are still fresh, and its causes are still with us.

Politicians as well as monetary authorities seem deeply impressed with the perils of the situation. The Kennedy Administration professes its determination to bring the balance-of-payments deficit to an end, and in considering ways to speed up the domestic economy it is painfully aware of the need to keep up the appearance of fiscal integrity. The Federal Reserve and the central banks of Western Europe have taken steps to cooperate in meeting any speculative movement that might threaten the dollar.

Such defensive measures are reassuring, but the fear of crisis will persist and can be banished only by a positive policy that leads to a profound reform of the international monetary system.

The aim of such reform must be to establish order in the monetary relations of the U.S. and its trading partners in the Atlantic family of nations.

The essentials of monetary order can be summed up in three conditions:

First, the guarantee of unqualified freedom in international payments—i.e., no controls or threat of controls on the exchange of one currency for another.

Second, a fixed relationship among the various currencies so that businessmen can plan their trade and investment operations ahead without fear that their money will suddenly change in value.

Third, a means of bringing the balance of payments of every country quickly into equilibrium so that some countries do not go on suffering chronic deficits while others keep building up embarrassing surpluses.

My contention is that these conditions of order can be brought about only by a restoration of the gold standard—in its classic sense, with currencies unconditionally redeemable in gold at home and abroad, and with the settlements of international accounts made in gold and gold only. In my judgment, this move will have to be accompanied by a revaluation of gold.

The return of gold to its once preeminent position as the base of money and credit is the only way of insuring against wide fluctuations in the values of currencies and restrictions on free exchange. And the sensitive response of the money supply to the flow of gold in and out of a country would be the most effective discipline on national economic policies.

The steps back to the gold standard should be taken in unison by all the advanced industrial nations of the West, but it is fitting and proper that the initiative should come from the U.S. A bold and imaginative approach to monetary order would be a natural companion policy to President Kennedy's trade program, for free trade cannot flourish on weak and uncertain financial underpinnings.

TO GOLD IN TWO PHASES

As I envision it, the return to the gold standard would be accomplished in two phases. Phase I would be an agreement by all the nations in the van Lennep group [1]—meaning, in effect, the whole Atlantic Community—henceforth to pay off all balance-of-payments deficits in gold and gold only. Countries that based their currencies in part on reserves of dollars or sterling would continue to do so for the time being, but further accumulation of such reserves would be halted. This step would bring to a halt the perniciously deceptive spread of dollar holdings abroad under the gold exchange standard. The U.S. would be compelled to get its payments into balance in a hurry—or face immediate and continuing losses of gold. This transition would give the participating nations a chance to get used to the new discipline, and to begin synchronizing their monetary and interest-rate policies.

Phase II would comprise three separate but simultaneous moves:

1. A decision by the U.S. to pay off in gold all short-term dollar obligations held by foreigners. This would finally get rid of the gold exchange standard and put the dollar once again on firm footing. No longer would an uncertain threat hang over U.S. gold, encouraging speculation and threatening financial crisis.

2. An agreement by the nations in the van Lennep group to make all their currencies fully convertible into gold. Convertibility is, of course, the essence of the gold standard. The U.S. would have to repeal the New Deal monetary legislation and restore private ownership of gold. Quite apart from other considerations, this would be a welcome reaffirmation of a property right that has been denied Americans for a quarter of a century.

3. Joint action, again by the van Lennep group, to double the price of gold in terms of all currencies. For the U.S. this would mean raising the price from $35 to $70 an ounce. My motive is not, I must emphasize, to get the U.S. out of its present scrape. Nor do I share the view of economists such as Sir Roy Harrod that a rise in the gold price, by itself, would solve our monetary problems by increasing international liquidity; the root of these problems is not shortage of liquidity but disorder. My reason for revaluing gold is that, otherwise, the transition to a true gold standard would be impossible. For one thing, if the U.S. were to pay off immediately its dollar debts abroad at $35 an ounce, it would lose so much of its reserve that none would be left to support the domestic currency.

1. [A subcommittee of the Organization for Economic Cooperation and Development. *Editor.*]

For another thing, though there is no real liquidity shortage in the world today, one might eventually develop when the expansion of money and credit became tightly linked to gold. Just as it did after World War I, the price of gold has remained unchanged while the prices of everything else have risen sharply. As a result, gold production has been discouraged, and additions to the world gold supply have lagged far behind the expansion in world trade. Over the past decade, newly mined gold provided only about one-third—and since 1958 one-fourth—of the annual increase in currency reserves (not including those of U.S.). The difference was made up by gold from U.S. reserves (which dwindled from $23.2 billion worth in 1952 to $16.4 billion worth this year) and by increased dollar holdings abroad.

MANY PEOPLE WILL BE PROVOKED

When the gold standard is re-established, nations will no longer be able to augment their reserves by increasing their dollar holdings. When gold becomes the exclusive means of international payment and the exclusive backing for currency, therefore, it will become crucially important that the supply of new metal keep pace with the growth of trade. The present price of gold is inadequate to ensure such a supply.

The proposal to revalue gold will provoke a number of objections. Some people will see it merely as a devaluation of the dollar. This is such an explosive issue that hardly anyone in a responsible government position will even admit that it is being considered. But a careful distinction must be made between a unilateral devaluation of the dollar, undertaken in panic, and a readjustment of the gold price, accomplished by international agreement as part of a plan to restore monetary order.

A second objection that will be raised is that revaluation will have a great inflationary effect because, rightly or wrongly, people associate any jiggering of the gold price with inflationary finance. But this danger will be averted under my proposal because revaluation will be accompanied by full gold convertibility of the dollar, the best possible safeguard for stable money.

Finally, critics will point out that any change in the gold price will have to be approved by Congress, which might spend many months in debating the matter; meanwhile there would be such a mighty run on U.S. gold reserves as to precipitate the very crisis of confidence we have been so fearful of. This is a telling objection, but it is not insurmountable. If all the countries in the Atlantic Community undertake these reforms in the proper international spirit, it should be possible for central banks to take the joint action needed to stem a run on gold during the time revaluation is under public discussion. This will require considerable ingenuity and skill, but the stakes of lasting monetary reform surely justify the effort.

FREEDOM OF ACTION

The most serious objection to the whole idea of reviving the gold standard is that it would deprive governments of their freedom of action in dealing with cyclical unemployment and recession. In fact, however, the gold standard would allow governments considerable leeway in fiscal policy. For example, the U.S. could run a deficit to counter a recession if it met the deficit by borrowing at high enough rates of interest to tap genuine savings —and not, as has been the case in the past, at such low rates that it was in effect pumping inflation into the economy. The gold-standard discipline would not prevent the U.S. from coping efficiently with domestic problems; it would merely narrow the choice of methods used.

Those who believe that the U.S. should be free to inflate its way out of recessions will doubtless feel frustrated; perhaps it is high time they were. Americans still suffer, as a nation, from a hangover of economic nationalism from the days when we were a much less important economic and political influence on the world scene. We have learned a great deal about our international role in the past forty years. This is one more lesson.

Once these reforms have been carried out, the great edifice of free trade can at last be completed—on a foundation of stable money. The U.S. will play its role as the world's greatest creditor nation with a currency that inspires universal confidence. The whole non-Communist community of nations will take on greater political and economic strength with which to protect its freedom and assist the backward countries to improve their lot. By reinstating gold as the heart of the international monetary system we shall be drawing upon successful past experiences, rather than taking a hazardous flight into the unknown. We shall have built a bridge over the half-century of disorder.

Exchange-Rate Flexibility

J. E. MEADE

J. E. Meade is Professor of Economics at Cambridge University in England. In this essay, first published in the June 1966 issue of the Three Banks Review, *he extols the virtues of exchange-rate flexibility and suggests a solution combining a widening of the band within which rates can fluctuate with a sliding parity.*

EXCHANGE-RATE FLEXIBILITY covers a multitude of sins and of virtues. My main purpose in this paper is to catalogue the various forms of sin and virtue and to comment as objectively as is possible upon the merits and demerits of each form. But I will not disguise the fact that I am one of those who favour a much greater measure of exchange-rate flexibility than is practised by the countries of the free world today. Accordingly, I shall arrange my paper in the following three parts. First, I will outline the reasons why in my view we need to consider very seriously the adoption of a greater measure of exchange-rate flexibility. Second, I will catalogue the various forms which exchange-rate flexibility can take and will note the arguments for and against each form. Finally, I will describe the form of exchange-rate flexibility which I would personally advocate in present circumstances and will try to put it into the framework of the present discussions on the possible reform of the International Monetary Fund (IMF).

THE CASE FOR GREATER FLEXIBILITY

The basic case for variations in exchange rates is fairly familiar and I have myself on other occasions argued it at some length. I shall, therefore, on this occasion state the case very briefly.

When a country has a surplus in its overall balance of international payments, it can go on accumulating foreign-exchange reserves indefinitely. If it is in deficit, it can go on as it is so long as its foreign-exchange reserves last or so long as it can beg, borrow, or steal additional reserves from some external source. But there are very good reasons for rejecting such do-nothing solutions. Overall surpluses or deficits in international *payments* are, broadly speaking, indications of maladjustments in the general structure of relative *money* prices, incomes, and costs in the various countries; and there is no reason to believe that a desirable use of the world's *real* resources is obtained if the countries which happen at any one time to have international surpluses of *money* receipts automatically continue indefinitely to finance those countries which happen to have international *money* deficits. It is, for example, very possible for wealthy countries which are rich in capital to find themselves in deficit, while poor countries are in surplus, on their balance-of-payments current account. A continuation of such a situation could mean a continuous flow of real resources from the poor and underdeveloped to the rich and developed countries.

One can tackle the problem of adjustment of balances of payments through direct interventions or controls of a more or less drastic kind on international trade, capital movements, and foreign aid. The authorities in deficit countries can restrict imports from lower-cost sources by import quotas or import surcharges; they can subsidise their own exports against the better quality or lower-cost goods of their competitors; they can restrict or tax the flow of capital funds from their own country where capital is plentiful and the rate of return on it is low to countries where capital is scarcer and rates of return higher; they can cut down on their foreign aid; they can insist that the aid which they give must be spent on their own products even though some other country's products might be even more suitable for the recipient's needs. But to those of us who, like myself, sincerely wish to see the principles of the market mechanism and of the competitive price system appropriately extended not only within the countries of the free world, but in the economic relations between those countries as well, these methods of balance-of-payments adjustment should be anathema. Particular goods should be imported or exported according to their relative costs and qualities, not in order to adjust an overall balance of payments. Countries should give or receive foreign aid according to their real wealth and real needs, not according to the state of their overall balance of payments. Capital should move to the place of highest economic return, not necessarily to the country with the largest overall balance-of-payments deficit. Funds received in aid or by loan should be spent on the goods which are most efficient for the recipient's purposes, not necessarily on the goods of the country which happens to have a deficit. And so on and so on.

Balances of international money payments should be corrected by adjustments in the general levels and structures of money prices, incomes, and costs in the countries of the free world. Such general adjustments can be effected either by a general upward movement in surplus countries of their domestic prices, incomes, and costs in terms of their domestic currencies combined with a general downward movement (or at least a slower upward movement) in the deficit countries' prices, incomes, and costs or else by an adjustment in the rate of exchange between the domestic currencies of the surplus and the deficit countries. Let us briefly consider these two methods.

The truly orthodox type of solution is that the authorities in the deficit countries should by restrictive monetary and budgetary policies reduce money expenditures on goods and services within their countries, while the opposite expansionary policies are adopted in the surplus countries. If all domestic prices and costs, and in particular money wage rates, were readily and quickly adjustable, this orthodox solution might well be the most desirable one. The deflation of demand in the deficit country leads to a reduced demand for labour; there is some increase in unemployment and underemployment of both men and machines. But if a short period of very moderate slack is all that is required to obtain a considerable weakening of all money prices and costs, and if correspondingly in the surplus countries a short period of very moderate excess demand suffices to obtain a large rise in the basic structure of money prices and costs, an international system could well be built on this foundation.

But the facts of life are otherwise. You may well have a situation in the modern world in which there is considerable slack in the domestic economy of a particular country, but the whole structure of domestic money prices and costs does not as a result decline. If at the same time this country is internationally in deficit, there is a tragic dilemma. It will be desired to expand demand for domestic reasons to encourage growth and full employment; but it would be necessary to restrict demand and to increase unemployment still further in order to put sufficient downward pressure on money wages rates and other prices. May this not have been the position of the United States in some recent years?

Such is the simple, straightforward, and in my view decisive argument against the orthodox solution. There is possibly a secondary argument against it which is worth mentioning in passing. Suppose that a relative downward pressure on money prices, incomes, and costs is needed in one country on balance-of-payments grounds. Suppose that the authorities in that country do adopt the severe deflationary policy necessary for this purpose, but that money wage costs do not respond very rapidly. During this process, the profitability of industry will be greatly reduced since each producer's selling market is restricted but cost per unit is not immediately reduced. This profit squeeze may induce owners of capital to invest in other countries where no such profit squeeze is in process, with the result that during the perhaps prolonged process of adjustment the outflow of capital makes the balance of payments worse. Of course, when the process of downward adjustment on wage and other costs has been successfully concluded and the deflationary policies are ended, the country's balance of payments will be in better shape. Its price-income-cost structure will have been adjusted and the profit squeeze will have ceased. But during the process of adjustment the strain of the capital items on the balance of payments may be very great. May it not be that there has been an element of all this in the United States' experience in some recent years?

Many persons who recognise the force of these arguments would nevertheless still hope to be able to use successfully the method of adjustment of domestic price-income-cost structures to remedy balance-of-payments problems. They hope that we can learn to make the necessary adjustments of money prices—and in particular of money wage rates—by means other than prolonged deflations of demand. This is called nowadays the use of an "incomes policy." I am afraid that I am very sceptical about the efficacy of such an approach to the problem. Consider once more the problem of a country which already has considerable unemployment and at the same time is in deficit. One needs expansionary fiscal and monetary policies to promote growth and full employment. Could one really hope to combine with that an incomes policy which will cause this *greater* level of employment and output to take place at a *lower* level of money wage costs and prices? If it were seriously proposed to exercise a strict governmental control over a myriad of wage rates of different types of labour in different occupations and over a myriad of prices of products of various kinds and qualities, I would reject the policy on other grounds. It may be possible to achieve something by moral suasion and by much less severe measures of governmental interest in wage-bargaining and price-fixing, but surely one cannot hope to achieve the main instrument for balance-of-payments control by such innocent means.

If this assessment is correct, we are left with the possibility of adjusting relative price-income-cost structures by adjustment of the rates of exchange between the various national currencies. The basic principles of this method are simple. The authorities in each country should use their monetary and budgetary policies and whatever influence they can exert over the fixing of money wage rates and prices to attain the best combination within their powers of the domestic goals of full employment, economic growth, and price stability. Long-run adjustments in the balance of payments can then be facilitated by variations in the rates of exchange between their own national currency and those of other countries. This does not, of course, mean that there is no connection between domestic financial policies and the balance of payments. On the contrary, there is a very close connection.

Consider a country which domestically is in equilibrium but suffers from a balance-of-payments deficit. A depreciation of its currency by making its exports cheaper in foreign currencies and its imports more expensive in terms of its own currency may successfully increase the value of its exports relative to its imports. But if foreigners now spend more on its export products and if its own citizens now spend less on imports and more on home products, there will have developed an excess demand for its own products. To prevent domestic inflation, some degree of restriction in domestic financial policies is now necessary. In this way, to reduce a balance-of-payments deficit without leading to domestic inflation requires a combination of exchange-rate depreciation with deflationary domestic financial policies.

Or consider a country which has an unemployment problem domestically but is in balance-of-payments equilibrium. It needs to adopt expansionary domestic financial policies to engender the necessary degree of economic expansion domestically. But this expansion will cause its balance of trade to deteriorate as the demand for imported goods rises and as goods which would otherwise have been exported are sucked into the expanded home market. The rise in domestic incomes may also mean that its citizens have more savings available for investment abroad; but on the other hand, as we have already observed, the greater measure of profitability of industry at home may attract for domestic investment some funds which would otherwise have been invested abroad. Thus the net effect of the domestic expansion on the balance of payments may be unfavourable or favourable. If, as is most probable, it is unfavourable, then the domestic expansion must be accompanied by some depreciation of the currency; if favourable, then by some appreciation.

It is not possible to trace all the possible permutations and combinations of appropriate policies. But the general principles of such a system are clear. There are three targets: full employment, price stability, and balance-of-payments equilibrium. The authorities have three weapons: domestic budgetary-cum-monetary policies; incomes policies; and the rate of exchange. Three stones can be used to kill three birds. (1) More or less inflationary domestic policies as the level of employment threatens to fall or rise; (2) more or less restraint in incomes policy as the general level of money prices threatens to rise or fall; and (3) an upward or downward movement of the exchange rate as serious long-run surpluses or deficits appear on the balance of payments—such a threefold prescription will make possible a serious attempt (not merely a pious hope) to attain all three targets simultaneously.

THE VARIOUS FORMS OF EXCHANGE-RATE FLEXIBILITY

So far I have noted the merits of exchange-rate variations and the demerits of other instruments for balance-of-payments adjustment. This is, of course, not playing fair. Life in this wicked world is a choice of evils and it may be that the evils of exchange-rates variation, when one comes to look at them, are worse than those of some of the other methods. I do not myself believe this to be the case, but it is only fair to have a good look at the difficulties. Accordingly, in this section of my paper, I will consider in turn each of the six main forms which, in my view, a system of exchange-rate flexibility might take and shall search for the snags in each case.

1. The first is what has come to be known as the *Adjustable Peg* system, and is the system under which we are supposed to be living at the present time according to the rules of the IMF. Each country fixes the value of its national currency (within very narrow upper and lower limits) in terms of some common unit (such as an ounce of gold) and undertakes to maintain the value of its national currency at this level by buying it (with gold or other foreign currencies) if it tends to fall below its par value and by selling it (for gold or other foreign currencies) if it tends to rise above its par value. But if a country's balance of payments falls into fundamental disequilibrium, then it can make a suitable adjustment in the rate at which it pegs its currency to gold— raising the price of gold in terms of its own currency if it is in deficit, and *vice versa* if it is in surplus.

As this system has in fact developed, the stress has come to be put upon the fixity of the peg rather than upon its periodic adjustment. Certainly exchange rates have been very much less variable than many persons hoped at the initiation of the Fund. One reason for this is probably the very grave disadvantages of this method of exchange-rate adjustment. Its use builds a paradise for anti-social speculation. A country is in balance-of-payments deficit: if it is widely known that such countries are very liable to raise the pegged price of gold (and so of other currencies) in terms of their own currency, speculators have every reason to sell the currency of the deficit country and hold other currencies; the currency concerned may be depreciated, it is certain that it will not be appreciated; if the peg is changed, they gain a quick and large profit; if the peg is not changed, they lose at the very most a small margin on their money.

As the present rules of the IMF are drafted, countries must in general obtain the permission of the Fund before adjusting their pegs. If such a Fund decision were to be based upon a profound international inquiry into the alleged "fundamental disequilibrium" of the country wishing to adjust its peg, the system would become wholly unworkable. The idea of a really meaningful inquiry and discussion in an international organisation of the pros and cons of altering, for example, by a large percentage the value of the dollar or sterling while all holders of dollars or sterling proceeded to take their one-way speculative option is so ridiculous as not to be capable of being taken seriously. Permission of the Fund must mean little more than overnight snap agreement with a decision which a handful of the responsible men have brooded over in extreme secrecy in the inner councils of the country concerned.

Such adjustments will tend to be rare events. In order to discourage speculation against its currency, the improbability of change will be stressed and change will appear improbable if it is in fact infrequent. If, however, as a last desperate resort a change is made, it is likely to be very large for two reasons: first, because a great deal of disequilibrium must be built up before the fatal step is admitted to be inevitable; and, second, because a new fixed peg must be chosen and—hung for a lamb, hung for a sheep—if a depreciation is undertaken it will be considered wise to err on the safe side and to choose a rate which really will insure a surplus for the depreciating country—and, therefore, incidentally a deficit for someone else.

It is not perhaps inevitable that the IMF system should have developed in this way. With a looser and in my view more useful interpretation of the phase "fundamental disequilibrium" one can imagine a state of affairs in which a regular use was made of exchange-rate variation as an instrument of balance-of-payments control in the form of frequent small movements in the pegs—a currency being put up or down by, say, 2 per cent without any implication that it might not next month or next quarter be moved by another 2 per cent in the same direction if a greater movement seemed necessary or back to its original position if developments suggested that the former move had been unnecessary. Such a system would to some extent keep the speculators guessing; there need never build up those positions in which a huge potential one-way option is presented to operators in the foreign-exchange markets; only small movements would be expected and they might quite well be reversed. Nevertheless, even in this form the system would be subject to grave disadvantages. It would still present speculators with substantial opportunities, since it would still be clear from time to time that a currency's peg might be moved in one direction but not in the other. And the system would need very close, continuous, and intimate cooperation between the representatives of the main national monetary authorities to reach agreement upon the frequent small adjustments.

2. The present IMF system is thus one of pretty rigidly fixed rates subject from time to time to substantial and disturbing adjustment. Let us next consider a system at the other extreme, namely one of *Freely Floating Exchange Rates* in which the prices of the various currencies are determined from day to day by the free play of competition between private buyers and sellers of currencies in foreign exchange markets which are subject to no controlling intervention either by national monetary authorities or by any international institution. With such a system, the national authorities would devise and use their monetary, fiscal, and wage-determining institutions in whatever way they considered to be most appropriate to achieve full employment and economic growth and to avoid instabilities and fluctuations in money incomes and prices. They would let the balance of payments look after itself.

Now the advocates of this system argue that the balance of payments would satisfactorily look after itself. Consider, for example, a country—such as the United States or the United Kingdom in recent years—which develops a deficit on its balance of payments. There will be an excess of domestic purchasers of foreign currencies to make payments abroad over the foreign purchasers of the domestic currency to make payments to the country in question. Foreign currencies will appreciate in terms of the currency in question. This will reduce the money price-income-cost structure of the country concerned relative to that of other countries. All over the world, within and outside the country concerned, people will be encouraged to shift their purchases from the goods and services of other countries on to the goods and services produced by the deficit country.

It is, of course, well known to the advocates of this system that such shifts of demand which are needed to restore equilibrium will take time. Purchases will be shifted only as the new opportunities are appreciated, existing contracts run out, new plans are matured, and so on. But in the meanwhile, so it is argued, the private foreign-exchange speculator will play a useful and social role in supporting the currency of the deficit country. In the absence of the speculator, the country's currency might depreciate very heavily indeed during the period when there was an excess demand for foreign currencies and before the consequential alteration in relative price-income-cost structures had had time to have its effects on imports and exports. But the speculator would realise that this period of acute difficulty was temporary; he would expect the currency to recover its value as time passed and the necessary adjustments in imports and exports were made; the speculator would, therefore, have a straightforward profit incentive to buy up the currency concerned in exchange for foreign currencies while it was extra cheap in order to make a gain on its subsequent appreciation. In short, it is argued that a system of freely floating exchange rates (i) brings about long-run structural adjustments in balances of payments through appropriate changes in relative price-income-cost structures and (ii) induces private speculators to give the necessary temporary support to currencies under pressure, a support which under other systems would have to be given by the use of official reserves of gold and foreign exchange.

There is only one possible snag to this system. Could one rely upon private speculation to fulfil adequately this vital role? True, speculators buy when they expect prices to go up. But on what do they base their expectations of future prices? Is it always on a correct anticipation of what is going to happen to the basic underlying elements of long-run supply and demand? But it is never easy to tell what the future holds in store for a country's imports, exports, and international capital movements. Some speculators may base their expectations of future exchange rates mainly on what has happened recently to exchange rates; and when a currency falls in value because of some new strain on a balance of payments, they may expect a further fall simply because there has been a recent fall. Such speculation will intensify, not mitigate, the fall; the speculators' sales are added to the other pressures on the balance of payments. Then other speculators may sell the currency, although they realise that it has already fallen below its long-run value, simply because they expect this first group of less-well-informed speculators to go on selling. In other words, speculation could take a form which made completely free exchange rates subject to excessive fluctuations. And this could bring with it a further danger. An excessive depreciation of a currency could lead to a sharp rise in the price of imports. Such a price rise—particularly if, as in the United Kingdom, imports of food and other necessities make up a large element in the cost of living—could itself engender a rise in money wage claims and thus a rise in the domestic price-income-cost structure. And this rise in turn would justify increased pessimism about the future value of the currency.

3. Now whether these fears be justified or not—and I would not myself be ready to assert that they are wholly imaginary—it is most unlikely that national governments would be prepared at one fell swoop to take the risk of letting the exchange rates go to fluctuate freely without any intervention. If the currency pegs were removed and exchange rates were allowed to fluctuate, the national authorities would undoubtedly insist on standing ready with their reserves of gold and foreign exchange to intervene in the exchange market from time to time. This we may call the system of *National Exchange Equalisation.* The system would work in the following way. As in the case just examined, currency pegs would be removed; national currencies would fluctuate in terms of each other; long-run adjustment would thus be achieved by changes in money price-income-cost structures due to alterations in the exchange rates between different domestic monies; and speculators would be free to speculate and—it would be hoped—to provide short-run support for the currency of a deficit country. But national monetary authorities would not rely wholly on private speculation. They would set up National Exchange Equalisation Funds, endowed with resources in terms of their own currencies and of gold and foreign currencies. If private speculation appeared to them to be driving down excessively the value of the national currency, they would themselves support the currency by selling foreign currencies or gold and buying the domestic currency through their own Exchange Equalisation Account, and *vice versa* if private transactions seemed to be raising the short-run value of the domestic currency excessively.

This system has in my view a great deal to recommend it. But it has its own peculiar difficulties which became obvious in the late 1930's when—so far as sterling and the dollar were concerned—something like it was in operation. At that time there was a fear that a national monetary authority would use its Exchange Equalisation Fund to engage in competitive exchange depreciation. For example, the U.K. authorities by selling sterling and buying dollars could depreciate unnecessarily the value of sterling in terms of the dollar, thus enabling U.K. manufacturers to undercut U.S. manufacturers even though there might be no underlying deficit on the U.K. balance of payments and no need, therefore, for such undercutting. The dangers of such action were undoubtedly much more real in the late 1930's than they would be in present conditions. Then there was mass unemployment; and national authorities were tempted to give employment to their own resources by beggar-my-neighbour international policies which stole markets from their neighbours even though their balance-of-payments position did not require such action. Nowadays there is not mass unemployment; and in any case national governments realise that they can give employment by measures which expand their own domestic markets, using measures which expand their exports and contract their imports only if they have a balance-of-payments deficit.

But even if competitive exchange depreciations are a much less real danger nowadays, it is pretty clear that the system of National Exchange Equalisation must be supplemented by an extensive system of international co-operation. To put it simply, if the U.K. exchange equalisation account is intervening to control the dollar-sterling rate of exchange, it is clear that they would be well advised to co-ordinate their actions. But the obvious way to co-ordinate their actions is to agree on the rates at which they will peg their currencies and only to change the pegs from time to time in agreement; and this is, of course, in essence the present IMF system of the Adjustable Peg with which we started our discussion. In fact, it was the fear of competitive exchange depreciation engendered in the 1930's, combined with the obvious need to co-ordinate the actions of independent National Exchange Equalisation accounts, which led through the Tripartite Monetary Agreement of 1936 to the Articles of Agreement of the IMF and the present excessively rigid exchange-rate structure.

4. Thus National Exchange Equalisation cries out for international co-operation which appears to imply the system of the Adjustable Peg, which—as we have seen—is likely to imply a rigid exchange-rate structure. A possible escape from this dilemma is through *Supranational Exchange Equalisation*. Under this system, national monetary authorities would renounce the use of national exchange equalisation accounts; exchange rates would be allowed to vary to give long-run balance-of-payments adjustments; private speculation would be supplemented not by the

operations of a number of national exchange equalisation accounts but by a single Supranational Exchange Equalisation authority which—like the present IMF—would be endowed with a large fund of the various national currencies, but—unlike the present IMF—would be empowered on its own initiative to buy and sell these currencies in otherwise uncontrolled foreign exchange markets in order to control short-run fluctuations in exchange rates.

If I am frank, I must admit that I regard this as technically the best possible solution in the present circumstances. For at heart I believe that in the free world we should develop real supranational authorities. It is in my view a quite mistaken form of monetary supranationalism to start by fixing rigidly the exchange rates between national currencies as a first step towards a supranational currency. We are at a very early confederal stage in our affairs. It is the national governments which have the great taxing powers and so the instruments for controlling budgetary inflations or deflations of demand; it is the national governments which have the great central banks which control the issue of money and so interest rates; and the nations have their own different modes of wage-rate determination. It is a wise and sensible division of powers in our present confederal stage that the national governments should exercise these budgetary, monetary, and wage-fixing influences to control their own employment, growth, and price stability. This implies, I am sure, some variations in the rates of exchange between their monies. It is in the necessary Exchange Equalisation between these monies that the first tentative supranational steps should be taken.

However, I am sufficiently realistic to admit that this supranational solution is politically not a starter in the year 1966. So reluctantly I pass on from Supranational Exchange Equalisation to other possible measures.

5. If we abandon the heroic solution of Supranational Exchange Equalisation, can we do some useful but more mundane tinkering with the present excessively rigid Adjustable-Peg system? I believe that we can. First of all, we could introduce *Wider Bands* within which fluctuations could take place. I have so far treated the present system of Adjustable Pegs as if each currency were precisely and exactly pegged to gold. But this is, of course, not the case. The present IMF obligation is for each member country

to settle a par value for its currency in terms either of gold or of the dollar with its fixed gold content and then not to allow the value of its currency to vary by more than 1 per cent above or below this par value. This means that if a country is in deficit, it can allow the value of its currency to depreciate by 1 per cent before having to support it from its own reserves; if it is in surplus, it can allow the value of its currency to appreciate by 1 per cent. Such small variations [1] do not allow the exchange rate to be a significant instrument of long-run adjustment; but they can exercise an important and in general a beneficial effect on speculation in the exchange rates. Thus if a country is in deficit and the value of its currency has depreciated by the permitted 1 per cent, speculators (provided that there is no risk of a change in the currency's par value) will have some speculative incentive to purchase the depreciated currency; it cannot depreciate any further; it might, however, appreciate in the future by anything up to 2 per cent. This consideration will prompt speculators to support a currency when it is under pressure and thus helps the authorities to maintain the exchange rate with a smaller loss of reserves than would otherwise be necessary. This feature of a system which sets upper and lower limits to the Band within which exchange rates may fluctuate gives it an advantage over the system of National Exchange Equalisation without any upper or lower limits. For a monetary authority to support its currency when it has fallen by x per cent will be much easier if speculators know that it will not fall any further than if they realise that at any time it may be still further reduced. As against this there

---

1. Consider two countries both of which have fixed the par values of their currencies in terms of gold. Suppose country A is in surplus and its exchange rate is 1 per cent above parity, while country B is in deficit and its exchange rate is 1 per cent below parity. Then B's money is 2 per cent devalued in terms of A's. If later B is in surplus and A is in deficit, B's money may be 2 per cent appreciated in terms of A's money. The maximum swing in the rate of exchange between the two currencies is, therefore, 4 per cent. The maximum conceivable swing could be somewhat greater if A had fixed its parity in terms of gold and B in terms of the dollar and if there were a margin between the United States' buying and selling prices of gold in terms of dollars. The swing in the rate of exchange between A's and B's currencies would be enlarged if (i) the dollar happened to be weak in terms of gold when A's currency was at its strongest (in terms of gold) and B's at its weakest (in terms of dollars) and (ii) the dollar happened to be strong in terms of gold when A's currency was at its weakest (in terms of gold) and B's at its strongest (in terms of dollars).

must, of course, be set the reduction in the range of variations which can be used as an instrument of balance-of-payments adjustment.

But there is nothing sacred about 1 per cent. Suppose that the rule of the IMF were altered so that each member country were obliged only to prevent the value of its currency from deviating by more than 5 per cent from its par value. Changes in exchange rates could now begin to exert some, though still a moderate, influence on basic price-income-cost structures. Consider two currencies both of whose par rates were fixed in terms of gold. The most extreme permitted swing in the exchange rate between the two currencies would now be 20 per cent,[2] though generally much smaller changes would be the rule. The possibility of these enlarged swings would also increase the incentive to speculators to aid the authorities in the support of a currency under pressure. For when the currency did reach its lower level there would, as before, be no possibility of a further fall in its gold value, but there would now be a possibility that its gold value might rise by anything up to 10 percent instead of only 2 per cent.

The wider the Band within which the exchange rate can vary, the greater its power as an instrument of basic adjustment of price-income-cost structures and the greater its power to induce the support of speculators when a currency is weak and at its lower level. Why then not advocate much Wider Bands? Why not 20 per cent above or below par? Unfortunately, in this wicked world one cannot have one's cake and eat it. Fluctuations within the Band raise all the problems already discussed of Freely Floating Exchange Rates or of Exchange Equalisation controls over fluctuations, of competitive exchange depreciation, and of the co-ordination of National Exchange Equalisation policies. If the Band is kept reasonably narrow, one could without danger have a system in which exchanges were allowed to float freely without any official intervention within the permitted Band. Or, as a second-best alternative, if National Exchange Equalisation were permitted within the Band, one could perhaps leave the necessary co-operation between national authorities in the Exchange Equali-

2. At one extreme, A's currency would be 5 per cent above par with B's 5 per cent below par; at the other extreme, A's would be 5 per cent below par and B's 5 per cent above. The swing could be somewhat greater if A's parity were fixed in terms of gold and B's in terms of dollars. See the preceding footnote.

sation use of their national reserves of gold and foreign exchange to be worked out by suitable *ad hoc* arrangements. Simply because the Band is limited, the dangers of anti-social speculation or of the misuse of National Exchange Equalisation funds will also be limited. Permission to fluctuate by 5 per cent either side of par value combined with freely floating exchange rates or with the uncontrolled national use of national monetary reserves within those limits might well provide a better mix than at present between international restraint and freedom of national action.

6. There is one other way in which the present IMF rules might be modified in order to give a somewhat different mix between international restraint and national freedom in exchange-rate matters. At present, the rule is that a member country can alter the par value of its currency only if it is in fundamental disequilibrium and only with the permission of the IMF, except that it can make an initial 10 per cent adjustment on its own initiative. These rules might be revised in the following way. Basic adjustments to meet a fundamental disequilibrium would be hedged around with even more safeguards and would be made even more exceptional than at present. The allowance of an initial 10 per cent adjustment would be abolished; but in its place member countries would be permitted to alter the par value of their currencies by not more than ⅙ per cent in any one month; moreover, they would undertake to depreciate their currencies by ⅙ per cent in any one month if, but only if, they were faced with a continuing balance-of-payments deficit and to appreciate by this amount if, but only if, they were faced with a continuing surplus in their balance of payments. This system might perhaps be called that of the *Sliding Parity*. For, if the right to change the parity were exercised every month, the exchange value of the currency would be changed continuously at 2 per cent per annum.

Such a system is not, of course, a panacea. But it could be used as a partial but very useful supplement to other measures to achieve long-run equilibrium. If a country were in continuing balance-of-payments deficit, it could by this means lower its price-income-cost structure by anything up to 2 per cent per annum— that is, by 10 per cent over a five-year period. If, at the same time, some other country were in continuing surplus, it could have raised its price-income-cost structure through exchange-rate appreciation by anything up to 10 per cent over the same five-year period. A 20 per cent adjustment in five years is by no means to be despised. But this would be the very maximum, and clearly reliance could be placed on this method only if the countries concerned had very ample reserves of gold and foreign exchange to tide them over the fairly prolonged processes of adjustment.

The system raises also important problems of exchange-rate speculation. For this reason, to operate the system the monetary authorities would have to use their short-term interest rate policies for balance-of-payments reasons. Let us take the extreme possible case. Suppose that A's currency is confidently expected to appreciate at the maximum rate of 2 per cent per annum while B's currency is confidently expected to depreciate at the maximum rate of 2 per cent per annum. B's currency would then be expected to depreciate in terms of A's currency at the rate of 4 per cent per annum. To prevent the wholesale movement of short-term funds from B to A to take the prospective 4 per cent profit on the exchange rate, the short-term rate of interest would have to be maintained in B four points above the level in A—for example, at 6 per cent per annum in B and 2 per cent in A. This means that to work a system of this kind, the national monetary authorities would have to co-operate in setting their short-term interest rates in the interests of preserving balance-of-payments equilibrium. They would have to rely on budgetary policies and—in so far as they can be determined independently of short-term rates—upon long-term rates but not upon short-term rates, for the control of domestic economic expansion.

If a system of this kind were adopted, it might be sensible for the monetary authorities in each country to give a gold guarantee in respect of balances of its own currency which were held as monetary reserves by other monetary authorities. This is not an essential feature of the proposal, and the decision whether or not to give such a gold guarantee could be left to each individual country. If such guarantees were given, there would develop a structure of more or less uniform short-term interest rates in all the main financial centres for such currency balances as were backed by a gold guarantee, while divergent short-term rates would appear on balances of national currencies not subject to a gold guarantee—the short-term rate being higher in those centres where the exchange rate was expected to depreciate and *vice versa*.

CONCLUDING PROPOSALS

Let me sum up by putting forward proposals for the arrangements which in view of the above considerations I would myself advocate. There is no reason why a *Wider Band* should not be combined with a *Sliding Parity*. This could be achieved by two straightforward changes in the IMF rules.

1. As at present, member countries would fix a par value for their currencies. But their obligation would be to prevent deviations by more than 5 per cent (in place of the present 1 per cent) each side of this par value.
2. As far as alterations in par rates were concerned, the present allowance of a 10 per cent initial alteration at their own discretion would be removed and, in its place, each country would be permitted at its own discretion to change its parity by not more than ⅙ per cent per month.[3] Member countries would undertake to make such adjustments if, but only if, their balances of payments were in their view in continuing deficit or surplus.

Let us consider how such a system might operate. Suppose that we start in equilibrium with exchange rates at parity and that then some change in conditions occurs which puts country A into serious deficit and country B into serious surplus. As a result of the Wider Band, A's currency would then depreciate by 5 per cent and B's would appreciate by 5 per cent. This would give at once a 10 per cent adjustment of relative price-income-cost structures which could begin to have a significant effect in bringing about the necessary basic adjustments. As long as the imbalance in international payments continued, as a result of the Sliding-Parity arrangements, A's currency could further be depreciated at a rate of 2 per cent per annum while B's was appreciated at a rate of 2 per cent per annum, so that at the end of two and a half years there would have been another 10 per cent adjustment —or 20 per cent in all—in relative price-income-cost structures.

Thus these proposals could make a very serious contribution to the adjustment of balances of payments. At the same time, they

3. At this rate, it would take it five years to achieve an initial 10 per cent change.

need not lead to insoluble speculative problems. As far as fluctuations of the exchange rates within the Wider Band were concerned, exchange rates could best be left to the free play of market forces. If speculators expected a fall in a currency, they could by their sale of it drive it down at once to its lower limit. Beyond this, they would know for certain that it could not fall by more than 2 per cent per annum and might rise at any moment by 10 per cent. The expectation of a steady fall of 2 per cent per annum could induce speculative pressure and so loss of reserves on the deficit country, unless this was offset by a 2 per cent differential in short-term interest rates between the deficit country and other countries. For this reason, the fully successful operation of the system would require real co-operation between the main central monetary authorities so that short-term rates were set at a lower level in surplus countries whose currencies were expected to appreciate and at a higher level in deficit countries. The financial authorities would have to rely rather on their fiscal policies and long-term interest-rate policies for the control of their domestic economies. Apart from this set of problems, there is in my opinion very little to be said against the proposed system; and, in my view, this set of problems should not prove unmanageable. The degree of exchange-rate flexibility which the system would introduce would very greatly reduce the probability of there being (as at present) every now and then a huge once-for-all disturbing exchange-rate adjustment. It is the fear of such once-for-all government-determined devaluations of 10, 20, 30, or 40 per cent which cause the really big speculative runs on a currency; and with the new system, such runs should quickly become a thing of the past.

I do not put these proposals forward as a cure-all. Although the amount of price-income-cost adjustment that it would make possible would, as we have seen, be really significant, there would, of course, be pressures on balances of payments while currencies were at their lower and upper limits on the edges of the Wider Band. Such pressures would have to be met by the use of national reserves of gold and foreign exchange or, if such reserves were not adequate, by the more drastic and more quickly operating measures of import restrictions or of otherwise undesirable deflations of domestic demand. The proposed system is not an alternative to other reforms of the international monetary mechanism designed to ensure that the amount and the nature of international liquid reserves are appropriate to modern conditions. It is a well-recognised fact that those methods of balance-of-payments adjustment which operate quickly (such as import restrictions or severe domestic deflations) are objectionable on other grounds, whereas acceptable methods of adjusting balances of payments through adjustments of relative price-income-cost structures (such as incomes policies or alterations in exchange rates) operate slowly and with considerable time lags. One can, therefore, rely on these better policies only if there are adequate resources of international liquid reserves to tide over the periods of adjustment; and this is particularly true when, as with the present proposals, the changes in exchange rates are themselves expressly designed so as to be both moderate and gradual.

Epilogue

Where the Rainbow Ended

THE ECONOMIST

This fable is the work of the staff of The Economist, *originally published in the December 1960 issue. It implicitly argues for the demonetization of gold and for the transformation of the International Monetary Fund into something resembling a world central bank.*

BY A DEFT STROKE, THE ECONOMIST HAS GOT HOLD OF THE MEMOIRS OF DR PER JACOBSSON TEN YEARS BEFORE THEY ARE WRITTEN. CHAPTER FOUR, *"The Brainwave of 1961,"* HAS A CERTAIN TOPICAL INTEREST.

It was in the words of that firm exponent of stable money, the Duke of Wellington, a damned close run thing. Speculation against the dollar, momentarily quietened by President Kennedy's inauguration, flared up suddenly again in March. The main cause seems to have been the bid made by General Motors for British Motor Corporation, to which the United Kingdom government gave its approval on condition that the bid be deemed to cover British Railways as well. This was fine for Britain, but it pushed the United States gold reserves below $16,000 million, and the fact that no more than two-fifths of the world's gold was buried under the United States naturally shook everyone's confidence in the stability of dollar prices.

Soon the pressure proved too much for the loose understanding that had been reached about management of the London gold market. The dollar price of gold shot up and on April 1st was quoted at $49. This time it could not so easily be brought back under control. Investors the world over, disillusioned with dividend cuts on their growth stocks, reverted to more ancient habits, and bought gold.

Plainly something had to be done. The economists, rising to the occasion, called a world conference in Fiji to thrash the matter out. After meeting all through the Easter vacation they issued a considered statement of 10,000 words which pointed out that fundamentally there was no problem. In a closely argued minority report, Sir Ralph Hawtrey identified the trouble to the undervaluation of sterling in 1949.

Still the exchange and bullion markets seethed. Samuel Montagu opened a recruiting office in Coventry. In June the directors of the International Monetary Fund unanimously agreed that there should be no annual meeting that autumn. The markets heaved a sigh of relief. Soon after, however, an eavesdropper to a meeting of the National Temperance Council at Haywards Heath, England, reported a mystifying discussion about par values and fundamental disequilibrium. Worst suspicions were confirmed when it was found that fifteen Professor Skinners had registered at the Station Hotel.

So it appeared, that bleak and rainy summer, as though the world's currencies would after all have to succumb. The world's best economic brains, its most eminent practical bankers, had thought hard and long; but none had found a means of breaking the speculators' grip. More and more of them, privately, were beginning to think that the only way of getting rid of the speculators was to give in to them. The dons, back with their Fiji tans, were turning over the problem that had eluded them to their students. "Explain in 500 words what you consider to be the best means of checking the present flight from the dollar into gold." It livened up the seminars. But by one of those strange strokes of coincidence that go to the making of history, the paper of one of the students, a certain Joe Plain, did very much more.

It all happened because Mr. Plain discussed his paper one evening with his father, a principal in overseas finance at the Treasury. For two days Mr. Plain senior did nothing. Then, in the most tentative way, he passed up a memorandum to his assistant secretary. In the ordinary course of events, I have no doubt, matters would have stopped there. But this assistant secretary happened to be an old pupil of Professor J. K. Galbraith, now chairman of the Federal Reserve Board; and he felt it permissible, on an academic rather than an official level, to pass on to his old teacher the academic musings of his junior's no doubt unworldly but ingeniously minded son. On Friday, July 7th, he airmailed a copy of the paper to the professor's home address.

Who will ever forget the Monday that followed? It came as a thunderbolt not only to the public at large but to the whole financial community, from Treasury officials to central bankers. It came in the form of a short statement by the Federal Reserve Bank of New York, acting as agent for the U.S. Treasury.

In recent months doubts have been thrown on the continuance of the policy of the Federal Reserve in buying and selling gold at the parity of $35 an ounce, on the ground that market forces are inexorably pressing towards a higher price. The Federal Reserve has no wish to hold back the forces of the market. Forthwith, therefore, its undertaking to buy and sell gold at $35 an ounce, or at any other price, lapses.

In three sentences, the Fed had demonetised gold. The financial markets were knocked dizzy. The event was too large for men to take in. As they began working it out, they fastened on another statement which on my own initiative I put out for the International Monetary Fund:

The Federal Reserve Bank of New York announced today that it is ending its undertaking to sell gold to central banks at $35.08¾ and buy gold from any source at $34.91¼. The Fund approves this step. As an interim arrangement, until December 31, 1961, the Fund is taking over the commitments of the Federal Reserve, with certain differences. It will buy gold, at $35 less commission, only from central banks of its member countries, who will receive in return deposits with the Fund which can be used for all international payments; and it will be happy to sell gold at $35 plus commission to anyone. It assumes no obligation to buy gold after December 31st.

So, as the City editors quickly explained, anybody who held gold had better sell it quickly. For six months gold still had a value near $35, provided one's national central bank agreed to act as intermediary between the public and the International Monetary Fund. From the new year on, gold would be just a commodity, and busy calls went round to try to establish just what, as a commodity, gold would be worth.

Not everyone was happy with the discovery. The Zurich nursing homes had to open emergency wards: "It is the shock, the shock" the harassed doctors were heard to mutter. Kuwait decided to postpone its new retirement pension plan for all Arabs anywhere. Other countries saw their problems solved. In India the peasants were already carrying their gold into the banks; within three days the finance minister announced that the Indian government now had sufficient reserves at the IMF to dispense with all external aid for the third year plan. The Bank of France, too, enjoyed a windfall from its own people, and General de Gaulle's first impulse to make a proper hydrogen bomb gave way to a grand plan for full integration with Algeria at the French scale of social services, accepted by the Muslims by popular acclaim.

There were of course certain problems. South Africa was thunderstruck by the ruthless devaluation of its most important export commodity; it would not object to selling all its gold to the Fund but could not possibly dig it all out of the Rand in six months. The Fund offered special arrangements, the only condition being that South Africa should abolish *apartheid;* and after a bloodless *coup d'état* South Africa gratefully accepted. The other hard-hit gold producer, Russia, chewed over the problem a little longer. Here the Fund was asking simply that Russia should become a member and, in accordance with Article VIII, end all restrictions on current payments. The Old Guard fought passionately against; but Mr. Khrushchev—"Are we going to let the capitalists rob us of the value of our tens of billions of hard-dug gold?"—prevailed, and announced the decision on the same day as the cession of one thousand square miles of Mongolian desert to China. Most dramatically of all, even Switzerland decided to break with all precedent and join the Fund, though two cantons preferred to set up their own central banks; since the gold in their balance sheets has no ascertainable value it is to this day recorded in ounces.

This revolution in international finance of course transformed at one stroke the status of the International Monetary Fund. "The Fund," one commentator wrote, "now stands to the central banks of its member countries as does the Federal Reserve Board to its member banks." Possibly this was somewhat premature. At any rate the Fund secured a new hold on the public mind. In the vernacular, there was a rush to jump on the bandwagon. In response to strong pressure, I myself agreed to serve a second term as chairman and managing director. And recently we have been fortunate enough to persuade Lord Cromer to give up his promising start as governor of the Bank of England to return to his old and now highly coveted post as executive director of the Fund.

We have of course outgrown our new building, and at an early stage it was thought appropriate to move west, to a splendid new glass structure built over Fort Knox. In the early days visiting finance ministers were comforted by the sight of the bars of gold on which, as they still saw it, the security of their IMF deposits rested. But such out-moded thinking soon lost sway, and when at a recent annual meeting the governor for the United Kingdom, under pressure at home to economise in his budget, pointed out that no less than $2.50 an ounce for gold could be obtained from dentists, the meeting decided there and then to put the whole lot out for public tender; a running income was assured by leasing Fort Knox to a grateful U.S. Defence Department for underground nuclear tests. The base of world liquidity at last broke free from its golden chain, and was determined instead by the hydraulic calculations provided free of charge by Professor Kendall of the London School of Economics.

So the operation that may well have saved the economy of the western world was brought to its triumphant conclusion. For the student of affairs, it brings two striking lessons. The first concerns the means by which the change was brought about. I well remember how the governor of a European central bank, who must be nameless, told me a few years ago that much the same scheme had been suggested by one of the less experienced delegates at that Haywards Heath gathering. "And what happened? It was laughed out of court." The central banks would refuse to co-operate; they would hang on to gold, which history had endowed with value, rather than part with it in exchange for a typewritten entry in the books of IMF. So much for the view of the men of the world, for whom money was a fixed and unchanging thing.

Yet just in those years Professor Sayers and the Radcliffe committee in England had reminded the public that money was whatever the public chose to accept as such. The same is true internationally. That is my second lesson. To those who doubt this, to those who feel that positive control over the course of economic events must for some reason stop short at the terms of international exchange, I need only say: remember The Year We Demonetised Gold

Suggested Further Readings

Adler, F. M., "The High Cost of Foreign Investment Restraints," *Columbia Journal of World Business*, May-June 1968.
Aliber, Robert Z., *The Future of the Dollar as an International Currency*, (Praeger, 1966).
Balassa, Bela, "American Direct Investments in the Common Market," *Banca Nazionale del Lavoro Quarterly Review*, June 1966.
———, *Trade Liberalization among Industrial Countries: Objectives and Alternatives* (McGraw-Hill, 1967).
Ball, George, "Cosmocorp: The Importance of Being Stateless," *Columbia Journal of World Business*, November-December 1967.
Bator, F. M., "The Political Economics of International Money," *Foreign Affairs*, October 1968.
Birnbaum, E. A., *Gold and the International Monetary System: An Orderly Reform*, Essays in International Finance, No. 66, April 1968, International Finance Section, Princeton University.
Clendenning, E. Wayne, "Euro-dollars: the Problem of Control," *The Banker*, April 1968.
Cooper, Richard N., *The Economics of Interdependence* (McGraw-Hill, 1968).
Curzon, Gerard and Victoria, *After the Kennedy Round: What Trade Policies Now?*, The Atlantic Trade Study (1967).
Curzon, Gerard, *Multinational Commercial Diplomacy* (Michael Joseph, 1965).
Diebold, John, "Is the Gap Technological?" *Foreign Affairs*, January 1968.
Fellner, William, Machlup, Fritz, and Triffin, Robert et al., *Maintaining and Restoring Balance in International Payments* (Princeton University, 1966).
Fleming, J. Marcus, *Guidelines for Balance-of-Payments Adjustment under the Par-Value System*, Essays in International Finance, No. 67, May 1968.
Future United States Foreign Trade Policy, Report to the President Submitted by the Special Representative for Trade Negotiations (U.S. Government Printing Office, 1969).
Gilbert, Milton, *Problems of the International Monetary System*, Essays in International Finance, No. 53, April 1966.
Grubel, Herbert G., ed., *World Monetary Reform: Plans and Issues* (Stanford University, 1963).
Halm, G. N., *International Financial Intermediation: Deficits Benign and Malignant*, Essays in International Finance, No. 68, June 1968.
Hansen, A. H., *The Dollar and the International Monetary System* (McGraw-Hill, 1965).
Harris, S. E., ed., *The Dollar in Crisis* (Harcourt, Brace, and World, 1961).
Johnson, Harry G., *The World Economy at the Crossroads* (Oxford University Press, 1965).
Joint Economic Committee, *The Future of U.S. Foreign Trade Policy*, 90th Congress, 1st Session (United States Government Printing Office, 1967).

Also, *Hearings* on same (1967).

———, *Next Steps in International Monetary Reform*, 90th Congress, 2nd Session (United States Government Printing Office, 1968). Also, *Hearings* on same (1968).

Kenen, Peter B., *Giant among Nations* (Rand McNally, 1963).

Klopstock, Fred H., *The Euro-dollar Market: Some Unresolved Issues*, Essays in International Finance, No. 65, March 1968.

Krause, L. B., *The Common Market, Progress and Controversy* (Prentice-Hall, 1964).

Kravis, Irving B., *Domestic Interests and International Obligations* (University of Pennsylvania Press, 1963).

Lary, H. B., *Problems of the United States as World Trader and Banker*, National Bureau for Economic Research (1963).

Machlup, Fritz, *Remaking the International Monetary System: The Rio Agreement and Beyond*, Committee for Economic Development (1968).

Massel, Mark S., *Non-Tariff Barriers as an Obstacle to World Trade*, Brookings Institution (1965).

Maxwell Stamp Associates, *The Free Trade Area Option: Opportunity for Britain*, The Atlantic Trade Study (1967).

Organization for Economic Co-operation and Development, *The Balance of Payments Adjustment Process* (August, 1966).

Polak, J. J., "The New Facility in the IMF," *The Banker*, November 1967.

Powers, John J., Jr., "The Impact of U.S. Controls on Foreign Investment," *The Atlantic Community Quarterly*, Fall 1968.

Reuss, Henry S., *The Critical Decade: An Economic Policy for America and the Free World* (McGraw-Hill, 1964).

Robertson, David, *Scope for New Trade Strategy: Dimensions of Free Trade*, The Atlantic Trade Study (1968).

Rolfe, Sidney E., *Gold and World Power: The Dollar, the Pound, and the Plans for Reform* (Harper & Row, 1965).

Roosa, Robert V., and Hirsch, Fred, *Reserves, Reserve Currencies, and Vehicle Currencies: An Argument*, Essays in International Finance, No. 54, May 1966.

Salant, W. S. et al., *The United States Balance of Payments in 1968* (Brookings, 1963).

Swerling, Boris, *Current Issues in Commodity Policy*, Essays in International Finance, No. 38, June 1962.

Triffin, Robert, *Gold and the Dollar Crisis* (Yale University Press, 1961).

———, *Our International Monetary System: Yesterday, Today and Tomorrow* (Random House, 1968).

Vernon, Raymond, "International Investment and International Trade in the Product Cycle," *The Quarterly Journal of Economics*, May 1966.

Williamson, John H., *The Crawling Peg*, Essays in International Finance, No. 50, December 1965.

———, "Exchange Rate Policy of the Future," *Moorgate and Wallstreet*, Spring 1967.

The Editor

BELA BALASSA *is Professor of Political Economy at the Johns Hopkins University and Consultant to the Economics Department of the International Bank for Reconstruction and Development. He is a native of Hungary and came to this country after the 1956 revolution. Mr. Balassa has a doctor's degree in law and political science from the University of Budapest and a Ph.D. in economics from Yale University. He taught at the universities of Yale, Berkeley and Columbia and has been consultant to various international and government organizations. Mr. Balassa is the author of numerous articles in professional journals. His books include* The Hungarian Experience in Economic Planning (1959), The Theory of Economic Integration (1961), Trade Prospects for Developing Countries (1964), Economic Development and Integration (1965), Trade Liberalization among Industrial Countries: Objectives and Alternatives (1967).

Date Due